Dynamic Memory Revisite

Roger Schank's influential book *Dynamic Memory* described how computers could learn based upon what was known about how people learn. Since that book's publication in 1983, Dr. Schank has turned his focus from artificial intelligence to human intelligence. *Dynamic Memory Revisited* contains the theory of learning presented in the original book, extended to provide principles for teaching and learning. It includes Dr. Schank's important theory of case-based reasoning and assesses the role of stories in human memory. In addition, it covers his ideas on nonconscious learning, indexing, and the cognitive structures that underlie learning by doing.

Dynamic Memory Revisited is crucial reading for all who are concerned with education and school reform. It draws attention to how effective learning takes place, and it provides ideas for developing software that truly helps students learn.

ROGER C. SCHANK is John Evans Professor of Computer Science, Education and Psychology, and Director of the Institute for the Learning Sciences at Northwestern University. He also serves as Chairman and Chief Technology Officer of Cognitive Arts.

Dynamic Memory Revisited

Roger C. Schank

Northwestern University

CAMBRIDGE
UNIVERSITY PRESS

CAMBRIDGE UNIVERSITY PRESS
Cambridge, New York, Melbourne, Madrid, Cape Town, Singapore, São Paulo

Cambridge University Press
The Edinburgh Building, Cambridge CB2 2RU, UK

Published in the United States of America by Cambridge University Press, New York

www.cambridge.org
Information on this title: www.cambridge.org/9780521633024

First published 1999

A catalogue record for this publication is available from the British Library

Library of Congress Cataloguing in Publication data
Schank, Roger C., 1946–
Dynamic Memory Revisited / Roger C. Schank.
    p.   cm.
Includes bibliographical references.
ISBN 0-521-63302-8 (hardcover). – ISBN 0-521-63398-2 (pbk.)
1. Memory. 2. Learning, Psychology of.   I. Schank, Roger C.
1946-   Dynamic memory.   II. Title
BF.371. S365   1999
153.1 – dc21   99–11983
                                                            CIP

ISBN-13 978-0-521-63302-4 hardback
ISBN-10 0-521-63302-8 hardback

ISBN-13 978-0-521-63398-7 paperback
ISBN-10 0-521-63398-2 paperback

Transferred to digital printing 2007

Contents

	Preface to the Second Edition	*page* vii
1	Introduction to Dynamic Memory	1
2	Reminding and Memory	21
3	Failure-driven Memory	41
4	Cross-contextual Reminding	75
5	Story-based Reminding	89
6	The Kinds of Structures in Memory	107
7	Memory Organization Packets	123
8	Thematic Organization Packets	137
9	Generalization and Memory	155
10	Learning by Doing	172
11	Nonconscious Knowledge	195
12	Case-based Reasoning and the Metric of Problem Solving	212
13	Nonconscious Thinking	237
14	Goal-based Scenarios	255
15	Enhancing Intelligence	270
	References	289
	Index	299

Preface to the Second Edition

The first edition of this book was about artificial intelligence (AI). This second edition is about education. It is hard to see how this could be. Are these two subjects really in any way the same? My answer is that fundamentally they are, but of course, I recognize that such a notion would not necessarily be accepted as gospel truth. The common element is *learning*. Without learning there are neither intelligent machines nor intelligent people.

The subtitle of the original *Dynamic Memory* was "*a theory of reminding and learning in computers and people.*" In the late 1970s and early 1980s, I was fascinated by the idea that computers could be as intelligent as people. My assumption was that if we could figure out what intelligence was like in people, then we could get computers to model people. Detail the process sufficiently and – *presto!* – intelligent machines. I no longer hold such views.

Since 1981, not as much has happened in AI as one might have hoped. The goal of building a dynamic memory, a memory that changed over time as a result of its experiences, has proven to be quite difficult to achieve. The major reason for this is really one of content rather than structure. It is not so much that we can't figure out how such a memory might be organized, although this is indeed a difficult problem. Rather, we simply were not able to even begin to acquire the content of a dynamic memory. What does a person know? We can attempt to detail the facts an adult might know, as indeed Doug Lenat has attempted to do, but the fact is that facts aren't all there are. For instance, we may know a lot of facts about cars but, even more important, we have a great many experiences with cars, ones that have informed and modified our view of cars over time such that what we really know about cars includes the smell of the back seat of the family car when we were five, the difficulty of dealing with a date when we were teenagers, and fear about changing a tire on an open road. These ideas are not about cars at all. Each experience we have with a car is also an experience with a person, or a problem, or a life issue. Each informs the other and contributes to what we know about the world.

Content is the primary issue both in building intelligent machines and in helping to form intelligent people. Workers in each of these disciplines sometimes act as if they would just like the content problem to disappear. AI researchers want learning to come for free somehow, either by statistical methods or by making lots of connections. But, any way you look at it, someone has to get a computer to know what a human knows about using a toaster or playing baseball.

We hope we can educate people by simply presenting content or by avoiding the issue altogether and having students learn principles apart from content. It is the details that matter in both cases, and these details must be acquired, unfortunately, through repeated experience. In a dynamic memory, change is the norm and static facts are meaningless; therefore, it is not just the acquisition of content that is the issue. Whatever you learn changes over time. Dealing with change is an important part of intelligence for both machines and people.

When the first edition of this book appeared, I was attempting to lay out the groundwork for building intelligent machines. I did so by attempting to observe and to codify what I could about the nature of the memory that underlies human intelligence. Today I am concerned less with computers and more with people. And today I am concerned more with what it means to learn than with what it means to be smart. I have come to realize that intelligence without learning is not intelligence at all.

In 1981, I had two small children, a daughter who was nine and a son who was six. They were in school and they were learning, but the learning that mattered most in their lives was not taking place in school. What I learned about learning in working on this book was that school as it was constituted (at least in my children's lives) could not possibly actually contribute to learning, at least not in the way one assumed it was supposed to.

Making students memorize and then seeing if they have successfully done so through tests makes no sense in the context of computer learning. We can easily get a computer to know lots of facts. But, in what sense does it really *know* these facts? It is the utilization of information that constitutes knowing, not the recitation of information. Although schools pay lip service to this idea, AI people cannot. No one cares what a computer knows. We care what it can do. The same is true of students, but schools fail to recognize this in any important way.

When I would ask my children what they had learned in school, they occasionally mentioned the factual instruction they had received that day, but more often they talked about the other kids, their relationship with their teachers, and the worries and concerns about social interaction that were truly the instructional material of school. Their dynamic memories were working, and school was causing them to think, ponder, wonder, and generalize, but not about history or mathematics. I began to understand that what I knew about learning wasn't known by the school system as a whole. Schools were trying to teach things that children had no interest in knowing.

The issue is not whether kids are interested in topics like math and history. Presented properly, almost everything is of interest to children, and my kids were no exception. But they weren't generally interested in the way these topics were taught in school, namely, in a non-doing learning environment that was devoid of reference to real-world relevance and to their lives.

All my work in AI until 1981 had been about getting knowledge into computers. But, we didn't try to teach history or mathematics, we tried to teach how to function in a restaurant, or how to understand the interactions of foreign diplomats. Of course history and mathematics were valuable to know on occasion in some contexts, but the real issue was the acquisition of the mundane knowledge that people take for granted. And watching my children grow, I could see them acquiring this knowledge. They acquired it even in school sometimes, since they acquired it wherever they were, but such knowledge was simply not the material that counted in school, although it counted in life. Something was radically wrong with what the schools were trying to teach.

In 1989 I moved from Yale to Northwestern. This was not simply a change in venue. The move occurred because of the issues just raised. I felt that we were not likely to build intelligent machines any time soon but that we might help create more intelligent people. The major point of the original *Dynamic Memory* was that humans have complex and constantly changing memories and that if we wanted to build intelligent machines we would have to figure out how each experience that a machine involved itself in would alter its existing memory structures. To accomplish this, we would need to study how people acquired and stored memories and how they constantly learned from new experiences. In short, if we wanted to build machines that learned from experience, we would have to study how people learn from experience. To make dynamic memories in computers, we needed to know what dynamic memories looked like in people.

This is easier said than done. Real people aren't very willing or able to discuss their memories. We could get a machine to acquire experience in only one of two ways. Either it would have to grow naturally through experience as a child does, or it would have to have knowledge spoon-fed into it. The former approach, though obviously the "right" one, is very impractical: The computer would need to be able to operate in the world, to have needs it had to satisfy, and to find ways (on its own) of satisfying them. The prospect is exciting but daunting. The alternative approach, spoon-feeding all there is to know about the world, is equally daunting, but for different reasons. What do we know? How can we find everything that a given entity knows and put it in a memory that can dynamically reorganize itself with every new experience? That, to some extent, was the question behind the first version of *Dynamic Memory* and it is still discussed here.

Although these subjects are still of great interest – we will always want to know how we acquire knowledge and how we could get a machine to acquire knowledge – they have been supplanted in my mind by a more important, but quite related, issue. In order to get machines to acquire knowledge, I began to wonder about how humans acquire knowledge. As I looked into this issue, I began to wonder about the question of how we could help humans acquire knowledge better.

In the late 1980s, I began to seek funding to help me take what we had learned about learning in the context of the creation of intelligent machines and apply that knowledge in building learning environments that would enhance the learning of people (especially children). What had we learned about learning? In the first *Dynamic Memory*, the main points were that learning depends upon expectation failure and the attempt to explain that failure, and that reminders that come from our store of memories are instrumental in helping us create explanations and are therefore critical to learning. We process new experiences in terms of prior experience, and our memories change as a result. To translate this into a teaching environment, we must set up situations in which students can have their expectations fail and can either be reminded or be instructed about how not to fail next time. To put this another way, learning takes place if, while one is attempting to do something, something else inhibits the doing and causes one to wonder why what one thought would work, didn't.

One key problem addressed in the original version of this book is how the process of abstraction and generalization from experience works. Abstraction and generalization are integral parts of the learning process. In order for an entity to learn, it must be able to generalize from experience. But, more important – and I realize this seems obvious – in order to generalize from one's experience, one must have an experience. The obviousness of this point has not prevented computer scientists from failing to provide proper real-world experiences for their so-called learning machines, nor has it pointed educators toward the idea that learning will require actual experience.

The key idea here is doing. John Dewey and others have noticed that most learning occurs in the context of doing. While I was considering how computers might learn, I came face-to-face with the realization that computers weren't doing much of anything. We were trying to get them to learn about restaurants because they were reading about restaurants. They weren't eating in restaurants, nor were they really likely to be very interested in restaurants. Of course we could remedy this by having them learn to cook or something practical like that, but in fact AI, as a field, never really did such things. AI never concentrated on getting a machine to do something practical and learn about it by doing it.

For that matter, although children learn by doing all the time in their daily lives, they hardly do it in school at all. They learn mathematics or history because they have to, not because they are trying to do something for which such information might be valuable. Thus, both for computers and for people, environments would need to be created that allowed them to do something they wanted to do and allowed learning to take place in the context of that doing. The ideas in *Dynamic Memory* are critical to understanding how learning takes place in a doing environment.

This new version of *Dynamic Memory* is about translating what the original version said about how computers might learn into a more direct version that addresses the issues of enhancing human learning. I am concerned with how to change education. It is necessary to understand how learning works, and because the job of learning is to change memory, we need to understand how memory works. Armed with that understanding we can begin to rethink school.

The work of the last nine years that underlies the rewriting of *Dynamic Memory* was supported in large part by Andersen Consulting. It was a tumultuous relationship, different than the typical federal grant by quite a bit. Nevertheless, they enabled me to build the Institute for the Learning Sciences (ILS) and this created the venue for building the software that embodies many of the ideas described here. ILS was, at its height, an exciting place filled with many brilliant people. I especially want to thank Alex Kass, Gregg Collins, Ray Bariess, Larry Birnbaum, Kemi Jona, Michael Korkusca, Chris Riesbeck, and a host of others who contributed to building software and playing with ideas about learning. Also, I want to thank Franci Steinmuller, who read early drafts of the manuscript and made copious notes, rewrote sentences, challenged ideas, and occasionally wrote a sentence or two as a suggested improvement. I also want to thank Adam Neaman and Heidi Levin for their help in the preparation of the manuscript of *Dynamic Memory Revisited*.

Roger C. Schank
Palm Beach, Florida
February 1998

CHAPTER 1

Introduction to Dynamic Memory

What is a dynamic memory? It is a flexible, open-ended system. Compare the way an expert stores knowledge about books in his field to the way a library catalog system does the same job. In a library, an initial set of categories is chosen to describe a domain of knowledge. Within those categories, titles, authors, and subjects of the books are recorded. Such a system is not *dynamic.* Eventually, the categories will have to be changed; overutilized categories will require updating; other categories will have to be created to handle new subjects and subject divisions.

A library does not have a dynamic memory. It changes with great difficulty. More important, to change it requires outside intervention. An expert has neither of these problems. He can change his internal classification system easily when his interests change, or when his knowledge of a particular subject matter changes. For the most part, these changes are not conscious. The expert may relate one idea to another or he may fail to do so. He knows when he knows something, but there is a lot he doesn't know he knows. He may be able to categorize without knowing the categorization scheme he uses. He can make observations about what he knows and thus can alter the memory structures that catalog what he knows. He can do this without even realizing he has done it. He has a dynamic memory.[1]

Libraries require physical space, and decisions must be made about how to use it and when to leave certain areas open for future use. Knowing where you want to put a book, or information about this book, requires having some preconception of the possible places available for it in the library. But there would be disastrous consequences if our memories got stuck with "empty floors" awaiting collections that never materialized. Worse yet, imagine if we didn't have room in our category schemes for unanticipated new materials. We need a category

---

[1] For an example of research on category formation, see Ross, 1996a; Ross, 1996b.

scheme that can change not only as we acquire new knowledge, but also as we change our understandings (and thus classifications) of our knowledge.

The problem for libraries in this regard is no doubt great. People, on the other hand, seem to be able to cope with new information with ease. We can readily find a place to store new information in our memories, although we don't know where or what that location is. This is all handled unconsciously. We can also find old information, but again we don't know where we found it and we can't really say what the look-up procedure might have been. Our memories change dynamically in the way they store information by abstracting significant generalizations from our experiences and storing the exceptions to those generalizations. As we have more experiences, we alter our generalizations and categorizations of information to meet our current needs and to account for our new experiences (Wattenmaker, 1992; Ross, 1996b).[2] Despite constant changes in organization, we continue to be able to call up relevant memories without consciously considering where we have stored them. People are not aware of their own cataloging schemes, they are just capable of using them.

Consciousness does not extend to an awareness of how we encode or retrieve experiences. Our dynamic memories seem to organize themselves in such a way as to be able to adjust their initial encodings of the world to reflect growth and new understanding. Our memories are structured in a way that allows us to learn from our experiences. They can reorganize to reflect new generalizations – in a way, a kind of automatic categorization scheme – that can be used to process new experiences on the basis of old ones. In short, our memories dynamically adjust to reflect our experiences. A dynamic memory is one that can change its own organization when new experiences demand it. A dynamic memory is by nature a learning system.

Thinking about Artificial Intelligence

Prior to the writing of the first edition of this book, my primary focus in artificial intelligence (AI) had been on the problem of getting computers to be able to read. I had selected this focus because I felt that language and its use were a window into human understanding. After the first edition of this book was written, and in response to the

---

[2] Also Metcalfe (1993).

issues it raised, my colleagues and I began working on the issues of knowledge acquisition, learning, memory, and what came to be called case-based reasoning. Although we were successful in getting computers to read stories (see DeJong, 1977; Cullingford, 1978; Wilensky, 1978; Dyer and Lehnert, 1980 for descriptions of some of the programs we wrote at Yale), the creation of the programs themselves forced us to reconsider what reading a story means. Being able to answer questions about what was read, or summarizing or translating what was read, which were the tasks we chose for ourselves, was not sufficient to convince us or anyone else that these programs were actually reading.

The reason we were unconvinced was that these programs didn't remember, in any real sense, what they had read. Our programs were successful enough that we would show them off regularly. To do this, we had a ready supply of newspaper stories that we knew the computer would read accurately. I began to worry, however, that our programs never got bored. They read the same story about an earthquake in Iran over and over again, but never once exclaimed that there had been an extraordinary number of Iranian earthquakes lately or that they were mighty tired of reading the same story repeatedly.

It is hard to swallow the idea that a computer program that fails to remember what it has just read can be said to be comprehending. We tried, during the course of our work in creating computer programs that understand language, to avoid the issues of memory and learning. Language is hard enough to get a computer to process; did we have to work on memory and learning too? Well, yes, we did. The separation of language and memory is quite artificial. Linguists have always tried to separate the two to make their lives easier. Because I came from that tradition, it seemed reasonable to me to do the same. But the differences between people and computers began to nag me. People don't read yesterday's newspaper a second time unless they were powerfully impressed with it the first time or else have nothing else to read. People get bored and irritated by being asked to read something again and again, but our computer programs never did. They didn't learn from what they read. They merely coped with the mechanistic problems of language. That is, they were trying to piece out meanings without enhancing the meaning of those meanings to themselves. To put this another way, they didn't want to know the information contained in the stories they read.

Language is a memory-based process. It is a medium by which

thoughts in one memory can, to some extent, be communicated in order to influence the contents of another memory. It is only one of several vehicles used to pass information from one memory to another. All of the senses can affect memory; language is an encoding of one kind of sense datum. Any theory of language must refer to a theory of memory, and any theory of memory is a theory of learning. No human memory is static; with each new input, with every experience, a memory must readjust itself. Learning means altering memory in response to experiences. It thus depends upon the alteration of knowledge structures that reside in memory.

In the work that preceded the original *Dynamic Memory*, we attempted to provide some view of how knowledge structures might represent information about events. In Schank and Abelson (1977), we developed the notion of a script. We defined script as a knowledge structure useful in the processing of text to the extent that it directed the inference process and tied together pieces of input. Input sentences were connected together by referring to the overall structure of the script to which they made reference. Thus, scripts were, in our view, a kind of high-level knowledge structure that could be called upon to supply background information during the understanding process. As embodied in the computer programs we wrote, they were essentially sets of predictions of event sequences. A script was constituted as a list of events that compose a stereotypical episode. Input events that matched one or more of the events in the list would cause the program to infer that the other events in the list had also taken place.

Since the publication of Schank and Abelson in 1977, some psychologists have found the notion of a script useful in explaining the behavior of children (Nelson, 1979; Nelson and Gruendel, 1979; McCartney and Nelson, 1981; Fivush, 1984; Slackman and Nelson, 1984; Adams and Worden, 1986; Hull Smith et al., 1989) and adults (Bower, 1978; Jebousek, 1978; Smith, Adams and Schorr, 1978; Graesser, Gordon and Sawyer, 1979; Graesser et al. 1980) engaged in the language comprehension process. Thus, some of the representations we proposed seem to have some psychological validity (Abelson, 1980; Graesser, 1981; Ratner, Smith and Dion, 1986; Bauer and Mandler, 1990; Farrar and Goodman 1992).

Considering language as a memory process changed our view of how understanding works. We now see language understanding as an integrated process. People don't understand things without making reference to what they already know and to what they think about what is being said. We don't break down the task of understanding language into small components. Rather, understanding is entirely a process of relating what we are hearing or experiencing to what we already know. In contrast to this, our early models were modular in nature, breaking the task of understanding into discrete and serially executed components. For example, SAM, our original story comprehension program, had a modular organization (Cullingford, 1978). After translating a sentence into Conceptual Dependency, the meaning representation scheme described in Schank (1972), SAM began the process of script application, which involves the recognition that a given script applies in a situation.

When a script was successfully identified, a set of predictions was made about what events were likely to transpire. We knew that such a modular approach was unrealistic – surely people begin to understand what a sentence is about before it is completely uttered. We built SAM in a modular fashion because that was the easiest way to work out the mechanics of script application; divorcing the parsing process from the process of script application simplified matters. But scripts are the sources of memories, and how we understand is affected by what is in our memories. A coherent theory of the structures in memory must naturally precede a complete theory of language understanding.

To solve problems involved in building understanding systems, we needed first to understand the kinds of high-level knowledge structures available in the understanding process. An important question that guides this work is, What else is available to an understanding system besides scripts? In the computer programs PAM (Wilensky, 1978) and POLITICS (Carbonell, 1979), we used plans and goals as high-level structures that control understanding. They served to help these programs make predictions based on story fragments. Certainly any memory must have access to such structures. But how many different sources of predictions are there? How can we find out what various knowledge structures are like?

The focus of the original version of this book was on building computer systems that understand. It became clear that to build such systems, we needed to build systems that learned as well. We know memories change over time. A person is changed in some way by every new sentence he processes. Smart computers would have to learn as well. However, we weren't (and aren't) interested primarily in computers. Computer programs help us make precise theories. They provide the rigor that is sorely lacking in most psychological theories. But, in the end, it is people who are the interesting subject. And, it became clear that if we wanted to know about how people processed language, we were going to have to study learning. So, we needed to study how the mind adapts to new information and derives new knowledge from that information. To do all this we needed a coherent theory of adaptable memory structures. We needed to understand how new information changes memory. We realized that learning requires a dynamic memory.

A dynamic memory would have to rely upon some scheme for structuring and restructuring its knowledge, a way of altering the structures it had previously found useful if their value faded or, alternatively, became more important. What is this system of organization, what do these structures look like, and how did they develop? It is unlikely that high-level structures in memory are innate. They develop because they address the needs that arise during processing by the individual understander, and different individuals have different needs. We know that our experiences affect the development of memory structures.

Scripts Revisited

In this book, I develop a theory of the high-level memory structures that constitute a dynamic memory. As mentioned, this theory of dynamic memory has its base in the older theory of processing natural language developed in Schank and Abelson (1977). From that earlier work came an idea critical to understanding how humans decide what to do and how they understand what others do – the concept of scripts described previously. In those days, scripts were intended to account for our ability to understand more than was being referred to explicitly in a sentence by explaining the organization of implicit knowledge of the world we inhabit. Thus, when John orders sushi, we assume that he is in a Japanese restaurant, that he might be seated at a sushi bar, and that he is probably using chopsticks and not a fork; we can even assume he is drinking Japanese beer. We assume these things because we know the sushi bar script. If we do not know this script, we cannot make such assumptions and thus might have difficulty understanding various sentences that refer to things we might be assumed to know.

Scripts enable people to understand sentences that are less than complete in what they refer to. When we hear "John ordered sushi but he didn't like it," we know that this sentence is referring to eating and to John's reaction to a type of taste sensation that he doesn't like. We know this because of what we know about restaurants (the restaurant script) and because of what we know about a small specification of the restaurant script, namely "sushi tasting." When we hear "John flew to New York, and he was very unhappy with the meal," we now must invoke the airplane script to understand the sentence. We do not imagine John flapped his arms to get to New York, nor that he was in a flying restaurant. We can explain what happened to him by saying that "airline food isn't very good," because we know the details of the airplane script, which include that kind of information.

We were originally interested in how a computer might process an experience such as this, and in that spirit we proposed that scripts and other knowledge structures were part of the apparatus that a knowledgeable entity would have to bring to bear during understanding. We endeavored to find out what kinds of structures might be available for use in processing. In general, we ignored the problems of the development of such structures, the ability of the proposed structures to change themselves, and the problems of retrieval and storage of information posed by those structures. We concentrated instead on issues of processing.

However, it seems clear in hindsight that no computer could simply be spoon-fed a script and be able to effectively function with it. What we know of restaurants is acquired in part by going out to eat, and by a process of constant reexamination of one's expectations in the light of their utility in processing a current experience. Thus, learning itself is at the heart of any knowledgeable entity because whatever knowledge might be attained by that entity would have to be malleable enough to be found and changed as a result of experience.

It is in this spirit that we must reexamine the notion of a script. Scripts have been taken to mean *some high-level knowledge source* and thus, given that there are probably a great many varieties of possible knowledge sources, different claims have been made for scripts that on occasion conflict with one another. In our early research we differentiated between plans and scripts, for example, but that distinction has not always been clear. Frequently, when we presented the issue of plans and goals, we were asked why *robbing a liquor store* was a plan and not a script, or why *reading the Michelin Guide* was not a script. The link between scripts and plans seemed fuzzy. For *liquor store robbing* to be a script and not a plan, it would have had to have been done a great many times. Of course such a thing might very well be a script for some people. We had chosen it as an instance of a plan because we were trying to illustrate the process of plan application, which was very different in nature from that of script application. In plan application, inferences about goals are made in order to establish the connections between input actions and the achievement of some goal. The most important point about script application is that often such goal-related inferences cannot be made. For example, without knowledge of the Japanese restaurant script, there is no way to determine why customers take off their shoes when they arrive.

The difference, then, between scripts and plans or any high-level knowledge structure resides in the amount of processing needed to come to understand a situation. The less one knows about a situation, or the less familiar one is with a certain kind of situation, the more inference work one has to do in order to process inputs dealing with that situation. Using scripts involves less work; planning implies more work. Scripts are a kind of mindless mental structure that allows one not to have to think too hard.

Our initial definition of a script was *a structure that describes an appropriate sequence of events in a particular context* or *a predetermined stereotyped sequence of actions that defines a well-known situation* (Schank and Abelson, 1975). The archetype that used scripts was SAM (Schank, 1975; Cullingford, 1978), a program to understand stories that used restaurants as their background. The idea was that we could short-cut the inference process by having certain inferences "come for free" because a script had been found to be relevant. When it was known that a story took place in a restaurant, all kinds of inferences – from table settings to check paying – became just that much easier to make.

Restaurant stories being neither plentiful nor very interesting, we began to look for new domains after we had initially demonstrated the power of script-based processing in our computer programs. We chose car accidents because of their ubiquity in the newspapers and their essential simplicity, and we began to alter SAM to handle these. Immediately we ran into the problem of what exactly a script was. Is there a *car accident* script? A computer could certainly use one to help it process such stories, but that would not imply that most people naturally would have acquired such a script. People who have never been in a car accident would not have a car accident script in the same sense that they might be said to have a restaurant script. Certainly the method of acquisition would be vastly different. Furthermore, the ordered, step-by-step nature of a script, that is, its essential stereotypical nature due to common cultural convention, was different.

This was emphasized in the way that a car accident script actually could be used to handle newspaper stories. Whenever a car accident occurred, we had to expect at least an ambulance script, a hospital emergency room script, a police report, possibly a subsequent trial script, and perhaps others as well, to be present. Were all these things really scripts? And, if they were, why was it that they seemed so different from the restaurant script in acquisition, use, and predictive power? To put it another way, it seemed all right to say that people know that in a restaurant you can either read a menu and order, or stand in line for your food. We felt justified in saying that there were many different *tracks* to a restaurant script, but that each of these tracks was essentially a form of the larger script. That is, they were like each other in important ways and might be expected to be stored with each other within the same overall outer structure in memory.

But what of accidents? Was there a general accident script of which collisions, accidental shootings, and falling out of windows were different tracks? Alternatively, was there a vehicle accident script of which those involving cars, trucks, and motorcycles were different tracks? Or was there a car accident script of which one car hitting an obstruction, two cars colliding, and chain reactions were different tracks?

It turned out for the purpose of creating SAM that none of this mattered. We encoded it all as scripts and allowed certain scripts to fire off other scripts to handle the sequence. However, the fact that we could make it work on a computer this way is basically irrelevant to the issue of the ultimate form and place of scripts in human memory. Did the fact that it worked in SAM really suggest that for people the emergency room script is in some important way a part of the car accident script? Although the idea of a general accident script seems to contradict an experientially based definition of scripts, that would have worked in SAM as well.

Gradually then, a practical definition of scripts was beginning to emerge that bore only surface similarity to the theoretical notion of scripts as a knowledge source for controlling inferences and tying together texts in highly constrained and stereotypical domains. This practical definition was that a script was a data structure that was a useful source of predictions. Scripts were supposed to depend on issues related to development based on repeated experience. But our use of scripts was not in agreement with our theory.

Whenever a script was accessed and an initial pattern match for an input made, the script could be used to predict what was coming next, or to take what did come next and place it within the overall pattern. In SAM's terms, a script was a gigantic pattern that could be matched partially in a piecemeal fashion.

This problem of precisely defining scripts became even more difficult when work began on FRUMP (DeJong, 1977). FRUMP is a program that was intended as a practical script-based approach to story understanding. SAM was rather slow and exceedingly fragile, since it made every inference within a script that was there to be made and, in doing so, had to rely upon an immense vocabulary and world knowledge store. Because the stories SAM read came from the newspapers, an unexpected vocabulary item was not only possible, it was rather likely. SAM had very little ability to recover from problems caused by missing vocabulary or missing world knowledge. (Later, a program was designed to take care of this to some extent; Granger, 1977.)

FRUMP got around these problems by relying more heavily on the predictive nature of scripts and less heavily on what the text actually said. FRUMP did not actually parse the input it received. Rather, it predicted what it would see and went about looking for words, phrases, or meanings that substantiated its predictions, relying upon what we termed *sketchy scripts* to do so. Examples of sketchy scripts included earthquakes, breaking diplomatic relations, wars, arson, and snow-storms. In other words, nearly anything at all could be considered a sketchy script (including robbing a liquor store, which put us back to square one). The theoretical difference between SAM's scripts and FRUMP's sketchy scripts is negligible. FRUMP's scripts are simply shorter and contain less information.

FRUMP's scripts are essentially just a set of "requests" (Riesbeck, 1975), which is another way of saying that they constitute a set of predictions about what might happen, and a set of rules about what to assume if those predictions are, or if they are not, fulfilled. But the concept of a script as an organized set of predictions is not exactly what we originally had in mind. It is easy to see why – for FRUMP – earthquakes and breaking diplomatic relations can be scripts.

But if earthquakes are scripts, then what is a script, anyway? Few of us have ever actually been in an earthquake; even fewer of us have, for example, broken diplomatic relations. But we do have knowledge about such events that can be used to understand stories about them or to handle similar situations. This knowledge can be encoded as sets of rules about what happens in general in disasters or in negative relationships between countries. Are such sets of rules scripts?

It really doesn't matter what we call them. Clearly both people and computers need knowledge structures in order to process what goes on around them. You need to know you are watching baseball in order to know that a man swinging a hunk of wood has done a good thing by swatting some small white thing a great distance. Knowledge structures help us make sense of the world around us. So, the issue is, what knowledge structures do we have and how do we acquire them?

Understanding how knowledge structures are acquired helps us understand what kinds of entities they are. Learning depends upon knowledge and knowledge depends upon learning. What kind of knowledge do we have about negative relations between countries? To understand how such knowledge resides in memory, we must find out how that knowledge was first acquired. Most likely, it was acquired through our knowledge of the methods we use to deal with someone else in a negative way, and then abstracted in such a way as to be relevant to international relations. We know, for instance, how we deal with other people, and we can use that knowledge to drive our understanding of international relations. But experts at international relations need to become more sophisticated. They need to take what they know and embellish it with generalizations of their relevant experiences in a new domain. Similarly, outside of the knowledge specifically associated with car accidents (e.g., that crashes can be caused by drunk drivers; that the police will file an accident report), most of our initially relevant knowledge in a car accident is true in any serious accident or, in fact, in any negative physical event. But, later, after we have had a few accidents, we embellish what we know.

The distinction then between scripts and other high-level knowledge structures hinges upon the notions of abstraction and generalization. Scripts are specific sets of information associated with specific situations that frequently repeat themselves. Scripts are a source of information, naturally acquired by our having undergone an experience many times. A script can be considered to be a very specific set of sequential facts about a very specific situation.

But people also have general information associated with general situations such as negative relationships between countries or natural physical disasters. This general information is very likely related to specific script-related information. The usual method of acquisition of script-based information is direct, repeated experience, but people also acquire general information in a more complex fashion by abstracting and generalizing from multiple experiences and from the experiences of others.

In addition, if there are two different kinds of information in memory (specific structures based directly upon experience and general structures containing more abstract information), it follows that the methods of storage in memory and retrieval from memory for both kinds of structures might also be different. In comprehending the breaking of diplomatic relations, we can use information stored under the historical relationship between two countries, their position in the world political situation, or their economic relationship, as well as information about what individuals say when they are angered or want to protest another's actions. All of this information cannot logically be stored in only one place in memory; rather, it must be obtained from multiple sources by many different retrieval methods. To not do this, to have all this information stored in only one location, is to have a script.

The difference, then, between a script-based memory and a memory based upon more general structures is that, in the first case, what we know in a given situation comes from what we have experienced in more or less identical situations. In the second case, using more general structures allows us to make use of information originally garnered from one situation to help us in a quite different situation. General knowledge structures save space and make information experienced in one situation available for use in another. One disadvantage of the script-based method is its lack of usability in similar but nonidentical situations. Reliance upon scripts inhibits learning from experience (Slackman and Nelson, 1984; Hudson and Nelson, 1986).

But scripts do have an advantage. We have knowledge specific to particular situations. People can remember individual experiences and use those experiences to help them in processing similar experiences. Generalized information that eliminates particular differences will lose some information, and this lost information may be valuable (Slackman and Nelson, 1984; Farrar and Goodman, 1990). But without generalizations, we learn very little. Human memory constantly attempts generalizations in order to learn, and abandons them when they fail.[3] Our task is to understand how that process works.

In summary, one can say that in any knowledge-based under-

---

[3] See Adams and Worden (1986), Hudson and Nelson (1986), and Hudson, Fivush and Kuebli (1992) for work on how children utilize scripts.

standing system, any given set of facts can be stored in either a script-based or a non–script-based form. If we choose to give up generalizability, we buy efficiency in the short term. Knowing a great deal about the domain we are in, and that domain only, will work for any system that never transcends the boundaries of a given domain. Any knowing system must be able to know a great deal about one domain without losing the power to apply generalizations drawn from that knowledge to a different domain. We must ask ourselves what human memory is like, how it got that way, and why it functions the way it does. By answering this question we can more effectively determine the relevance and place of any knowledge structure in memory.

Generalized Scripts

Before we begin our examination of issues in memory from a purely observational perspective, there is a piece of psychological evidence derived from more conventional experimental methods that bears on what we shall have to say. This work was done by Bower, Black and Turner (1979). For our purposes, in addition to the demonstration that scriptlike considerations are relevant in story understanding, one of the most valuable things to come out of that work was a problem it presented that led us to the realization that there are different types of organizing knowledge structures in memory. Recognition confusions were found by Bower and his colleagues to occur between stories that called upon similar scripts, such as visits to the dentist or doctor. In no intuitive sense can this result be called surprising; most people have experienced such confusions. It seems plain that in order to confuse doctor visits and dentist visits, some structure in memory is used by both stories during processing. However, if we posit a *visit to a health care professional* script in order to explain the confusion, we will have created an entity that has considerable drawbacks. In our 1977 terms, such an entity could not be considered a script because scripts were supposed to reflect knowledge derived from specific experiences in specific situations. To form the *health care professional* script, the general parts of some similar scripts would have to have been abstracted and stored at some higher level. Such a suggestion plays havoc with the original idea of a script.

The assumption here is that scripts are not merely useful data structures for processing, but that they are memory structures as well. As a memory structure, we might ask why, if we used the dentist script (hence $DENTIST) to interpret a relevant story, the remembrance of the story would get confused with one that used $DOCTOR. After all, two different structures used in processing ought not to get confused with each other. But if we assume that some structure that was a superset of those two was used, for example, $HEALTH CARE VISIT, such a structure would not account for the possible confusion of a dentist story with a visit to an accountant's office. It might be that an even more abstract structure such as $OFFICE VISIT was being used, but that kind of entity is getting more and more separated from any specific experience or reasonable group set of experiences. If information is stored at such a high level of abstraction, then understanding a story becomes much more complex than we had initially imagined. We cannot get away with simply applying the most relevant script, even in what appear to be very stereotyped and script-based situations, because a great many entities such as $OFFICE VISIT are likely to be relevant at one time.

If we can get confused between events that occurred in a dentist visit and those that occurred in a visit to an accountant's office, then the phenomenon observed by Bower, Black and Turner is too complex to be handled by invented generalized scripts such as $HEALTH CARE VISIT. On the other hand, we are certainly not storing new inputs about dentists in terms of a visit to an accountant. One possibility is that there is no dentist script in memory in the form we had previously suggested. At the same time, generalized scripts such as $HEALTH CARE VISIT probably do not exist either.

Any solution one proposes to the problem of what the correct kind of memory structure is, must be formulated in human memory terms. Clearly one can construct a program that uses a dentist script to understand stories where a dentist's office is the background context. That is not the issue. The issue is one of extensibility. Just because one can construct a program to do something in a particular way using a particular method, does not indicate that that program will be naturally extensible. If it is not naturally extensible, then it is unlikely to have much value as a psychological theory. Its only value as a program is as a test for the viability of its basic assumptions as process models (or as a program with practical value, if it turns out have any). So henceforth I will evaluate the notion of scripts in memory terms, rather than considering their value in a program. Furthermore, I shall consider scripts and other memory structures from the point of view of their ability to change through experience. A script, and any other memory structure, must be part of a dynamic memory. Any structure proposed for memory must be capable of self-modification. If it is not, then one must question its psychological validity. Thus, when I ask if there is a dentist script, I mean to ask, Is there one unique structure in human memory directly containing the information necessary for processing a story about a visit to a dentist? And, if such a structure does exist, what is the method by which such a structure would be modified as a result of experiences relevant to that structure but not completely predicted by it?

To answer these questions, one must examine the kinds of information that need to be stored in memory, as well as the likely methods of storing that information. The overall issue here is the level of generality of the information that is stored. One must ascertain what the most economical storage scheme is and whether such a scheme is likely to have psychological plausibility.

To start, therefore, I ask, What kinds of things is a person likely to remember? Obviously, a person can remember in some detail, for a short period of time, a particular experience. But after a while, the details will be forgotten, unless those details were interesting or unusual in some way.

Consider an experience of mine, a trip to Palo Alto, a place I have traveled to many times, and also have lived in. During the trip, I could answer questions about what hotel I was staying in; what my room number was and how much the hotel cost; what kind and color car I had rented and from what agency, and so on. In short, the details of the trip, even the petty details, were available immediately during or after the experience.

After a week or two, most of the details of my trip were probably completely forgotten. Indeed, after an hour or two, details such as what song was playing on the car radio, or the color of the rent-a-car pick-up van, were certainly forgotten. Why? How is it some parts of the experience are forgotten and some are not?

Psychologists have differentiated between short-term memory and long-term memory. Short-term memory lasts seconds, not hours. It is likely that there is a kind of intermediate-term memory that utilizes temporary memory structures. Whether an intermediate-term memory item gets retained in long-term memory depends on the significance of that item with respect to other items already retained in long-term memory. That is, we remember only what is relevant. The memory of some events in an episode last forever; others are forgotten almost instantly. Clearly there is a kind of selection process at work that picks some memories for special treatment by retaining them for long-term memory. It is the nature of this selection mechanism and the nature of the types of memories that do not fade quickly that are the key problems before us.

After a year or more, I only remembered a few particularly interesting details of this trip. If I had taken many trips to Palo Alto that year, then it is even more likely that the details of one particular trip would be unretrievable.

Some of the details could be reconstructed, however. For example, although I might not remember which rental car company or which hotel was used, it is often the case that people asked to answer such questions can do so with the following kinds of reasoning:

a) I always stay at the Holiday Inn, so that's where I would have stayed.
b) There are only two rent-a-car agencies that I have ever used and I had received my Hertz discount card around that time, so it would have been Hertz.
c) I can't recall the room number but I remember where it was and I could take you there (or nearly there).

Such answers are instances of what is commonly called reconstructive memory. The questions for a reconstructive view of memory are these:

1. What is actually stored in memory and how is that information stored such that reconstruction can take place?
2. What different kinds of reconstruction are there?

The three answers about my trip require very different kinds of reconstructive capabilities. For each question, the methods that effect the recall are very different and the places searched are very different.

Among the kinds of structures searched in reconstruction would seem to be those that encode a general, abstract view of how things happen in some category of events. In this way, particular instances in that category can be assumed to have followed the general rule. In our memories there are facts about certain things in general – what a hotel is like, how to rent a car, what a dentist visit is like – that are crucial to the reconstructing process, and these facts form an important part of our ability to remember (really, to reconstruct). Thus, we can recall something by recalling the prototype for that event rather than the event itself and *coloring* the general memory with whatever specifics might be available. Such prototypes exist because people have experienced these events so often that they have generalized them.[4] Even when a specific episode is chosen, the smallest details will usually not be available. Thus, with either recall approach, general memory structures are used for reconstruction (Slackman and Nelson, 1984; Myles-Worsely, Cromer and Dodd, 1986; Farrar and Goodman, 1990).

The role of such general memory structures in processing is to understand input events by noticing that they completely match the default representation present in the general structure. When an identical match is noticed, an episode can be forgotten. *Hearing the radio in the car* is so normative for some people, that is, it matches their general structure for *car driving* so well, and is of so little consequence, that it can be forgotten.

The use of such general structures in memory is twofold. On one hand, these structures help us decide what to pay attention to: If an item is matched by a general structure, it is understood as being of no use to remember. On the other hand, when an experienced event differs from the general structure, its difference may be noted. Noticing and recalling differences enables learning. We modify our old structures on the basis of mismatches. This is what dynamic memory is all about. The process of learning by explaining expectation failures engendered by predictions encoded in high-level memory structures is the subject of this book.

Finding Relevant Structures

I am suggesting, then, that by utilizing general structures to encode what we know in memory, we can learn – particularly if our experiences differ from those general structures. Thus, what is actually stored in long-term memory are those episodes that differ from the norm.[5] I am further saying that, given enough differences from the norm, it is necessary to adjust our memory structures accordingly, so as to begin to create new general structures that account for those differences. That is, just because an episode is new once, it does not fol-

---

[4] For examples, see Fivush (1984), Hull Smith et al. (1989), Bauer and Mandler (1990), and Farrar and Goodman (1992).
[5] For examples, see Adams and Worden (1986), Hudson and Nelson (1986), De Graef, Christaens and d'Ydewalle (1990), and Hudson, Fivush and Kuebli (1992).

low that it will be forever new. Eventually we will recognize what was once novel as "old hat." To do this, we must be constantly modifying our general structures, which is what I mean by a dynamic memory.

Thus, one must be concerned with the issue of how a memory structure is changed. In order to do this, one must address the issue of how a memory structure is found to be relevant in the first place. That is, how do we decide to use a given memory structure when we read a story or undergo an experience?

To consider this problem, imagine trying to answer the question, When was the last time you rented a car? It seems impossible to answer this question without asking yourself why you would have rented a car, establishing that it would probably have been on a trip, and then beginning to look for recent trips. In other words, *trips* provides a context in which to search for relevant general memory structures, whereas *rent a car* does not. How do we explain this? Why is *trip* a source of memories and *rent a car* not?

One possibility is that memory contains at least two kinds of entities, structures (that contain specific memories indexed in terms of their differences from the norm in that structure) and organizers of structures. One kind of structure is a *scene*. A scene provides a physical setting that serves as the basis for reconstruction. Some organizing entity must help point out the most appropriate scene. For example, in trying to answer a question about a previously rented car (e.g., color, make, or place of rental), the rent-a-car scene itself is of little use because it is not likely to contain memories relevant to specific aspects of the last car you rented. It would be possible to remember the color of the rental agreement by accessing the rent-a-car scene, however. One major difficulty in memory retrieval is finding the scene with the memory most relevant to the information being sought.

What kinds of things serve as organizers of scenes? What kinds of contexts are there? A scene is likely to be ordered by using different contexts. A *trip* structure in memory would indicate which scenes normally follow each other in a trip. *Trip* would also include information about hotel rooms or airports. Many other organizing structures can also point to these things. Thus, whereas a hotel room is a scene, it is a scene that can be expected to be part of a great many different structures. A hotel room can be part of the hotel structure, the trip structure, the visit structure, or a structure involving a place (e.g., a hotel room in Hawaii). There are also less physical kinds of structures of which hotel rooms can be a part (e.g., arguments, business deals, triumphs, frustrations). In other words, the scene *hotel room* is likely to have specific memories included in it, but those memories can be accessed by many higher-level structures.

In searching for a memory, then, we are just looking for an appropriate organizing structure. This structure provides a set of clues as to what scenes to look at, and, most important, how to set up those scenes so that we can find what we are looking for.

The Place of Scripts

What, then, has happened to specific structures, namely scripts? For example, what is the dentist script and where can it be found in memory? I will suggest that there is no dentist script in memory at all, at least not in the form of a list of events of the kind previously postulated. A more reasonable organization of memory would allow for scriptlike structures to be embedded as standardizations of various general scenes. For example, a *waiting room* scene might encode events in one or more standardized ways. Thus, we might expect that there is a DOCTOR JONES' WAITING ROOM script or a standardized DENTIST'S WAITING ROOM script attached to the waiting room scene. When available, such scripts would make specific, detailed, expectations that override more general expectations that come from higher-level scenes. We will see how this works in Chapter 6.

What I am saying, then, is that the dentist script itself does not actually exist in memory in one precompiled chunk. Rather, it, or actually its subparts, can be constructed to be used as needed from the various scenes connected with the experience of visiting a dentist. Thus, we have two kinds of information with respect to visiting a dentist. We have information about what scenes, or other general structures, compose a trip to the dentist, and we have information about what specific colorations of each scene are made because it is a dentist's waiting room (or a particular dentist's waiting room), and not a lawyer's. Specific memories, standardized as scripts or not, are thus attached to more general memories to which they relate.

The economy of such a scheme is very important. Scenes transcend the specifics of a situation, so they capture generalities. Specifics are added by other structures. The construction of what was previously called the dentist script is actually done on demand during processing time, by searching for information from general organizing structures that tell which scenes will be relevant for processing.

The main issues, then, are ascertaining which high-level structures are likely to be used in memory; explaining how the information contained in those structures gets used in processing new inputs and recalling old ones; explaining how the experiences that have been processed change memory; explaining how learning works; and understanding which of these processes are known to us and which underlie our conscious processing abilities. I shall now attempt to answer these questions.

CHAPTER 2

Reminding and Memory

Reminding

Any memory system must have the ability to cope with new information in a reasonable way, so that new input causes adjustments in the system. A dynamic memory system is altered in some way by every experience it processes. A memory system that fails to learn from its experiences is unlikely to be very useful. In addition, any good memory system must be capable of finding what is contained within itself. This seems to go without saying, but the issue of *what* to find can be quite a problem. When we process events as they happen, we need to find particular episodes in memory that are closely related to the current input we are processing. But how do we define relatedness? What does it mean for one experience to be like another? Under what labels, using what indices, do we look for related episodes?

The phenomenon of reminding sheds light on both the problem of retrieval and our ability to learn. This crucial aspect of human memory received little attention from researchers on memory prior to the first edition of this book. (For example, in a highly regarded book that attempts to catalog research by psychologists on memory [Crowder 1976], *reminding* does not even appear in the subject index.) Yet reminding is an everyday occurrence, a common feature of memory. We are reminded of one person by another, or of one building by another. More significant are the remindings that occur across situations. One event can remind you of another.

Why does this happen? Far from being an irrelevant aspect of memory, reminding is at the root of how we understand and how we learn. If a current event failed to remind us of a similar previous event, how could we possibly generalize and learn the lesson that the combination of both has to teach? If we encountered an experience and treated it each time as a new experience because we failed to relate it to our prior memories of that experience, we would seem stupid. We cannot continue to visit a restaurant, for example, and each time act as if we had never been there before. The restaurant must remind us of having been there before.

At the outset, it is important to distinguish the following broad classes of reminding, since they tend to have different effects in an understanding system and must be accounted for in different ways:

1. Physical objects can remind you of other physical objects.
2. Physical objects can remind you of events.
3. Events can remind you of physical objects.
4. Events can remind you of events in the same domain.
5. Events can remind you of events in different domains.
6. New experiences can remind you of prototypical cases that characterize such experiences.
7. Abstract ideas can remind you of related ideas.

To the extent that reminding can tell us about the nature and organization of the episodic memory system, the most interesting situations would be those in which, in the normal course of attempting to understand an event, we are able to find a particular event in memory that in some way relates to the processing of that event. The organization of a dynamic episodic memory system depends upon the use of that system in understanding. Reminding occurs as a natural part of the process of understanding new situations in terms of previously processed situations even though it is not always obvious to us why this happens (Ross, 1984; Ross and Kennedy, 1990). Understanding exactly how human memory controls processing and gets naturally reminded is important.

Why one experience reminds you of another is of primary importance to any theory of human understanding and memory. If people are reminded of things during the natural course of a conversation, or while reading, or when seeing something, then this tells us something of importance about the understanding process. Given the assumption that understanding an event means finding an appropriate place for a representation of that event in memory, reminding would indicate that a specific episode in memory has been excited or *seen* during the natural course of processing the new input. To be reminded of something, we must come across it while we are processing the new input. If the explanation of reminding is that we find an episode because we are looking for it, we must ask ourselves how we knew of that episode's existence and were thus able to look for it. If, however, the explanation of reminding is that we accidentally run into an episode, we must ask why that accident occurs, and whether that accident has relevance to our processing.

I will argue here that it is an amalgamation of these two explanations that provides us with the method by which reminding takes place. We are not consciously looking for a particular episode in memory during processing, because we do not explicitly know of that episode's existence. We have particular, unusual memories stored away, but they are not readily accessible. We are, however, capable of finding *types* of episodes. We may not be able to itemize every interesting restaurant we have ever been to, but we do know, for instance, what restaurants in general are like. In processing a new restaurant situation we seek this general knowledge. Our method of processing new episodes utilizes memory structures that point to the unusual episodes that are closely related to the new episode. Reminding occurs when the most appropriate structure in memory that will help in processing a new input is unusual in some way, when it is one of the weird experiences we have had and have stored away for just this eventuality. When no particular unusual episode is closely related to an input, we can process the input by using our general knowledge of that type of situation, and no reminding occurs. (If we are reminded of a prototypical episode, it doesn't feel like a reminding at all, and we may not notice it. We learn very little from such remindings, although they help us in the comprehension process.)

The more you know about a subject, clearly the more you can be reminded about it within the course of processing related inputs. Thus, experts in particular fields might be expected to have reminding experiences directly tied in with their expertise. For certain people, we might expect reminding experiences corresponding to

1. known chess patterns
2. known political patterns
3. previously encountered similar situations
4. patterns of behavior of a particular individual
5. relatedness of scientific theories
6. types of football plays
7. kinds of music or paintings

Why is it that some people are reminded of a famous chess game upon viewing another game and some people are not? The answer is that not everyone has knowledge of famous chess games. Obvious as this may be, it says something very important about memory: We use what we know to help us process what we receive. We would be quite surprised if a chess expert were *not* reminded of a famous chess game upon seeing one just like it. The fact that these are *famous* chess games reflects the fact that they are unusual episodes. We expect an expert to have categorized his experiences in such a way as to have these episodes available for aid in processing new experiences. Classification, then, is a mechanism used in the process of problem solving (Ross, Perkins and Tenpenny, 1990; Ross, 1996a).

Looked at another way, one can say that experts are experts because they are constantly learning about their domain of expertise. Thus experts are interested in acquiring sufficient cases so they can learn to detect nuances and be able to compare and contrast various experiences. To do this, they need to have had those experiences and to have properly labeled them. Thus, reminding is not a phenomenon that just happens to occur to some people at some times. It is a phenomenon that must occur in an individual who has a certain set of knowledge organized in a fashion that is likely to bring that knowledge to bear at a certain time. Or, to put this another way, there is no learning without reminding. We learn in terms of what we know. Trying to teach someone something for which they have no experiential base is likely to be an exercise in futility.

We are constantly receiving new inputs and evaluating and understanding them in terms of previously processed inputs – that is, in terms of what we have already understood. Seen in this way, understanding is an inherently creative process. An understander must identify relevant memories to match to a new input. In doing so, the understander can find items that are exact matches or can find memories that bear no obvious resemblance to the input. Bizarre matches can be seen as evidence of a thought disorder[1] or as brilliant insights, depending upon the circumstances. Exact matches can be seen as illustrating perfect understanding or extreme lack of creativity. Either way, a match with a memory must be made for understanding to take place.

An expert is someone who gets reminded of just the right prior experience to help him in processing his current experiences. In a sense, we are all experts on our own experiences. We may not have knowledge that is unique in a way that is interesting to the outside world, but nevertheless it is unique. We have a range of experiences, and we operate well in the world to the extent that we can determine which of our

---

[1] For example, in Williams (1993), work with learning disabled students.

prior experiences are most applicable to a current situation.

We all utilize some system of categories, as well as rules for modifying those categories, to help us find different things that we know when we need to know them. The categorization scheme therefore is a crucial detail. Understanding it will help us understand how one experience can be related to another. This will tell us a great deal about how learning takes place, since learning is, in essence, the process of assessing new experiences and categorizing them in a way that lands them in a place in memory where they will be found again when needed.

So, how do we get reminded? The answer to this question is strongly related to the problem of how we process new inputs in the first place. If reminding occurs naturally during processing by a dynamic memory system, how we get reminded and how we process ought to amount to different views of the same mechanism. Reminding is a natural, effortless phenomenon, so it must occur as a normal by-product of commonplace mental activity.

Consider an example of reminding. There was, at the time of the first edition of this book, an otherwise ordinary restaurant in Boston called Legal Seafood, where patrons were asked to pay their check before their food came. (This restaurant has since become a chain and no longer follows this policy.) If a person went to another restaurant where he paid before the food came, he should in theory be reminded of his prior experience at Legal Seafood even if he had been to this type of restaurant only once before. How would such a reminding likely take place?

A script-based view of the processing involved here has the restaurant script being called into play to help process the restaurant experience. In attempting to account for reminding within the natural course of script-based processing, it becomes clear that scripts must be *dynamic memory structures*. That is, given the phenomenon of reminding and what we have said about the relatedness of reminding and processing, a script cannot be a static (that is, unchangeable) data structure. Rather, the restaurant script must actually contain particular memories, such as the experience in Legal Seafood, and the script must be capable of accumulating new episodes processed with its help.

I am arguing that a script is a collection of specific memories organized around common points (Galambos, 1986; Hudson and Nelson, 1986; and Hudson, Fivush and Kuebli, 1992). Part of the justification for this modification of the old view of scripts is that it is not possible to say *exactly* what is, and what is not, part of any script. Particular experiences invade our attempts to make generalizations. To put this another way, I do not believe in the script as a kind of semantic memory data structure, apart from living, breathing, episodic memories. What we know of restaurants is compiled from a multitude of experiences with them, and these experiences are stored along with what we have compiled.

A script is built up over time by repeated encounters with a situation. When an event occurs for the first time, it is categorized uniquely (although things are rarely seen as being entirely unique). Repeated encounters with similar events cause an initial category to contain more and more episodes. Elements of those episodes that are identical are treated as a unit, a script (Ross and Kennedy, 1990; Ross, Perkins and Tenpenny, 1990; Spalding and Ross, 1994). Subsequent episodes that differ partially from the script are attached to the part of a script they relate to. The differing parts of the episode are stored in terms of their differences from the script (Hudson, 1988; Hudson, Fivush and Kuebli, 1992). In this way, such episodes can be found when similar differences are encountered during processing.

Thus, a script should be considered as an active memory organizer. It is this view of a script that is relevant in the Legal Seafood example. When we hit a deviation from our normal expectations in a script, and a previously processed episode is relevant to that deviation, we can expect to be reminded of that episode so that the entire episode can help us in processing the current experience.

One thing I am now arguing against is the notion put forth previously (Schank and Abelson, 1977) of the existence of a track, a script-like substructure that in form was just like any other script piece. It was called into play when some deviation from the norm was encountered. But, what really seems to happen is that, rather than finding new script pieces to help us when our expectations foul up, we find actual, real live memories that help us in processing. From these experiences, we formulate new expectations that help us to understand a new experience in terms of the relevant old one that has been found.

Scripts have a stronger role than previously supposed. A primary function of scripts is as organizers of information in memory. The restaurant script, for example, organizes various restaurant experiences such that when a deviation from the normal flow of the script occurs, the most relevant experience (the one that has been indexed in terms of that deviation) comes to mind. It comes to mind so that expectations can be derived from it about what will happen next in the new experience. Thus, reminding, in a sense, forces us to make use of prior knowledge to form expectations.

One important consequence of the reminding phenomenon is that it alters our view of what it means to understand. For example, when we enter Burger King for the first time, but after having been to McDonald's, we are confronted with a new situation we must attempt to *understand*. We can say that a person understands such an experience (i.e., he understands Burger King in the sense of being able to operate in it) when he says, "Oh I see, Burger King is just like McDonald's," and then begins to use his information about McDonald's to help him in processing what he encounters at Burger King. In other words, the person might be *reminded* of McDonald's. Understanding means being reminded of the closest previously experienced phenomenon. Such reminding behavior is not random. We are reminded of a particular experience because the structures we are using to process the new experience are the same structures we are using to organize memory. We cannot help but pass through the old memories while processing a new input.

Finding the *right* memory (the one most specific to the experience at hand) is what we mean by understanding. Episodic memory structures and processing structures are the same thing. It follows then that there is no permanent (i.e., unchangeable) data structure in memory that exists solely for processing purposes. Scripts, plans, goals, and any other structures that are of use in the understanding process must also be useful as organizing storage devices for memories. These structures exist to help us make sense of what we have seen and will see. Thus, memory structures for storage and processing structures for analysis of inputs are exactly the same structures (Reiser, Black and Abelson, 1985).

According to this view, it is hardly surprising that we are reminded of similar events. Since memory and processing structures are the same, sitting right at the very spot most relevant for processing will be the experience most like the current one. Thus, the discovery of a coherent set of principles governing what will remind a person of something particular is a crucial step in attempting to understand how memory is organized, how understanding works, and how learning takes place.

Types of Reminding

The word *remind* is used in English to mean a great many different things. Joe can *remind you of* Fred. You can ask someone to *remind you to do something*. We get *reminded* of a good joke, of past experiences, of things we intended to do, and so on.

The type of reminding I have been discussing is called *processing-based reminding*. This is the kind of reminding that occurs during the normal course of understanding or processing some new information as a natural consequence of the processing of that information.

In a broad categorization of reminding, two other types of reminding come up that bear superficial similarity to processing-based reminding, but which are not relevant for our purposes here. The first of these is what is termed *dictionary-based reminding*. Often when we look up a word in our *mental dictionaries*, we find an entire episode from our experience located with the definition, almost as if it were a part of that definition. Such dictionary-based reminding cannot occur for words that are in great use in our daily lives. But for words, concepts, or objects that we use infrequently, such reminding is likely to occur. The Yiddish word *zaftig* (buxom) is for me, for example, completely associated with a particular experience I had on a job interview where I happened to be accompanied by two women, one of whom my future employer characterized as "zaftig." The surprise associated with his saying this, together with the salience of the experience of getting this particular job, forever linked that word, that woman, and that experience in my mind. The word is defined by the experience.

Similarly, phrases, such as "I am not a crook" or "I am the greatest," bring to mind particular episodes. Dictionary-based reminding is easily accounted for. Our mental dictionaries do not look like Webster's. Information about how to use a word or phrase, which circumstances it first appeared in for you, who uses it, the classes of things it can be applied to, feelings associated with it, and so on, are part of our mental entry for a word. In a sense, the less that is there, the more we notice the word. As we gather a great deal of information about a word, the particular memories that we have associated with it tend to lose their connection to the word. Only the essential, user's definition remains.

Thus, dictionary-based reminding is a phenomenon that helps to define a word for us in terms of a particular memory. This is not very useful in the long run. In fact, if we treated every word like that, we would find it very difficult to actually process anything in a reasonable amount of time. Such reminding is an important part of initial concept formation, however. Thus, in a sense, when such reminding does not occur, we may well have understood better, since the concept is more universally, that is, less particularly, defined.

Actually, dictionary-based reminding is a processing type of reminding too, having to do with the processing of words (and sometimes objects). But, dictionary-based reminding is not very relevant to the operation of a dynamic episodic memory because it disappears with frequent use. Words are abstract ideas until they become more scriptlike as they are used every day. The more routinized an idea becomes, the more we have learned it and, ironically, the less we have to say about it and the less we notice it. Exceptions, after all, are the conscious remindings we have.

The second kind of reminding that is an aside from our discussion here is *visually based reminding*. Sometimes one thing just looks like another. Since our minds organize perceptual cues and find items in memory based on such cues, it is hardly surprising that such remindings should occur. As noted, the best reminding is the one we are least likely to notice. When we enter a restaurant we have been to before, our expectations about the events in that restaurant, and their subsequent realization, should remind us of that restaurant. In other words, we process what we perceive to be the closest fitting memory structure. We might not feel that we have been reminded if the fit is exact, because reminding occurs when the fit is approximate, not exact. Nonetheless, in the strict sense of reminding, we have been reminded of exactly the right thing.

The same thing occurs in perceptual processing. In processing John's face, the best fit is the memory piece that contains the perceptual features for John's face. We do not feel reminded by this, we simply feel that we have recognized the set of perceptual features. We feel reminded, too, when the fit is approximate. A new person can physically remind us of one for whom we already have features in our mind, because there is a partial match.

It is easy to confuse visually based reminding with processing-based reminding. Frequently, after an approximate perceptual match has been made, an episode from memory comes to mind that is associated with that approximate perceptual match. This is the visual analogue of dictionary-based reminding. Associated with the perceptual features of an object that has not been accessed a great many times will be one or more experiences connected to that object. Once the input has triggered a structure in memory that defines the input, memory is not overly concerned with whether the input was the perception of sights or sounds. However, the kind of reminding that is of interest is situation based. That is, in processing a situation, when one is reminded of another situation, the new situation should be quite relevant to our understanding of the original situation.

Types of Processing-based Reminding

I can now discuss different kinds of processing-based reminding. If we can determine some of the kinds of reminding experiences (from here on, when I say *reminding*, I mean *processing-based, situational reminding*) that exist, then we will have, at the same time, determined some of the possible organizational strategies that also exist in memory. Reminding is the result of similar organization, after all. Thus, one can help in the discovery of the other.

Reminding Based upon Event Expectations

The first type of reminding is the kind referred to in the Legal Seafood example. It is based on the assumptions about processing that were captured by the notion of scripts as presented in Schank and Abelson (1977). The relevant assumption is that, given an action, it is reasonable to expect another particular action to follow. Such assumptions are often based upon what we know about the situation we are in. Even infants appear to form these kinds of assumptions, and they react with heightened interest when their assumptions or expectations are violated (Hull Smith et al., 1989).

Whatever structural entities in memory actually have the responsibility for encoding expectations should serve both as memory organizers and as data structures used in processing. Such structures contain predictions and expectations about the normal flow of events in standardized situations. Whenever an expectation derived from that structure fails, its failure is noted. (Hudson, 1988; Hull Smith et al., 1989; De Graef, Christaens and d'Ydewalle, 1990; Hudson, Fivush and Kuebli, 1992; Patalano and Seifert, 1994). The deviation is remembered by its being indexed with a pointer to the episode that caused the expectation failure, the index being placed at the point of deviation. Thus, if ordering in a restaurant is handled by expectations derived from a restaurant structure, then the Legal Seafood experience would cause an expectation failure in that structure. The Legal Seafood experience would be stored in memory in terms of a failed expectation about ordering in a standard restaurant.

This kind of setup tells us a great deal about how we learn and what we are capable of learning. Normal schooling methods – at least the ones that do not involve doing – cannot entail any interesting failures in doing. Simply telling somebody something, and then assuming that he will remember what he was told, is a bad idea. People remember what surprises them, what makes their normal expectations fail, and what, as a result, they have had to think about. People learn while attempting to process the world around them and discovering that what they had expected failed to occur. They learn when they are trying to achieve a goal and discover that their methods to accomplish that goal have failed. And, they learn when, having become curious about what surprised them, they think about what went wrong.[2] People learn by doing, and by thinking about what they have done.

Reminding that is based upon expectations about events occurs when the structure that was directing processing produces an expectation that does not work the way it was supposed to. This kind of reminding occurs whenever a deviation occurs in the normal flow of events in a structure. At the end of these deviations are indices that characterize the nature of the deviation. A match on the index brings to light the memory stored there.

Consider a *ride in airplane* script. Under the event of serving drinks, we might find memories about *drinks spilled on lap, free drinks,* or *drunken party in next seat.* Each of these is a potential index, based on expectation failures from one's own experience, under which actual memories are found.

One would expect, then, that all of one's experiences inside an airplane are organized by some *airplane* structure (and by other structures that might also be relevant). These particular memories are indexed according to their peculiar attributes with respect to the event in the relevant script piece. From this come two key questions: What are the categories or classes of memory structures? How are indices formed and used in memory organization within a structure?

---

[2] See Chi et al. (1989), Chi and VanLehn (1991), and Lampert (1995) on the learning benefits of students' forming explanations for themselves.

But not all reminding is neatly restricted within a given memory structure that reflects one particular context (such as restaurants or airplanes). Sometimes reminding can occur *across* such structures. Thus there is a third important question: How does a memory organized in one memory structure remind you of something that would be classed in a different structure? The answer to this question is a key problem before us in the book. It is important to understand why this is so within the bounds of processing-based reminding.

Recall that in studying processing-based reminding, we are trying to discover how an extremely relevant memory can be brought to the fore in the natural course of processing. In the kind of reminding just discussed, it was suggested that one way such reminding occurs is this: In attempting to make predictions about what will happen next in a sequence of events, we bring in a relevant structure. In the course of applying the expectations derived from that structure, we attempt to get the most specific expectations to apply. Often these must be found by using an actual memory that has been stored under a failure of one of the expectations that is part of that structure. Thus, to get reminded in this way, there must have been an initial match on the basis of an identity between the structure now active and the one originally used to process the recalled episode (i.e., the one you were reminded of) (Gick and McGarry, 1992).

Now the question is, can we ever get reminded of something that is not from a close match in an identical structure? It is obvious that people do get reminded across contexts. A reminded event can have something in common with the initial event, but that common element does not have to be a physical or societal situation. But how can such reminding occur, if all memories are stored in terms of structures such as the scripts of Schank and Abelson (1977)? It is obvious that it cannot. As stated in the 1977 book, many different types of structures govern processing. Distinctions were made between plan application, goal tracking, and script application, often seeming to suggest that the *correct level of processing* flitted from one to the other. What seems clear now is that memories are stored at all levels and that processing of inputs must take place on each level. That is, at the same time that we are applying a scriptlike structure, we are also processing the same input in a number of different ways. To find out what those other ways are, we must take a look at other kinds of reminding.

Goal-based reminding

In processing an input, we are not only attempting to understand each event that happens as an event itself; we are also attempting to get a larger picture, to see the forest for the trees, so to speak. We want to know not only what happened, but why it happened. Thus we must track goals.[3]

An example will serve to illustrate goal-based reminding. Someone told me about an experience of waiting on a long line at the post office and noticing that the man ahead had been waiting all that time to buy one stamp. This reminded me of people who buy only a dollar or two of gas at a gas station. What could be the connection? One possibility is that I had characterized such motorists as *people who prefer to do annoying tasks over and over when they could have done them less often if they had purchased larger quantities in the first place*. Such a category is extremely bizarre; it is unlikely to exist in memory. The existence of so complex a structure would imply that we are simply creating and matching categories in our heads in order to be reminded, which seems unreasonable.

Recall that processing considerations are intimately connected with memory categorizations. If we ask what kind of processing issues might be in common between the post office experience and the gas station experience, we find that in the *goal-based* analysis of the kind proposed in Schank and Abelson (1977), there is a very obvious similarity. Both stories related to goal subsumption failures (Wilensky, 1978). In processing any story, we are trying to find out why the actor did what he did. Questions about the motivations of an actor are made and answered until a level of goal-based or theme-based explanation is reached. In this story, why the person bought a stamp is easy, as is why he stood in line. But good goal-based processing should note that this story is without a point if only those two goals are tracked (Schank and Wilensky, 1977). The *point* of the story is that the actor's behavior was somehow unusual. This unusualness was his failure to think about the future. In particular, he could have saved himself future effort either by having bought more stamps before or by buying more stamps at this time. But he failed to *subsume* this goal. Thus the story is

---

[3] Seifert (1990), found evidence that "goal, plan and action inferences are likely to be made during reading and become a part of the memory representation that is indistinguishable from explicit information" (p. 120).

telling us about a goal-subsumption failure of a particular kind. Understanding this story involves understanding the kind of goal-subsumption failure that occurred.

There is a set of memories organized by *goal-subsumption failures* in much the same way that memories are organized by scriptlike structures. Here too, there is a set of indices on particular kinds of goal-subsumption failures. One of these has to do with waiting in line for service, which is where the gas station experience sits in memory. The new post office experience is processed by using structures that track goals, as well as by using structures that carry expectations based upon particular contexts. There are no relevant processing predictions that come from the scriptlike structures here. The contexts in the reminding are quite different. But the goal tracking causes a reminding that can have potentially useful consequences if it is desirable to attempt to understand the motivations of the actor in the events that were described. My assertion is that we always seek an understanding of why people do what they do. Reminding that occurs in response to our questioning ourselves about why an actor did what he did can be useful for making significant generalizations (i.e., learning). In other words, attempting to understand at the level of goals can lead to a generalization that may be valid in future processing.

Consider another example of goal-based reminding. My secretary once took a day off because her grandmother died. My previous secretary had had a great many relatives die and was gone a great deal because of it. It is not surprising that one experience reminded me of the other. Furthermore, I could not help but make predictions based upon the first secretary's subsequent behavior with respect to the second's future behavior. Consciously, I knew that these predictions were useless since there was no similarity between the two people, but the reminding occurred nevertheless. What could a memory structure be like in which both these experiences would be stored? Again, we do not want to have static nodes in memory such as *employee's relative dies* (the hierarchical superset in both cases). Our memory connections must have processing relevance that may or may not be semantic-superset relevant. (In this example, I had had other employees' relatives die, but I was not reminded of those experiences.)

Here again, goal tracking causes a recognition that goal-subsumption failure has occurred. I had processed both of these situations with respect to how they related to me. They both caused the same goal subsumption of mine to be temporarily blocked. The temporary blocking of having my secretarial work done, due to the death of a secretary's relative, is an index under goal-subsumption failure. The reminding that occurred had the possibility of applying what occurred in the first situation to the understanding of the second. The recognition of like patterns from which generalizations (and thus predictions about the future) can be made is very important for a knowing system. The fact that the particular reminding was of no use here does not negate the general significance of such goal-based remindings.

One key issue in the reminding and memory storage problem, then, is the question of what higher-level memory structures are used in processing a new input. Some of these structures were discussed in Schank and Abelson (1977) (see also Wilensky, 1978, and Carbonell, 1979), which recognized structures such as Goal-Blockage, Goal-Failure, Goal-Replacement, and Goal-Competition, not to mention the various structures associated with satisfying a goal. Each time one of these goal-based structures is accessed during normal processing, that structure becomes a source of predictions that are useful for future processing and learning via reminding. Structures based upon goal tracking are thus likely to be of significance in a memory that can get reminded.[4]

Plan-based Reminding

If goals are being tracked, then it follows that so are the plans created to satisfy these goals. If we are to learn from our remindings, and that does seem to be one of the principal uses of reminding, then we must learn at every level for which we have knowledge. It follows, then, that there should be a plan-based reminding that facilitates our construction of better plans.

Consider the following example. My daughter (age 8 at the time) was diving in the ocean looking for sand dollars. I pointed out where a group of them were, yet she proceeded to dive elsewhere. I asked why and she told me that the water was shallower where she was diving. This reminded me of the old joke about the drunk searching for his lost ring under the lamppost where the light was better.

People quite commonly undergo such reminding experiences – jokes or funny stories are common types of things to be reminded of. What types of processing does such a reminding imply?

[4] Both Trzebinski and Richards (1986) and Seifert (1990) found that people had better memory for goal-related information than for non–goal-related information in stories.

The implication is that, just as scriptlike structures must be full of indices to particular episodes that either justify various expectations or codify past failed expectations, so are plans used as a memory structure. How would this work in this case? Here, the similarity in these two stories is that they both employ some plan that embodies the idea of *looking where it is convenient*. But it is not the plan itself that is the index here. One could correctly pursue that plan and not be reminded of the drunk and the lamppost. The reminding occurs because this plan has occurred in a context where it should have been known by the planner to be a bad plan. I shall discuss the difficulties involved in this example and what they imply later on. For now, the main point is that memories are stored in terms of plans, too. Hence, reminding can also be plan based.

Reminding Across Multiple Contexts

Reminding can take place in terms of high-level structural patterns that cut across a sequence of events, as opposed to the reminding that has been discussed thus far – reminding that occurs at particular points in the processing of individual events. This kind of reminding occurs when a pattern of events, as analyzed in broad, goal-related terms, is detected and found to be similar to a previously perceived pattern from another context.

Imagine a head of state on a foreign affairs visit getting into an argument that disrupts the visit. Hearing about this could remind you of arguments with your mother on a visit. It could also remind you of a rainstorm during a picnic. Recall that any given input is processed on many different levels simultaneously. Imagine a context in which our hypothetical head-of-state visit took a great deal of planning, went smoothly at the outset, was expected to have great ramifications for future efforts at consummating an important deal, and then went awry because of some capricious act under the control of no one in particular that caused the argument and the subsequent diplomatic rift. The same sort of thing could be happening at a well-planned picnic that was intended to have important personal or business ramifications and then got fouled up because of the weather, which in turn permanently ruined the pending deal.

A less fanciful example of the same phenomenon occurs in watching a play or movie. If you have seen *Romeo and Juliet* and are watching *West Side Story* for the first time, it is highly likely that at some point in the middle of *West Side Story* you will notice that it is the *Romeo and Juliet* story in modern-day New York, with music. Such a realization is a reminding experience of the classic kind. It represents true understanding, of the kind mentioned earlier between McDonald's and Burger King. The reminding matches the most relevant piece of memory and brings with it a great many expectations that are both relevant and valid.

But the complexity in matching *West Side Story* to *Romeo and Juliet* is tremendous. In the Burger King example, it was necessary only to be in some sort of *fast food* script and proceed merrily down the script. But in this example, everything is superficially different. The city is New York, there is gang warfare, there are songs. To see *West Side Story* as an instance of *Romeo and Juliet*, one must not only be processing the normal complement of scripts and goals. One must also be, in a sense, summarizing the overall goals, the events of their actions, the interpersonal relationships that are affected, and the eventual outcome of the entire situation.

Morals

When a new input is received, we also – in addition to all the other analyses suggested – tend to draw conclusions from what we have just processed. Often these conclusions themselves can remind us of something. A moral derived from a story, the realization of the *point* of the story, and so on, can each serve as an index to memories that have been stored in terms of the points they illustrate or the messages they convey. These are, in essence, the lessons learned from the experience. Such lessons are important because knowing them is good and because they serve as indices for processing future experiences.

Such reminding depends, of course, on our having made the actual categorization or index for the prototypical story. In other words, unlike the other kinds of reminding that have so far been discussed, here we would have had to analyze the prototypical story in terms of its moral message or point. Why would we choose to remember a joke or story unless it had a point we were particularly fond of?

But finding the relevant adage or joke can be a problem. We found the *drunk* joke, mentioned earlier, because the plans being used were the same. Similarly, we can find morals when physical or situational structures such as scripts are the same. But what do we do when the only similarity is the moral itself? To find memories that way implies that there are higher-level structures in memory that correspond to such morals. This also involves being reminded across contexts. We shall have to come up with structures that can account for such remindings.

Intentional Reminding

The last type of reminding I shall discuss is what I label *intentional reminding*. Sometimes one can get reminded of something by just the right mix of ingredients, by the right question to memory, so to speak. In those circumstances, reminding is not directly caused by the kind of processing we are doing at the time. Rather, processing is directed by the desire to call to mind a relevant past experience. It is as if we were trying to be reminded. If we are trying to answer a question, the reminding would be in the form of getting the answer. If we are simply trying to understand a situation, intentional reminding represents our attempt to come up with a relevant experience that will help us to understand our current situation.

Not all intentional reminding represents our attempt to come up with a relevant experience that will help us to understand our current situation, nor is all intentional reminding consciously intended. Much of it comes from just thinking about what is happening to us at a given time, without any conscious feeling that we wish we were reminded of something. Our thinking of a way to solve a particular problem often causes us to be reminded.

I was once asked by a friend, as we were about to walk along a beach, if he should take his dog along. This reminded me of the last time I had been visiting someone and we had gone for a walk and had taken the resident dog along. I had objected, but my host said that we had to take it, and with good reason (protecting us from other dogs), it turned out. This reminding experience caused me to ask myself the next time if we would *need* the dog on the beach in the same way. I thought not and said so.

This is an example of intentional reminding. Had I not been reminded at all, I would have simply responded that I didn't want to take the dog, since I don't especially like dogs. Instead I posed a problem to myself. Knowing how and when to pose such problems is a complex matter, which is discussed in Chapter 4 and in Schank (1981).

Intentional reminding is extremely common. It forms the basis of a good deal of our conversation and of our thought. We try to get reminded by narrowing the contexts that we are thinking about until a memory item is reached. This narrowing is effected by a series of indices that are often provided by the input, but also by the person doing the thinking in an attempt to consciously narrow the context.

In the situation just discussed, two contexts were active: *visiting a colleague at his home* and *taking a walk*. Each context alone had too many experiences in it to come up with any actual memories. But the index of *dog* changed things; it focused the search. Here, *taking the dog* was a sufficient cue for me because I so rarely did it.

Reminding in School

The process of searching memory depends upon having a set of structures that adequately describe the contents of memory and a set of indices that point out the unusual features of the structures. Given such entities, it is then possible to search memory intentionally. Intentional reminding seems to have great relevance to education because education so typically involves looking for answers to satisfy the requirements of some test. In those moments, we try to get reminded, but quite often we fail to find the answer we need.

Reminding in an educational context should be either unintentional, in the goal-based sense (we get what we need because we naturally "ran into it") or intentional in the sense that we learn to ask ourselves the right questions to allow relevant memories to come into play to help us solve problems. Either way, the real issue is labeling memories in such a way that makes locating them trivial.

A serious problem in education, the transfer problem, depends entirely upon reminding. We can teach students something, they can memorize it and spit it back to us on a test, and yet, they still don't "know it" in the sense that, when a real use for that information comes up in their lives, they fail to be reminded of it. How can this be?

For example, many students learn when studying chemistry that acetone, the chemical in fingernail polish, dissolves glue. But when faced with a glue spill in their basement at home, few students can access this knowledge to help them with their problem. Instead they resort to whatever *home-repair* script they may have available. The way students store the information they learn in school usually does not relate to the way they create and use scripts in daily life. But in a real-world sense, not having knowledge available at the moment you need it is about as valuable as not having it at all.

Knowledge that is unavailable is *inert*; it is simply knowledge improperly stored. Storage techniques are not conscious; storage and labeling are automatic processes. The only way they can be controlled is by our providing new information in the proper context and in the right way. What this means exactly will be discussed in further chapters, but the bottom line is this: Simply telling someone something is no assurance that the new information will be retained at all; however, if it *is* retained, it is highly likely that it will not be available when needed unless it has been stored as part of a script and labeled in such a way as to ensure a goal-based or intentional reminding. The kind of memorization that constitutes most studying (and most schoolwork) usually ensures only that the information learned will be available in school-like contexts.

A Perspective on Reminding

Reminding, then, is a highly significant phenomenon that has much to say to us about the nature of memory. It tells us about how memory is organized and about learning and generalization. If memory has within it a set of structures, it seems obvious that these structures cannot be immutable. As new information enters memory, the structures adapt, initially by storing new episodes in terms of old expectations generated by existing structures. Eventually, some expectations that used to work will have to be invalidated. Indices that were once useful may cease to be of use because the unique instances they indexed are no longer unique. New structures will have to be built.

Reminding serves as the start of all this. As a result, looking at reminding gives a snapshot of memory at an instant of time. After that snapshot has been taken, memory must adjust by somehow combining the old reminded episode with the newly processed episode to form a generalization that will be of future use in processing. Thus, reminding not only tells us about memory organization, it also signals memory that it will have to adapt to the current episode. Reminding is the basis for learning.

CHAPTER 3

Failure-driven Memory

At the root of our ability to learn is our ability to find the experience we have in our memory that is most like the experience we are currently processing. Most learning doesn't look like learning at all. For instance, consider a situation in which we drive down a road and remember to take the first right after the public library. We do not seem to be learning; we simply feel we're either following directions (if this is the first time we have taken this particular trip) or recalling (if we have made this trip before). But, in either case, we are learning. On the other hand, consider a situation in which someone gives us directions, we try to memorize them, and then say we have learned the way to a place. Because we have been socialized in a particular way, this feels like learning. Understanding why the former situation is learning (even if it doesn't seem like it) and the latter is not (even if it does seem so) is critical to understanding the nature of the comprehension process and its modification through experience. Memorizing is not learning in any real sense.

Imagine you are a small child and your parent believes you should learn how to make toast. Your parent can sit you down and give you a lecture on the art of toasting, but this is probably not the best way to teach you. Three better choices are showing you how it is done while you pay careful attention; telling you to do it and then observing the outcome; or guiding you in doing it by providing advice prior to catastrophic failure. Which of these alternatives is best from a pure learning point of view? (I mean to discount here what are often quite relevant emotional issues.) The method good parents might typically choose is showing or advising, because these involve the parent and are good means of parent–child interaction. I am by no means suggesting that these are not the right thing for a parent to do, but from a pure learning point of view, the best method is simply telling the child to do it and observing the outcome of the child's actions.

The reason for this can be seen in the driving example. Reading directions helps us get to a place, but without reading them again the next time, there is a good chance we will not recall all their nuances and we might get lost if the directions are complicated enough. Nevertheless, after enough repetitions we will learn to get where we're going without thinking at all, because the set of directions will have become an internalized script. Clearly, this is learning in its purest form. One goes from knowing nothing to having a procedure so internally known that little thinking is required. How do we get to this state? Where and when exactly does the learning take place that allows someone to be an expert at something?

These are not easy questions. But, one thing is absolutely clear. The first experience at something guides the second. Whenever you do something for the first time, that experience is stored in memory and is used as a guide on the second try. Of course, it is possible to screw up this process by mislabeling the first experience so badly that it cannot be recalled when needed, or by having the second experience follow the first at too great an interval. It is also possible that the learner will not want to undertake the second experience because the first one was so painful. But, assuming that these motivational or timing issues are not present, most people learn if they practice something often enough. Our question is how this learning works.

There are some key elements in this process. First and foremost is *memory*. We must remember our prior experience. Second is *labeling*. We must be able to find our prior experience when needed. Third is *modification*. We take the first experience as prototypical. If we succeeded perfectly the first time, we need only remember every step we took. (This can be harder than it seems.) If not, then we must be prepared to modify the prototype to create a new prototype based on the new experience. Oddly enough, this process is facilitated if everything did not go perfectly the first time. This is the case because the fourth element of this process is *failure*. Each mistake we make must be remembered, or else we will make it the next time, too. But, remembering our failures isn't enough. We must understand them as well. This is the fifth element, namely the process of *explanation*. We must be able to explain to ourselves why whatever went wrong went wrong, so we will not fail in the same way again.

The learning process comprises all these elements. It is because learning works this way that the child is best off trying to make toast himself (but only from a pure learning point; because the child might hurt himself, it is not a good parenting point). The child needs to go through the process himself, explaining his errors to himself as best he can. Teaching comes in when he cannot make these explanations himself. Good teaching means supplying an explanation for an error to someone who cannot supply it themselves. Yet we seem to be able to recall our own explanations better than those that are given to us. For this reason it is very valuable to have one's own experiences and come to one's own conclusions.[1] The ability to form one's own explanations is critical to learning.

A good teacher might tell a student a good story that illustrates a point that would help to explain a failure. Alternatively, when the student is trying to explain to himself what went wrong, he is trying to recall a prior experience that will shed light on how one should act in a given situation. To bring exactly the right experience to mind at exactly the right time requires a memory organization capable of indexing episodes in such a way as to have them available for use when they are needed. This implies an indexing scheme that uses the procedures in operation as part of the labeling. Thus, we might have a "when making toast, first put in bread, then turn on toaster" rule that is indexed simply by looking at the toaster and the bread.

If a particular memory is relevant to processing at a certain point, it must be indexed in terms of that relevance. Processing relevance means the ability to recall a memory at just the point where that memory would be most useful for processing. Thus, what we are learning about making toast is the procedure cued by various aspects of the process. But something else is necessary when things do not go exactly as planned. When we have burned our hand because we forgot to use toaster tongs to remove the toast, we are reminded of this at just the point when we are likely to make that mistake again. Thus, we index memories in terms of their relationship to previous processing attempts.

Most failures involve prediction. Just before the child burns his fingers on the toast, he has made a prediction (albeit not a conscious prediction) that the act of picking up the toast with his fingers will be successful and will result in his having the toast in his hands ready to eat. Thus, after the child's fingers have been burned, the problem is not only that his fingers hurt but also that his predictive powers have failed. The next time he makes toast, one would hope, he would not

---

[1] Chi et al. (1989) and Chi and Van Lehn (1991) found that stronger and weaker students were different in their ability to form their own explanations.

predict the same outcome. Children who continue to burn their fingers have their intelligence called into question. Intelligence implies learning, and learning means changing predicted outcomes on the basis of experience. Thus, failed prediction leads to memory modification, which is what learning is all about.

Failures of the same sort cause us to contemplate why we have failed to notice that certain circumstances are identical. When making toast, we are forming a script, so we should notice the identity between what are very similar circumstances (after all, one toast-making experience, especially with the same toaster, is quite like the next). But, when circumstances are identical at a level higher than scripts, we feel we could kick ourselves for failing to notice the identity. For example, we can imagine someone who is dating who laments that he continually chooses the wrong kind of partner. Perhaps he is attracted to passive aggressive personalities, and always suffers from the attraction. The same predict–fail–remind–explain cycle is active; learning works in the same way here as it did in the case of the child learning to make toast. The complexity is in noticing that there is an identity. After all, one partner does not seem like another partner in the same way that one toaster is just like that same toaster a day earlier. In this case, indexing is the issue. Recognizing what we are dealing with is part of the prediction process. Thus, indexing depends upon prediction, and prediction depends upon the characterization we assign to the object in question. As long as we see a toaster as a toaster this is easy, and many predictions follow from that recognition. But, similarly, we need to be able to categorize types of people in order to make finer and finer predictions about how our relationships will fare. This categorization is an integral part of the learning process. Learning depends on failure, failure depends on prediction, and prediction depends upon the initial classification of the objects and events with which we are dealing.

At the root of all this is reminding. You can't learn unless there is something to base learning upon. No experience is brand new. We see everything in terms of predictions garnered from prior experiences we have called to mind because we believe these experiences will be germane to the current experience. We want to build up scripts and other processing structures that will enable us to correctly predict outcomes and to follow the rules we have set that will produce successful outcomes. So, when a failure occurs, either (1) the processing structure being utilized, which was derived from prior experiences, is made available for modification, or (2) there is no prior structure – that is, we are dealing with an experience for which we have only one or two somewhat similar experiences to guide us, and we then have the sensation of being reminded (Ross, 1984; Ross and Kennedy, 1990). In either case, memory is modified as a result of the failure. This is called *failure-driven memory*.

But how do we get our first predictions? Can every new experience really be guided by an old experience? How do we store each individual experience? Consider two restaurant experiences that are virtually identical except for what was ordered. We would expect that a person might not be able to distinguish between two such experiences months after the events. It would be easy to get confused about aspects of these two experiences – which waitress (if there were different ones in the same restaurant) served which food, for example. Such confusions indicate that people could not be storing every new experience as an entity in and of itself. We don't index chronologically, for example. Our memories just don't function that way. But then how do they function?

It seems likely that similar things are stored in terms of each other, that is, they are mushed together (Hudson and Nelson, 1983; Adams and Worden , 1986; Farrar and Goodman, 1992). We don't have to concentrate on the fact that silverware was used the last time we ate in a restaurant; instead we can invoke the standard script and reconstruct later, from memory, that silverware must have been used because it was a restaurant. We know that we can fail to pay attention and "remember" it anyway, because we can make it up by using the standard script (Slackman and Nelson, 1984; Myles-Worsely, Cromer and Dodd, 1986; Farrar and Goodman, 1990). It is as if we see something and say to our memories, "Oh yeah, that old thing again – pay no attention. We can reconstruct it later if it should turn out to matter, which I doubt it will."

One restaurant is like another. For the purposes of economy of storage, we need not remember the details of every restaurant we have been to. We can reconstruct from what we know about restaurants that we must have ordered or that we probably sat down to eat. This implies that what we are doing when we store something is checking for the features of that experience that are interestingly unique.[2] We then pay particular attention to those features in the storage scheme we employ. What we do not pay particular attention to is stored in

---

[2] De Graef, Christaens and d'Ydewalle (1990) have shown that people will predictably fixate on unexpected objects they find in a room they are entering.

terms of the normative flow of events, that is, the mush of memories that become the standard set of script actions, or the backbone of a script.

However, even what we pay attention to can be disassociated from an experience. If the silverware is especially fascinating to us – perhaps it is the same pattern our grandmother used and we are left with a flush of warm memories about our childhood – we would indeed recall it. But, even then, we might not recall it as part of that restaurant experience. We would update our silverware knowledge, we would rework our childhood memories about our grandmother, and still we might forget in what restaurant this occurred.

One of the purposes of reminding is to provide relevant predictions at a critical point in processing. A script is also a bundle of relevant predictions. It must serve as an organizational tool by which episodes with predictive value in processing can be stored in a way that facilitates the retrieval of those episodes at the right point in the future.

Script formation is a type of learning from failure, although it may not seem so. It is a kind of *learning from the denial of failure* that occurs by building up a stereotypical representation of a situation. Over time, in repeated encounters with that situation, the stereotypical representation is called up to help process new, seemingly similar events. In order to build a script, either we fail to pay attention to what has failed, or we modify the script. If the representation in memory provides an accurate prediction of the events unfolding in the current situation, then that representation is verified and the new situation becomes encoded in memory as simply a stronger confidence in the stereotyped representation to help in processing future occurrences (Hudson, Fivush and Kuebli, 1992).

Recall that we are trying to understand the organizational structure that integrates the structures of processing with those of memory. Episodes must be stored in such a way that each one of them can serve as a kind of script itself. Predictions are available from all prior experiences, not just those we have abstracted as scripts. People make predictions about what will happen next based both on particular episodes they have found in memory and on generalizations drawn from similar experiences. Scripts do more than simply govern processing by making predictions and filling in causal chain inferences. A person who has experienced something only once will expect the second time around to conform to the initial experience and will be surprised when the second experience does not do so. Scripts account for understanding based upon singular instances as well, because any atypical episode will have been processed by the structure most similar to it. In other words, a script will have been used for awhile in processing an atypical episode, and then will need to be revised. A dynamic memory is always changing as each processing failure causes learning to take place.

What we are dealing with here is the script acquisition problem. This is how scripts get put together in the first place: first one experience, then another on top of it, strengthening those areas of agreement and beginning to solidify the script. New experiences for which there is no prior experience can be understood only in terms of old ones because new experiences cannot be new in every way. The new parts of an experience can most certainly occur within well-trodden contexts. If they do not fit neatly into such a context, we attempt to force the fit. Thus, a train ride looks much like a plane ride the first time. We always try to understand by using our past experience.

I am proposing here that the significant parts of entire episodic memories are stored at critical script junctures. Memories can be organized by scripts, retrieved by scripts during reconstruction (Slackman and Nelson, 1984; Myles-Worsely, Cromer and Dodd, 1986; Farrar and Goodman, 1990), and found for processing use at just the point where the script-based predictions fail (Read and Cesa, 1991), which is when script-based reminding occurs. Thus, for Legal Seafood, the entire memory experience is available at the point of interruption or abnormality following the ORDERING scene. We are reminded of that episode when similar failures in prediction occur. We use those episodes to help us process new experiences that cause the same processing failures (i.e., that remind us of the same processing failures). This episode is used, just as any script is used, to predict what will happen next and to fill in the causal chain by making inferences.

Why does this matter for us when we study learning? Why should someone who cares about learning care about scripts? In the end, most of what we learn in life is procedural. We learn how to do things by extensive practice. Practice is about script building. When one practices a musical instrument, one is learning a very complex script with tremendous numbers of nuances and variations. We understand this when we teach music, since we ask music students to try and try again until what they do is effortless and does not require "thinking." Scripts are, in a way, *noncognitive*. We don't *think* when we use a script, we just *do*. This kind of rote learning is important, but, unfortunately it has

47

been generalized in schools to mean rote learning of nonprocedural tasks. Doing requires procedures, and procedures must be reinforced through practice. Exceptions to procedures require thinking, and exceptions are the true stuff of education.

It may not be obvious how "getting along with people" or "learning to sell" are scriptlike behaviors requiring practice, but they are. We start with sets of simple procedures in each case and make them more extensive through experience. We acquire nuances and subtleties through false starts and complications, and we gradually refine and expand our scripts to account for the oddball circumstances we have encountered and to include the explanations we have created for ourselves to guide us through them.

Learning subjects like biology and history ought to be procedural as well. But when these subjects are taught in schools today through rote memorization, the procedure being taught is simply memorization, which has little to do with real learning. Real learning means learning behaviors that become second nature and require little "thinking" to execute. Biology and history contain such procedures, but they are too often lost in modern-day classrooms, where efficiently delivering facts that can be tested is of the greatest importance. If we want real learning to occur in school, we need to find the scripts that matter in life and teach them (but not by telling them). Since learning is a continual improvement of scripts, school needs to be concerned with the introduction of new scripts that can be refined through practice (in the way I have described, with failure, reminding, and explanation).

We must look carefully at how script acquisition and refinement work in order to deeply understand the learning process. A script is more than a procedure for doing something – it is a container of all our records pertaining to doing that something. Deep within a script are links to every unique memory experience we have had that has been processed in terms of that script. (These pointers can be obliterated when an episode that we previously saw as unique recurs. At that point, a new script may be formed that combines the two and is independent of the original.) Thus script application is embellished by going down paths that the script itself organizes and that contain all prior deviant (that is, not completely standard) experiences (Hudson, Fivush and Kuebli, 1992). These experiences are functionally identical to scripts and thus are integral parts of the application process; they can occur within any script piece.

As an example of all this, consider Figure 3.1, a picture of a possible set of memory experiences tied to, or organized by, the restaurant script. This diagram illustrates the use of a script as an organizer of information in memory. Every important deviation from the standard script is stored as a modification of the particular scene in which the deviation occurred.

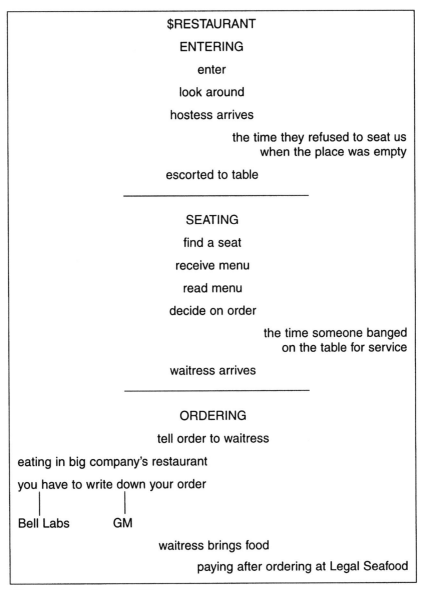

Figure 3.1 (*continued p. 50*)

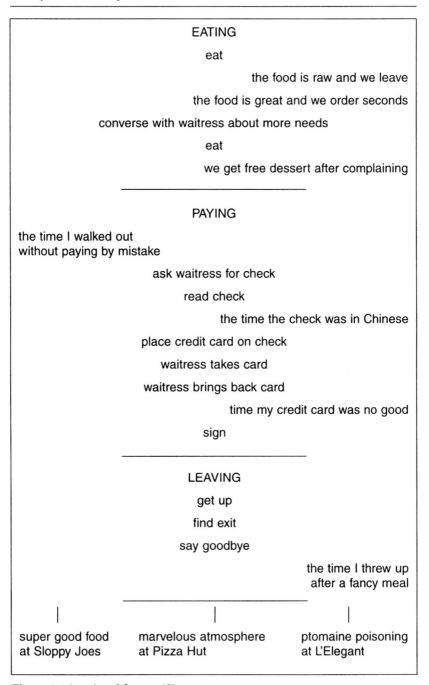

Figure 3.1 *(continued from p. 49)*

Information about a restaurant is processed by using the restaurant script as described in Schank and Abelson (1977) and Cullingford (1978). As long as the story fits current expectations (based upon the operating stereotype), no deviation from the usual default script is made, and no reminding occurs. Underneath the restaurant script's bare backbone, however, are all the memories that have ever been classified in terms of restaurants. As soon as an abnormal event occurs (i.e., one that is unusual to the extent that its occurrence is not predicted by, or is actually contradicted by, the normal flow of the script), normal processing stops (Adams and Worden, 1986; Hudson and Nelson, 1986; Hull Smith et al., 1989; De Graef, Christaens and d'Ydewalle, 1990; and Hudson, Fivush and Kuebli, 1992). At this point, an index must be constructed in terms of where the new episode will be stored. Constructing the index is complicated. It depends on finding an explanation for what went wrong with the expectation derived from a scene in the script. This will be seen in the cases discussed later in this chapter.

Figure 3.1 shows a number of deviations recorded in the various scenes. They include the experience in which someone repeatedly banged silverware on his plate to get service, the memory of having to write down my order at Bell Labs and General Motors (GM), and the experience in Legal Seafood of being asked to pay immediately after ordering.

The entire experience at GM can come to mind when a deviation from the norm of a similar type occurs. When I had to write down my order at Bell Labs, I was reminded of the GM ordering scene. That in turn reminded me of other scenes that day, which also became available for my consideration for their possible processing relevance. The recognition of the existence of these other scenes has two possible uses. First, relevant predictions, of the kind I have previously said were available from scripts, actually come from whatever prior experience is available. Thus, the rest of what happened at GM, even events that are in no way restaurant related, could be used to interpret what happened at Bell Labs.

The importance of this capability to be reminded cannot be overemphasized. People interpret new experiences in terms of old ones (Kolodner, 1993).[3] The only way to get the relevant older experience to be available is to have been reminded of it in the normal course

---

[3] Also Bransford et al. (1989) and Ghoulson et al. (1996).

of processing the new experience. Noticing that Bell Labs is like GM in the ordering scene can then allow for remembrances of GM experiences to guide future behavior at Bell Labs. Reminding is a catalyst for generalization.

Often there is no need at all for the remembered experience. Once one is reminded of GM, one can then ignore this reminding and return to normal processing by going back to the normal backbone of the script to handle future inputs. Alternatively, it is possible to never return at all to the normal script because its predictions are so standard as to be inappropriate in a novel setting. Instead, the predictions from the reminded events are used to guide processing.

Whatever choice is made, a new episode has been experienced and a decision must be made about how to store it. First, where are links made to the Bell Labs experience? Second, at what point is the Bell Labs experience broken up into pieces of episodes that lose their relatedness to each other? (This second question is critical; we can learn from pieces of an experience.) Third, what is the overall effect on memory and future processing?

The answer to the first question is that since the deviation ordering has been seen before, a pointer to the GM episode that existed previously at the write-down-order deviation is now joined by a pointer to that experience at Bell Labs.

With respect to the second question, I am assuming that a processor would have analyzed the new Bell Labs episodes in terms of all the relevant higher-level knowledge structures that were used to process it in the first place. We can expect that structures containing knowledge about lecturing, talking with colleagues, consulting, and so on, might all have been used in addition to a knowledge structure about restaurants. Some overall structure, such as a visit to a company to lecture, might well exist in the mind of someone who has frequently had such experiences. Thus, it might be possible to find memories contained in each individual structure during a reconstructive process utilizing a higher-level structure that connected them all together. As shall be seen later on, these high-level structures cannot be immutable across people as long as their role is to reflect (the differing) experiences that people have. Ordinarily, one would not expect these individual structures to be directly connected to any of the others. So the new pointer at the ordering deviation points to the part of the experience that contains restaurant and as many other pieces of that experience that may be causally connected to the restaurant part of the entire Bell Labs episode. Other parts of the Bell Labs experience would be stored in terms of the knowledge structures (such as scripts) that processed those parts. Thus, the entire experience is broken up into smaller pieces for processing and storage. It can all be put back together again, if appropriate high-level structures exist that contain information about which structures ordinarily link to other structures.

I asked about the overall effect on memory of an experience that deviates from the norm. Memory can be affected by such a deviant experience in two ways. First, if the deviant experience has no counterpart, for example, if there had been no prior GM experience or if the Bell Labs experience differed at the ordering scene in some significant way from the GM experience, then a new deviant path off of the ordering scene (in the first instance) or off of the GM deviation (in the second) would have to be created. This deviation would point to the relevant experience at Bell Labs with respect to ordering and would now serve as a new source of relevant predictions if that deviation were encountered again inside the restaurant script. All prior experiences, if classified initially as being interestingly deviant, serve as embellishments to the script of which they are a part and thus serve as a source of predictions (Adams and Worden, 1986; Hudson and Nelson, 1986).

If the new experience does have a counterpart, that is, if similar deviations have been met before, at some point these experiences are collected together to form a new structure whose prediction, like the higher-level restaurant script itself, is disembodied from actual episodes. Thus, at some point the understander notices that not only the GM and Bell Labs restaurants have you write down your own order, but so do various faculty clubs and other company lunchrooms. When enough (probably two is enough, but that remains an empirical question) of these are encountered, a new structure will be created such that the understander will not be reminded of particular experiences that caused the creation of this subscene. (These remindings stopped for me after awhile as I began to go to more company cafeterias and later to private dining clubs. Eventually this became a variation of the ordering scene for me, devoid of its original experiences. As I rewrite this book twenty years after the experiences at GM and Bell Labs, I find that I have no memory of them whatsoever. I do, on the other hand, expect to write down my order in a private dining room.)

As a new structure is used, the links to the relevant episodes that helped to create the structure become harder to find (Hudson, Fivush and Kuebli, 1992; Hudson and Nelson, 1986). In a sense, the new memory structure is broadened by more experiences at the same time that it is narrowed by the loss of its origins. These origins cannot be remembered in the face of many similar experiences. Thus, an argument at lunch at the Harvard Faculty Club might still be remembered, but it would not be possible to get at it through the deviation in the ordering scene of writing down your order, any more than it would be possible to get at it by the sitting down scene or any other scene that was now normalized. Thus, if you tripped and skinned your knee while eating in a restaurant, it might be wise to store this somewhere other than in the BEING SEATED scene unless, of course, it happened because of something that is really a property of all (or one or two) restaurants. Knowing where to store failures is an important part of understanding.

One last possible effect of a deviation from expectation is the abandoning of the original memory structure. Thus, if all restaurants begin to employ the written form of ordering, not only is a new structure created, the original one is seen as useless and of only historical interest. Often, such abandoned structures reflect views of the world that never were true in the first place, that were simply wrong generalizations from scanty data.

Thus, memory collects similar experiences from which to make predictions. Before structures are created that embody generalizations relating to a given situation, remindings of prior experiences serve as the source of relevant knowledge. Unique classifications of experience serve as a rich source of understandings about new experiences. Repeated experiences tend to dull people's ability to respond to the world around them by lulling them to sleep during processing, as it were. One problem here is knowing which items that are unique in an experience are also interesting and potentially relevant later on. Mushing two episodes tends to eliminate their differences. An intelligent processor must be careful not to eliminate interesting differences, nor to especially note dull ones.

Using Expectation Failures

One must now ask what general principles there are in all this. How does it happen that we store some memories at deviation points in scripts? Why does this matter if we want to understand how learning works? Is there something going on here that relates to the other kinds of reminding that were discussed, or is this phenomenon spe-

cific to script-based reminding? Is learning possible without reminding?

The primary advantage of reminding is its production of a maxi-
mally relevant memory for use in making predictions and generalizations. Such predictions can then be used in processing the current
episode. Any generalizations that are made can be used to process
future episodes that share something in common with both the current
episode and the reminded episode.

A script is a generalization. It is a structure with an implicit, built-
in assumption, namely, that because something has happened many
times in a similar way, one should expect that thing to happen in the
same way next time. When we are reminded of a memory at a juncture
in a script, we are prepared to make another generalization. We can
formulate a new script piece, based upon whatever identity we can
find in the two memories that have in common their placement at the
same junction in the script. For Legal Seafood, this might be:
Restaurants that make you sit at long tables also make you pay after
ordering. Clearly, some future encounter might remove this generalization from memory as invalid, but the point here is that we do enter-
tain such hypotheses. When they stand up over time, we have learned
a new script or piece of a script.

One can say that reminding is the basis for learning, at least as far
as scripts are concerned, but is there something more significant going
on? Stepping back to look at what is going on in script-based reminding, one can see that there is a feature common to the various kinds of
reminding that were discussed in Chapter 2; namely, in each of these
remindings there is a processing failure of some kind. We make a prediction about what will happen next, and our prediction turns out to
be wrong. At the point that we recognize that there is a prediction failure, we are reminded of a similar prediction failure.

Memory is failure driven. We expect our predictions about other
people's behavior and processes to be accurate. When they are not, we
make note of our error so that we can make better predictions when
we encounter the same situation next time. This notation forms a link
between the failure and the episode that caused the failure, indexed in
terms of the reason for failure (Johnson and Seifert, 1992). This is what
happened in the script-based remindings discussed, but it is far more
ubiquitous than that.

Lehnert (1979) developed a theory that questions were often best
answered by following a trace of the previous processing that had

occurred. Thus, in answering a question about a story, one would have to have saved some of the false starts and failed expectations used in processing that story. Some questions would be answered on the basis of those failed expectations (Granger, 1980).

The theory I am proposing is similar in spirit to Lehnert's proposal. I am suggesting that all of memory conforms to her view of question-answering in story processing. We try to make predictions about what will happen in any episode we are attempting to comprehend. When we detect a failure of an action to conform to our expectations, we remember that failure. In a sense, we are attempting to jot it down for next time, so that we won't fail that way again and so that we learn from our failures.

Viewed this way, reminding can occur when an expectation fails to materialize, or when something unexpected happens. Indexed under either of these two kinds of failure are prior failures of the same kind. We get reminded when we notice that we have failed in this way before. From this consistency of failure of the same type, we learn to create better expectations.

Of course, not all remindings are of this type, but failure-driven remindings are common enough, and significant enough, that I view memory from that perspective. Clearly, a memory that does not account for such remindings will be of little value in learning and generalization.

Kinds of Failures

What kinds of failures in processing expectations can there be? Clearly we have a great many low-level processing expectations from syntax, phonology, vision, and so on that can fail. Episodic memories are not necessarily indexed off all types of these failures. What we are looking for here are failures of predicted actions on the part of other people, or the world in general.

A large part of what we do in understanding is to attempt to predict other people's behavior. We want to understand why someone does something and what he will do next. When we fail in our predictions, we remember our failure for next time. Failure-driven reminding is based in failures in our prediction of other people's action.

To see the kinds of remindings I am talking about, and the way memory is required to deal with them, consider the following reminding experiences (one of which was discussed briefly earlier). They were collected for the most part by simply asking colleagues to report remindings they had.

A. The steak and the haircut

X described how his wife would never make his steak as rare as he liked it. When this was told to Y, it reminded Y of a time, thirty years earlier, when he tried to get his hair cut in a short style in England, and the barber would not cut it as short as he wanted it.

B. The sand dollars and the drunk

X's daughter was diving for sand dollars. X pointed out where there were a great many sand dollars, but X's daughter continued to dive where she was. X asked why. She said that the water was shallower where she was diving. This reminded X of the joke about the drunk who was searching for his ring under the lamppost because the light was better there, even though he had lost the ring elsewhere.

What do these reminding experiences have in common? They are both examples of a person's inability to correctly predict someone else's behavior. Jokes are frequently about people's unexpected behavior. To access them in our memories we must have indexed them by their particular type of failures. We retrieve them again when we encounter a similar kind of failure.

A large part of the problem of reminding can be explained by assessing the kinds of failures there are in expectations about other people's behavior. These failures seem to serve as indices to memories. The question is, how? Consider the kinds of failures exemplified by the two cases just cited: In A, we have a failure of a person to do what she or he was asked. In B, we have a failure to act in one's own best interest in the initial episode. The reminding is of someone's suggestion that a person failed to act in his or her own best interest.

Remindings of this sort suggest a view that memory involves our processing an episode on many levels at once. Essentially, we can view an understanding system as tracking the goals, plans, themes, and other high-level knowledge structures that are active in any situation. It is the understander's job to produce sets of expectations about what the next action to achieve a step in a plan should be, what the next plan to achieve a goal should be, what the next goal in a thematic relation should be, and so on.

This may seem to be a very complicated task. Are people really doing all this mental work when they are attempting to understand the world around them? Do they really have expectations at this many levels? I asked my graduate students to tell me stories from their school experiences that were particularly absurd. I will use some of them here as data to consider the points I am about to make. Consider the following story from the point of view of how you process it yourself:

C. British spelling in America

In sixth grade, I have very distinct memories of doing poorly in spelling. One of the big reasons was that, since my parents are from Australia and Canada, a lot of our children's books had British spellings. I had grown used to certain words being written in this way. Once, after having the word "theatre" marked wrong on a spelling test, I went to the shelf, grabbed the dictionary, and showed Mrs. Kroesing that, in fact, my spelling was given as an alternative. Surely the impartial dictionary was incontrovertible evidence that I was right. She said, "I don't care what the dictionary says. In my class, that's not the way it's spelled." I saw that, in that class, education was a power game in which she held all the cards. That impression lasted a long time.

What are some of the expectations here? That justice will be done, or that a teacher will be reasonable, or that dictionaries will be taken seriously, or that students have trouble convincing a teacher that she is wrong. We have numerous beliefs about the world, and every story or situation we encounter causes us to bring those beliefs to mind to make predictions about the behaviors we expect. We are constantly attempting to explain why our beliefs turned out to be wrong. The things we remember for a long time revolve around such expectation violations. The number of high-level expectations we have when we process anything is quite high. The fact that people handle this is an indicator of the mind's complexity.

Explanations

One of the most interesting facets of human beings is their desire to explain the mysterious. We want to know why a strange thing happened or why people do what they do. We are unhappy if a person pursues a set of goals we find incomprehensible, and, when a person fails to do what we expected, we attempt to explain it. When our view of what should happen next in a given situation is contradicted, we attempt to explain why. These explanations are the essence of real thinking. When we consider education in this context, it becomes clear that students must be put in the position of coming up with explanations on their own so they will learn how to think. But since the explanation process begins with failure, they must first fail. Explanation is the by-product of learning from failure and naturally leads to script revision or new script building. These failures ought to come from situations deliberately set up by the school and the teacher. Story C was an expectation failure that was unintentional on the part of the teacher. Here is a story involving an expectation failure that was intentionally generated by the teacher.

D. Liquid hydrogen

One of our labs had to do with liquid hydrogen and nitrogen. The professor was doing some demos of just how cold these liquids are. He placed a frog in the container, brought it out a second later, placed the now frozen frog on the table and hit it with a hammer, shattering it into pieces that went flying into the class. He did a similar demo with a rose, throwing it on the table and shattering it. He concluded our prep for the lab with something like, "So, this stuff is really cold and can do some serious damage if it isn't treated with respect. So be careful." He then commented about how tough it is on the throat to speak for lectures everyday, and said he'd really like a cold drink. He picked up the thermos with the liquid nitrogen in it, did a double take to the class, and proceeded to drink the entire contents. A few people in the class let out involuntary shrieks of horror, thinking he was going to completely freeze his mouth and interior. He was fine, with a smile on his face as he set the empty thermos down. He went on to explain that the liquid is so cold that the 98.6 [degrees] of the body is high enough to make it immediately boil upon contact, causing no harm. The trick, he explained, is in pouring it slowly enough that there is no "build up" in your mouth. It made a BIG impression on the class.

Although the explanation for this expectation failure was provided by the teacher, the event still made an impression on the student and was remembered. Next is a story in which the students made up the explanation and obviously remembered it, although what they remembered wasn't what the teacher was trying to teach.

E. Montreal, Ontario

One day, my teacher asked the class in what Canadian province Montreal was located. I had just been there with my family, so I knew the answer was Quebec. My hand shot up along with a few other children. The teacher picked another student, who answered "Quebec." "No, that's wrong," the teacher answered. Another student suggested Ontario, which the teacher affirmed was the right answer. Later, I went to the classroom globe, to see whether the teacher was right. I then figured out why the teacher made her mistake. Although the globe showed Montreal in Quebec, the actual word "Montreal," for lack of space, was written within the confines of Ontario. The teacher had used the globe to derive her answer!

So, we search for explanations. In school, to the extent that students can find their own explanations, they will remember their experiences. People remember what they think better than what they are told, and they remember what they are told only if it strongly relates to something they are really wondering about.

In general, we are satisfied with simple explanations; the less work they cause us the better. One of the simplest kinds of explanations is a script. If we understand that a person is doing what he is doing because he is following a script, we feel comfortable that we have explained his behavior. We can, of course, look for an explanation that is deeper than a script-based one, but we are usually content not to. Thus, an explanation of why one takes off one's shoes in a Japanese restaurant, or why religious Jews always have their heads covered, can be answered by "because that's the way it is done in their culture." Surely there exist better explanations: For example, because the Japanese sit and sleep on the floor, they are more fastidious about its cleanliness; or Jews come from the desert, where head coverings prevent sunstroke. Often the participants in these rituals (or scripts) do not themselves know or believe such explanations. People are usually content with script-based explanations when they are available.

Complex explanations are not always available to us. When no script is in operation, we look for explanations at the level of goals. Unusual episodes can be indexed by the point of failure in a script – for example, being asked to pay before eating poses a failure at the point of the ordering scene in the restaurant script. However, failures may also be indexed by the relevant explanations that are generated.

An episode can be encoded with multiple points of indexing. It all depends upon how much thought we choose to give to a subject. There is a reason the Japanese want us to take off our shoes when we enter their private rooms, but do we really need to know it? We can function well without the explanation. We choose for ourselves what to consider deeply and what to relegate to the world of scripts.

To explain why someone is doing something we didn't expect, knowing what goal he is pursuing may at least partially explain his actions. Understanding someone's goal does not always explain his choice of plan to carry out that goal, which may seem very strange indeed, even if we are perfectly cognizant of his goal.

Here is another student story, this time involving assessing the goal of the teacher and the plan brought forward by that goal.

F. Counting frog parts

In my tenth-grade biology class we were assigned to work in small groups dissecting frogs. Our objective was to excise parts of the frog, to pin them to a big slab of cardboard, and to write the name of the part next to tiny piece of formaldehyde-smelling flesh. We had at hand a reference book which showed in great detail all the names of frog parts. Our group conscientiously picked apart the frog, taking care to get the right names associated with the proper parts. We tried to not waste any time, since we knew we'd be graded on how many parts we correctly identified.

At the end, the teacher came around to the groups one by one and counted up the total number of parts on the cardboards. It seemed clear to everyone that he wasn't really checking to see if any of the part identifications were correct. As it turned out, our group got the lowest score. In chatting with students in other groups later, it became clear that they had been more astute than we in surmising that the best way to approach this assignment was as a race to get out as many parts as possible. My friend laughed that on several occasions, he had simply ripped out a part of the frog, chopped it up into several pieces, pinned down all the pieces, and looked for names in the reference book with which to label the pieces.

We look for explanations at the level of plan choice. Why does this teacher count the number of parts? Laziness. Sometimes a goal needs to be explained. We may not have any idea why someone would have this goal. In such a case, we look for thematic explanations. That is, we seek to explain goals in terms of higher-level goals or themes that obtain for this particular individual. If our teacher is so lazy we might wonder why he wants to be a teacher at all. Perhaps he wants the job to please his mother, or to get experiences to help him in a future career. We are satisfied by explanations that make odd behavior seem rational.

Here is another student's story. What beliefs can we imagine were held by the teacher who ran this class?

G. Memorizing the Periodic Table

In my eighth-grade science class, we were forced to memorize all of the elements on the Periodic Table. On test day, we had to write them down in order; if we did not get one hundred percent, we had to take the test again after school, and continue taking the test until we got them all right. In the first pass, I did not score one hundred percent, but that was okay, neither did the entire class. I didn't get them all the second time either, but wasn't worried about it because a large number of classmates also missed some. Each afternoon after school, I came to the classroom and took that test, and each day I made some stupid error and didn't get it perfect. By the end of the week, there were only a few people still taking the test: me, another guy who would remain in the eighth grade for several more years, and two people who would later drop out and get convicted. Finally, I got one hundred percent. Instead of feeling joy over my success, however, I decided that chemistry was the stupidest subject I had ever seen, and swore then and there that I would never take another chemistry class again in my life.

The student may have believed that chemistry is a stupid subject, but certainly this does not explain the behavior of the teacher. We are compelled by the mental discomfort caused by unsatisfied expectations to create some explanation and often to accept ones that are not so well thought out. (A good teacher can help in this process, of course. Indeed, helping a student create a good explanation of an expectation failure in an arena a student cares about is one of the most important things a teacher can do.)

At the root of our ability to understand is our ability to seek and create explanations (Chi et al., 1989; Scardamalia and Bereiter, 1991; Graesser, Baggett and Williams, 1996). Explanations of human behavior are always grounded in the beliefs of the person we are trying to understand. That is, what we are trying to do when we seek an explanation for an actor's behavior is to find a set of beliefs that the actor could hold that would be consistent with the actions performed. Explaining another person's actions requires us to try to take a look inside his head. Consider some possible explanations in the previously mentioned cases:

A. *The steak and the haircut:* The server must believe that X doesn't really want the extreme of what he asked for.

B. *The sand dollars and the drunk:* The planner must believe that the easier plan is the best plan, regardless of information to the contrary.

C. *British spelling in America:* The teacher must have felt that her job was to enforce the rules that she believed in.

E. *Montreal, Ontario:* The teacher didn't know the right answer and thought she did.

F. *Counting frog parts:* The teacher didn't want to work very hard at grading the students' work.

How carefully we examine what other people might believe depends on our need to know. This often reflects our estimates of our future predictive needs. Thus, in Legal Seafood, we can seek an explanation for the actions of the waitress, which are easily explained as doing what she is told to do because it is her job. We must then seek an explanation for the behavior of the management of the restaurant, as embodied by the waitress's asking for payment at an odd time. Doing this may require us to examine the history of the beliefs of the management, but our need to know is not that great. We are satisfied with an explanation that is script based, because we are not greatly outraged at what has happened in place of what we expected. "That's the way they do it here" will do when we are willing to put up with the inconvenience. We need only to mark our script so that we will be able to predict this next time, and we can go on to worry about something else. Of course, if the waitress's aberrant behavior had been to hit us for leaving a poor tip, "that's the way they do it here" would fail to suffice as an explanation.

The explanation of unexpected behavior by one's friends, parents, and teachers, and the explanation of odd situations that are important to us, require more careful attention than simple attribution to script-based explanations. When we fail to predict accurately in those circumstances, we may well want to assess the beliefs of the actor who failed to conform to our expectations. Often such assessments crucially affect our relationship with these people. We might not wish to be around someone who is willing to kill to get what he wants, for example, or we might want to provide him with a less drastic plan if we are in sympathy with his goal but not his method. Doing this, however, requires us to have correctly assessed his underlying beliefs. Thus, at the root of our ability to operate in the world is our ability to explain the behavior of others by examining their beliefs. (We also explain by examining other aspects of a situation. Thus, an explanation that someone was tired, drunk, or stupid will also suffice. In these cases, a person tends to modify what he knows about a given individual rather than what he knows about a given situation.)

Thus, I am suggesting that indices to memory, and hence our memory organization, are belief based. The explanations for the stories in this chapter are grounded in an understander's view of what someone else believes. We always attempt to explain an actor's behavior. Usually, we have pre-satisfied our need for an explanation by simply noting that the actor did what we expected him to do. When he does not do as expected, we must examine the possible belief structures that he may have had at the point of the expectation failure.

Of course, not every story in memory is based on the actions of other people. Sometimes we must create a belief about the physical world and use it as an index. But in either case, we are talking about beliefs. We index our memories according to our own beliefs about other's beliefs.

What we believe about the physical world, and what we believe about what others believe, drives our every action. When we walk across a street, with the green light, in front of oncoming vehicles, we believe the driver of the car coming toward us will stop, because we believe he believes he should stop at red lights and because we believe he would rather not injure us. We trust our beliefs, but we need to be vigilant about them. If an oncoming car fails to stop, we will mark this expectation failure and never again walk into the path of an oncoming vehicle. We will have learned our lesson. Much educational and psychological research indicates that the goal relevance of experiences is predictive of memory retention.[4] Self-preservation is, of course, a glaringly important goal, but other goals work the same way. In attempt-

---

[4] Adams and Worden, in their 1986 study, found that "relevance to a goal is a more important factor than typicality in determining recall for events" (p. 159). Also, Seifert, Abelson and McKoon (1986) and Pressley et al. (1988).

ing to achieve our goals, we must track the beliefs of the other people who might have an impact on these goals. Tracking beliefs is thus an organizing theme in memory. Learning depends upon this goal–belief interaction for the creation of indices to be used as labels to find relevant memories that can be predictive of future events.

This suggests an algorithm that has the following gross characteristics:

Utilize the appropriate high-level knowledge structure (i.e., scripts, plans, goals, etc.) to process input.

When an expectation generated by those structures fails, attempt to explain the failure.

To explain a failure of another person to act according to your predictions, attempt to figure out his beliefs. This entails

assessing the implicit beliefs you expect that person to hold in that situation;

producing an alternative belief that would be consistent with the behavior;

using the alternative belief as an index to memory to find other memories previously classified with that alternative belief; and

using other features of the situation as additional indices within the range of behavior delimited by the alternative belief to find an actual memory to be used for generalization and modification of predictions.

I am proposing that memory is organized, at least in part, by a classification of explanations of other people's behavior based upon our assumption of what it is that they must believe. Within that classification, memories from other, quite different, contexts can be found, indexed by explanations. A memory is found by noting an expectation failure, deciding upon an explanation, and subsequently noting that a similar explanation has been used before. Explanations are thus somewhat like keys to locked doors. Memory is organized in terms of explanations we create to help up us understand what we receive as input when that input differs from what we had expected.

Consider the steak and haircut example from this perspective:

1. Process with knowledge structure. The first problem in any understanding situation is to find the relevant higher-level knowledge structure (such as a script) to use for processing. Since I am arguing that memories are stored in terms of prediction failures, and that predictions are made by higher-level knowledge structures, clearly the decision about which knowledge structure to begin to use in processing is crucial. However, I also am arguing that processing, and therefore predictions, take place at many levels at once. Thus, the problem of which knowledge structure to use in processing is solely the problem of which structure to use for each level of processing. That is, we must decide what scripts, plans, goals, and other structures are applicable. For the purposes of this example, I shall just assume a structure that I shall term PROVIDE-SERVICE. (I shall discuss the validity of such a structure later.)

The assumption here is that PROVIDE-SERVICE will be a relevant source of predictions about why, how, and when a person in a serving role will provide service. This structure provides expectations about actions that are likely to come next in the story.

2. Expectation fails. The predictions contained in a structure such as PROVIDE-SERVICE are about the behavior of the participants in a situation governed by that structure. Thus, among other things, one predicts that someone who has voluntarily assumed the SERVER role in that structure will do what he has been asked to do, if he can and if what he has been asked is within the domain of the area in which he normally provides his service. In the steak story, making steak rare is within the range of abilities of the SERVER, yet she has failed to do so. Thus there is an expectation failure. My thesis is that such failures must be explained. An understander who does not attempt to explain such failures will never learn how to cope with new situations. Without the ability to explain expectation failure, no memory would be of any use for very long. Thus, this explanation-finding behavior is fundamental to understanding.

3a. Assess implicit belief. The next problem is to explain the prediction error. Why didn't the server do what he was asked? There are many possible explanations and there is no way to know which is correct; an understander must simply discover a reasonable one. This was evident in the student explanations for cases C, E, and F, in which students attributed bad motives to their teachers and made explanations that served their own purposes.

We might speculate on why people are not scientific about the explanation process. Certainly they could consider many possibilities, ponder the differences and then make more valid conclusions. But, in fact, they rarely do. One reason for this is that the process of explanation itself is actually much simpler than one would imagine. In *Explanation Patterns* (Schank, 1986), I point out that most people make explanations by copying ones they have already settled upon in other venues. They allow their prejudices about why people do things to constrain the search for original explanation. Although this might be seen as some sort of cognitive laziness, there really isn't that much time in the course of processing an event to consider all possible explanations. Teaching students to do this in circumstances that are worthy of the expenditure of lost time is a worthwhile educational goal. Without having learned a rigorous explanatory process, people naturally rely on a more sloppy one.

Recall that what we are trying to do here is to understand how Y got reminded of the barber story. Given the multiplicity of possible explanations, an understander need not be concerned with which one is ultimately correct. In attempting to establish the algorithm here, we need only show a possible path. The first task then is to assess the implicit belief held by the actor who has failed to behave as expected. On the road toward reconstructing that belief, we must make an assumption about what the server might have been thinking. In this example, Y assumed that the SERVER intended to do what the SERVEE wanted.

3b. Alternative belief. The alternative belief (AB) generated must explain what could have gone wrong. Here again, there are many possible explanations. Y seems to have used "SERVER must not believe that SERVEE wants what he said he wants; he must want something less extreme which is more in line with the norm for this service." The issue then is, how does someone actually construct such a belief? I will discuss this shortly.

4. Find memory. After the alternative belief has been constructed, it is used as an index in the memory structure PRO-VIDE-SERVICE at the point where the prediction that a server does what is asked has broken down. That point in the memory of Y is the barber story. It has the alternative belief proposed in (3b) as its explanation, as well. This implies that the AB had

been constructed previously, when the barber story was originally understood, and had been created as the index to that
memory.

Kinds of explanations

The kinds of failures there are depend entirely on the kinds of predictions there are. Since predictions can be generated from any knowledge structure, any predicted goal, plan, or action can fail. Thus, determining the kinds of failures there are is not the major problem. Most
significant is assessing which explanations can be made. How are
alternative beliefs generated? Since I am proposing that memory is
organized in part by alternative beliefs, this is clearly a key question.

The first question to ask, in the process of constructing an explanation, is, Why didn't the person do what was expected of him? There
seems an obvious split in the kinds of explanations one can find with
respect to this question. People can fail to do what they should have
done because they intended to, or the failure can be because of an error
of some kind. Thus, there are two kinds of explanations at this level:,
motivational explanations and error explanations.

Motivational explanations are concerned with figuring out the rea-
son(s) why someone would want to do what he did. To construct such
explanations, we must attempt to find the goals behind the action performed and attempt to relate those goals to the goal we thought was
operating.

Error explanations are concerned with establishing the reason(s)
why the actor could not accomplish the goal, given that the actor had
exactly the goal that we expected him to have. To find the reason why
a person fails in an attempt at a goal, we must assess the kinds of errors
that could have been made and attempt to establish an alternative
belief or personal characteristic that would have resulted in such an
error being made.

The first problem in constructing an alternative belief is determining
which is necessary: a motivational explanation or an error explanation.
In many cases this is determined somewhat arbitrarily. We can just as
easily assume that someone made an error as assume that someone
really wasn't trying to do what we thought. However, most situations
dictate that we seek error explanations before motivational explanations
because, if we can find no error, the problem must be with our assess-

ment of the person's goals. Trying to figure out goals is a highly specu-
lative business at best, and there is no decisive way of knowing that you
have succeeded at finding the correct explanation. So most often we
look for motivation before an error; we are likely to find the former and
thus never need to consider the possibility that an error occurred.

To find an error, we must examine the various standard reasons for
an error-based failure. Whatever questions we ask about why an error
occurred can be asked at every level of failure. Thus, we can ask why
someone didn't do what he should, why he didn't plan what he
should have, or why he didn't have the right goal. I shall return to this
point later.

We'll look first at why a person didn't do what we expected. The
reasons for this can be manifold:

a) misperception of situation (misunderstanding the situation)
b) lack of resources
c) disbelief (not believing he should do what you thought he should do)
d) lack of common sense (not knowing what to do)
e) lack of ability

In the steak and the haircut example (story A), we can easily dis-
miss (b) and (e) by considering the resources and ability that are necessary and finding them to be present. There is nothing nonsensible
about the actions of the SERVER, so (d) is not a reasonable choice
either. It is then our task to discriminate between (a) and (c). We do this
almost arbitrarily in this case. It would not be unreasonable to assume
that some misperception of what was expected occurred. The only
thing wrong about this analysis is that it would fail to produce the
haircut episode. As that is only one of many possible responses to that
story, all we can say here is that Y did not assume a misunderstanding
of what was wanted in his analysis.

In order to explain the haircut reminding, we assume that Y took
the path of choosing (c) as his initial explanation. So, the input to the
construction of the alternative belief is disbelief. From this we conclude that the SERVER must not believe that the SERVEE wants what
he said he wants; he must want something less extreme.

Part of the alternative belief is that the SERVER must not believe
that the SERVEE wants what he wants. This belief results from the
combination of the request, the PROVIDE-SERVICE structure, and the
noncompliance with the request. To construct the rest of the actual

alternative belief requires us to focus on the right feature of what the SERVER actually provided. Here the answer is, something less extreme. This finishes the construction of the alternative belief.

Planning Failures

In constructing an alternative belief as part of an error explanation, we must attempt to assess the reason for the prediction failure. Where this process starts depends upon where the prediction came from. In the aforementioned case, the prediction came from a rather abstract scriptlike structure that we called PROVIDE-SERVICE, but predictions can come from other structures as well.

The explanation process differs somewhat when we have a planning failure. Consider story B (the sand dollars and the drunk), which illustrates a failure to plan optimally. There is a distinction between plans that are different because the goal behind them is different and plans that contain errors in their method of achieving the goal we assumed they had. For error explanations of planning failures, the questions to be asked are analogous to those asked for actions. The failure of a person to plan the way we thought he would may be due to the following:

1. Having a different goal than we had thought.
2. Lack of information and resources. Lack of information can result in the selection of bad plans.
3. Different perception of optimum strategy. A person may be able to devise a better plan than the one we expected.
4. Lack of common sense. What may seem a reasonable course of action to us may not seem so to a planner. For example, when we believe hard work to be the necessary step in the solution, our planner may not care to work very hard to achieve his goal. Or, he may be so foolish as to plan a harder method because he failed to see the optimal and easier way.
5. Inability.

Story B shows an instance of (4), lack of common sense. The task for the understander is to perceive the girl who is diving for sand dollars as failing to do what was expected at the plan level. To do this, we must be tracking her goal of FIND (sand dollars). We expect her to employ LOOK and GET in the appropriate place. When she fails to do this, we check (1) through (5). We know our perception of her goal to be accurate; X has given her the information of where to look, and she has the ability to do so, as is demonstrable by her diving. So the choice is between (3) and (4). X chose (4).

To construct the alternative belief, we need attempt to explain only her lack of common sense. (Note that this explanation need not be grounded in the beliefs of the actor in the story. Drunkenness or childishness may suffice as explanations.) Using the possibility that the easiest plan may appear to her to be the best, we construct the alternative belief: Use the easiest plan despite information to the contrary. This is used as an index under the goal of FIND (X). At that point, the drunk and the lamppost are indexed as instances of the same phenomenon.

The value of such indexing seems clear enough. In the case of our own planning, we want to remember plan failures so we do not repeat a mistake. In observing others' plans, we may want to help them if their plans do not vitally affect us, or simply not allow bad planners to get the opportunity to partake in plans that do vitally affect us. For the father in case B, after explaining his daughter's failure, his reminding was rather useless. Drawing the analogy between drunks and small children may be amusing, but the learning there is negligible.

Goal Failures

One cannot have an error in a goal in the same way that one can pursue the wrong plan, or perform an incorrect action. Explanations are necessary when goals are involved if we have made a prediction error that was caused by our own problems in correctly assessing a situation. In other words, we need to know what we misunderstood about another person's goal. It is easy to misperceive someone else's goal. We can also believe that someone has the wrong goal for his needs. Perhaps more significantly, we can decide that someone's goals conflict with ours, and are wrong in the sense that they affect us negatively.

We seek a motivational explanation when we decide that a person knew exactly what he was doing and that no error was made. Thus motivations come into play when explanations are necessary to understand why people perform in a way that is unexpected because of our misperception of their goals or the motivations behind their plans. Motivations are also relevant when we predict poorly because our conscious assessment of an actor's goals turns out to be wrong.

The failure to accurately predict someone's behavior can often depend on our failure to accurately assess his goals. We may not be adequately prepared to deal with another person's goal. These are not exactly failures of prediction. We may not have been aware of a person's goal or even of that person's existence. Nevertheless, we can encounter difficulties in our lives that are the result of our not knowing about another's goals. In those cases, as well as in the cases already discussed, we need to record our errors and the explanation of those errors to help in future understanding and to enable us to learn from those experiences.

As an example of the kind of reminding that is relevant here, consider the following episode taken from an unpublished 1982 manuscript by Norman and Schank.

H. The suckering sequences

Norman and Schank went to one of the cafeterias at the University of California at San Diego for lunch. Schank got into the sandwich line, where the server, a young woman, was slicing pieces of meat off big chunks of roast beef, ham, corned beef, and so forth. Schank saw the nice-looking piece of meat that was exposed on the side of the cut roast beef, and ordered a roast beef sandwich. However, the server had previously sliced some beef off the side, and she took this previously sliced beef for the sandwich. It wasn't nearly as nice as the meat that was still unsliced.

When they sat down at the table in the dining room, Schank turned to Norman and said, "Boy, have I ever been suckered!" He explained what had happened. Norman said, "No, you haven't been suckered, because my impression of the word *suckered* is that it implies a serious attempt to defraud."

"You want a real suckering experience?" Norman asked. "On our trip to Spain, we were driving across the country and we came to this tiny little village. We went into a little store run by someone who looked just like a gypsy lady. We bought some cheese, and great bread, and really nice looking sausage, and some wine. Then we had it all wrapped up and we drove out of the town. We parked in a secluded location, found a hill with some trees, climbed up to the top, and sat down looking out over the beautiful countryside. Then we opened the wine and unwrapped the food. Garbage. All there was was garbage, carefully wrapped garbage. Now that was a suckering experience. The gypsy lady suckered us."

The question here is how Norman got reminded of his suckering experience. According to my theory, there had to be an explanation indexed under a prediction failure that was used by Norman to retrieve the memory. What failure is there here? The script necessary for understanding Schank's story went without a hitch. No error was made. Indeed, it was not Norman's hearing about the events that transpired that reminded him of his story. Rather, it was his reaction to Schank's analysis of what had happened to him that reminded Norman of his story. Norman did not believe that Schank's story was an instance of suckering. This disagreement caused the reminding. Now the question is, how?

Norman's disagreement was about the goals of the server in the cafeteria. He claimed that she did not have the goal of suckering Schank. Schank did not believe that she had that goal either and they later argued about the meaning of the word *sucker*, but that is not the point here. The point is that Norman believed that suckering referred only to the intent to defraud and not to the feeling of having been suckered. Because he believed this, he constructed in his head a scenario in which the food served to a customer turned out to be different (in a negative way) from what the customer had expected. Different from what he had expected is, of course, the key item in memory. Such differences must be explained. Norman had constructed an explanation of his gypsy incident that had the gypsy's goal being poorly assessed as PARTICIPATE IN NORMAL FOOD SELLER script where it was actually USE RUSE OF FOOD SELLER TO CHEAT CUSTOMER OUT OF MONEY script.

In creating a scene in his head that corresponded to his definition of suckering, he created a scenario with an expectation failure that needed explanation. In constructing a motivational explanation for that scenario, he came across a memory that had that motivational explanation as its index, hence the reminding.

It is important to point out here that Norman's suckering and Schank's story both involve not only misperceived goals and the feeling of begin suckered, but also the situation of being served food. They correspond to identities of context (food serving as the initial memory organizer for prediction and understanding), prediction failure (resulting in feeling suckered), and explanation (misperceived goals). This last identity is between Norman's belief in what suckering would have been (that is, not Schank's actual story, because Norman didn't view that as suckering) and Norman's experience with the gypsy.

Summing Up

I have outlined here a way of storing and finding memories based on prediction failures. Intrinsic to such a scheme must be a set of structures in memory that generate predictions for use in processing (understanding). The next question is, What are the structures that memory uses to process inputs and store memories? Once a sensible set of these structures has been isolated, the next step is to show how such structures are selected for processing, how memories are organized within them, and how failure-driven memories are used for explanation, generalization, and learning. Finally, it must be shown how reminding can cause these structures to change.

When an expectation fails, we need to explain that failure. In the examples, we saw some instances of how people can alter their mental structures as a result of some anomalous experience. Explanation is the impetus to the automatic modification of one's memory structures. Explanations are generated because of confusions caused by expectation failures and are helped along by reminding. Reminding is thus an integral part of understanding and learning. But, more significantly, it is the failures that matter most in determining what and how we learn. A memory that gets what it expects every time would never develop in any interesting way. Reminding, expectation failure, explanation, and learning are all intimately connected.

Any learning situation depends upon expectation failure. Expectation failure causes thinking, and our thinking has a great impact on us. To design good learning experiences, we must set up situations in which students can experience expectation failure, can wonder why their expectations failed, and can begin to think something different from what they originally thought. That is what learning is. But, be careful in understanding what failure is all about. The best failures are internal, ones others don't see, ones that are failures to predict or act properly, because quite often the failure that is obvious to others causes denial rather than reflection.

CHAPTER 4

Cross-contextual Reminding

Remindings can occur both in context and across contexts. To understand learning, we must attempt to understand the nature of the structures in memory that contain the episodes of which we are reminded. Educators especially need to understand the nature of these structures because teaching means facilitating changes both in mental structures and in the organization of those structures.

Change in memory depends upon reminding. We cannot alter a memory structure without somehow melding a current experience with a prior one. Reminding is also about prediction. When we find a structure in memory to help us process a new experience, that structure is, in essence, predicting that a new experience will turn out just like an old one. In a sense, too, learning is about predicting outcomes. When we enter a new situation, we are interested in how it will turn out. This can be just a passive wondering about how events will unfold, or it can be an active undertaking to make events play out in a certain way. When we learn, we are learning about which actions will cause which effects, and which events normally follow other events; we are also learning to distinguish between the long-term and short-term effects of an action.

Predictions come in a variety of forms and depend upon remindings that can occur across contexts. We see analogies. We make generalizations. We come to conclusions about how things will turn out. We do these things not only in response to experiences in physical places but also in response to experiences of a more abstract nature, such as engaging in contractual relationships or observing the effects of imperialism on a nation's military outlook. We can make predictions based upon remindings that are not necessarily direct mappings onto what we are trying to predict.

Predicting outcomes helps to organize memory. When our predictions have failed, we can expect to find memories of them (Read and Cesa, 1991; Gick and McGarry, 1992; Johnson and Seifert, 1992). We make correct predictions in the future by making appropriate general-izations (based on our memories) about the reasons for our prediction failures. When our predictions succeed, we solidify our belief in the memory structure that generated the prediction. Either way, we learn. Key questions are, How are the failures to be explained? and, In what kinds of structures are such predictions likely to reside?

There are actually two kinds of remindings worth noting here: remindings that serve to explain unusual events, and those that serve to facilitate the planning of an as yet unfinished sequence of events. We may want to note the patterns of these remindings so that we can avert expected, but undesirable, outcomes.

In processing new inputs, we attempt to understand what happened and why. A person seeks to learn from his experiences, to draw new conclusions, to make sense of the world. When an expectation failure occurs, we want to learn from our past experiences, to ask ourselves "why" this failure may have occurred. Similarly, when we are faced with a planning problem, we look to our past experience to ask ourselves something about why this sequence of events may be happening and how it could potentially unfold.

To see how this works in practice, consider the following: In 1979, President Carter made statements about the Russian presence in Afghanistan. Then he alluded to the Munich conference of 1938; "no appeasement this time – stop them now" seemed to be the point. In 1991, President Bush made the same point about Saddam Hussein and the invasion of Kuwait.

There are many issues here. Both presidents were attempting to predict outcomes. They were also trying to rally support from the American public by making an analogy to something any educated American would see as a historical mistake that should not be made again. Both presidents were reminded, themselves, and attempted to intentionally remind the public, about what we, as a nation, had learned from past experiences. They were trying to predict possible outcomes and to convince the public that certain outcomes would result if a certain course of action were not followed.

The question is, How is an input processed so as to draw out the *appeasement led to disaster* episode from memory? Abstractly, we might think that it is simply a question of finding relevant plans and goals. After all, we need to assess the beliefs of the actors – and knowing plans and goals can help get us to that assessment. Finding plans and goals means understanding what the Russians or Iraqis were doing.

Thoroughly understanding what invaders are doing, however, implies recognizing what they might want, what the eventual outcome might be. In essence we are trying to understand the goals of current actors by relying upon our memory of the goals of past actors who, we have decided, are similar to the current actors. The presidents are saying that understanding the Russians or Iraqis requires understanding the Nazis. By this, the presidents mean more than that these groups have the same goals; they mean to convey emotional reactions – "We cannot bomb Hussein without believing that he is mad" – and madness is best demonstrated by analogy. The presidents know that we are case-based reasoners, and they mean to provide us with the case from which to reason. How do we grasp that this is their real meaning?

I have been developing the thesis that inputs are not processed by totally abstract structures such as goals or scripts. I have argued that such structures are really organizers of episodic memory. Within each abstraction of a script or goal are sets of episodes organized by that structure. In order to get these memories out, we must find the correct index, or cue, under which these memories have been stored. We must, in other words, think about death camps and goose-stepping soldiers in order to get really mad at Hussein. Humans quite naturally reason this way – using cases, comparing one prior experience with another. But in addition to depending upon logic, human reasoning also depends upon case-based episodic reminding (Johnson and Seifert, 1992; Gholson et al., 1996).

The indices for the example seem obvious: an aggressive enemy, an invasion, and a setting of peacetime. But what kinds of structures in memory are these likely to be useful in searching, and how do we find them?

To answer these questions, we can consider some alternative situations and see if they would have been likely to remind us of appeasement in Munich. For example, suppose the Dutch invaded Luxembourg, citing a centuries-old claim to the land. Would there be cries of "Stop them now or else we'll have another Munich"? The answer seems clearly to be no. There is no match possible between Nazi Germany and The Netherlands unless The Netherlands is characterized in a way that is quite out of keeping with how the Dutch are viewed by Americans.

Now consider an instance in which a slumlord is buying up decrepit buildings for use as houses of prostitution. In each case, he makes a deal with the authorities that he'll buy only one last building if they just leave him alone to conduct his business, but later he says he needs another one. This circumstance is much closer in spirit to the Russian invasion. Further, understanding it would be enhanced if one had access to the moral drawn from appeasement in Munich.

Why would the slumlord example remind us of the Russian invasion whereas the Dutch example would not? In order for the slumlord reminding to occur, a very abstract structure must be available. We must find a structure about aggression that has as one of its stored episodes the story of the Russian invasion. But how would that structure be labeled? Certainly we would not find it by looking for *Russia*, because we don't know it's there. We would not find it by looking for *aggression* unless we had characterized the slumlord as an aggressor. This characterization is the index. In other words, we find a pattern of plans and goals that is the index to the aggressor structure, and then inside the aggressor structure there are details about kinds of aggression and ways of stopping it. The very nature of goal-based processing, namely, the need to know why something is happening the way it is, causes us to find complex structures that contain large numbers of memories that have been stored in those structures. So once we understand that we are dealing with aggression, we can begin to attempt to understand its nuances.

We seek explanations in terms of our experience. In order to feel satisfied that they have really understood what is going on, people need to relate what they are currently processing to what they have already processed. Telling someone just the facts of a situation never gives them the rich picture that a story embodying those same facts would. This is why Carter and Bush encoded their messages the way they did. It follows, then, that people must have the ability to find experiences in their episodic memories by searching some set of structures that encode those episodes.

The structures must be written in the most general terms. For the slumlord example to remind you of the Russian invasion, either an organizing structure that contains expectations such as "aggressor wants more" must be available, or you must be able to generate such a structure when needed. In order to learn across experiences with different contexts, cross contextually based structures must exist in memory. The expectations derived from them must have a fairly general scope. For instance, a memory structure containing expectations about slumlords won't contain the Russian episode within it. Although the Russian episode may be thematically linked to the slumlord example, it is not an example of a slumlord story and so has no business being stored in the memory structure for slumlord episodes.

The difficulty is finding the structure that does account for the relationship between the slumlord and the Russian episodes. One could make the argument that both Russia and slumlords are somehow pre-categorized as aggressors. If this were the case, then "aggressor" could be a thematic structure that functions in the same way that I have suggested goals and scripts function: as organizers of actual episodes.

A "slumlord" might be categorized as an aggressor after he has committed an aggression and after the understander has experienced the reminding of the Russian invasion. The reminding itself classifies the slumlord as an aggressor. Actions need to be processed in a way that brings remindings to light. These remindings then help us understand what we have already processed. This may seem somewhat circular, and it is. We get smarter by thinking about what we have been reminded of.

The real commonality of the two examples is the resultant prediction. In each case we expect a certain outcome, and these outcomes are the same. We expect that the actor who only wants a little now, will want more in the future. In processing both the Russia and the slumlord cases, we are considering the goals of the actors. As we speculate about future goals, we ask the questions, When will it stop? Why won't they want more? These questions express an expectation about future actions that is contained in the abstract structure that has been activated at that point. They serve as an index within that structure that causes the Russian experience to come to mind. We do not ask this sort of question in the Dutch case because a different structure is active in processing that story. Thus, no such reminding occurs.

I am saying that reminding across contexts can depend on speculations about possible outcomes. In failure-driven reminding, we seek explanations when an incorrect expectation is generated by an operating knowledge structure. We seek an explanation for the error. Here, in reminding across contexts, there is no error, merely an inquiry to know more. Whereas in failure-driven reminding the index that finds relevant memories is an explanation of odd behavior, here the index is a question or speculation about future actions. What structure in memory is directing processing at the point where the predictions are made?

I have claimed that expectations are the key to understanding. In a great many instances, these expectations are sitting in a particular spot in memory, awaiting the call to action. Frequently they are prepackaged like scripts. But generating relevant expectations is not always so simple. That is, on the basis of prior experience, it is not always all that obvious what to expect. In such situations, we can simply not expect anything, we can just take what comes, or we can work hard at creating expectations by whatever means we may have available. The first possibility is quite feasible. It is quite reasonable to suppose that some people do go through situations having no idea what to expect, even though there can be great value in generating expectations in novel situations because this facilitates learning from those situations. Learning means altering existing structures. If we have no expectations, we cannot easily notice that our prior view of the world was in error and needs to be corrected. That is, we will not alter memory structures as a result of an essentially uninterpreted experience.

More often, we do try to figure out what will happen in a situation we encounter. When we hear that someone has a goal, we attempt to figure out why they have that goal, what goal they might have next, what pattern their behavior implies, and so on. In a sense then, we are plotting possible scenarios in our heads about everything we are attempting to comprehend. In attempting to imagine what will happen next, we must construct a model of how things will turn out. (This model can often be quite wrong, of course.) Sometimes, during the construction of the model, we come across memories that embody exactly the state of affairs that we are constructing; this is an instance of outcome-driven reminding.

When we hear about goal-directed behavior, we attempt to predict an outcome of that behavior if that behavior can possibly affect us. To do this, we must have asked ourselves about the goals that were being pursued, found the plans that seemed to be operating, and used them to assess the likely outcome of those plans.

The problems are how to generate a question such as "When will their demands stop?" and how to use that question to find a relevant memory. For our knowledge of goals, plans, and outcomes to be accessible at the right times, that knowledge must be stored in a processing structure. Thus, a processing structure must be capable of providing us with possible outcomes for the set of situations organized by that structure. In order to find a relevant memory in a processing structure, we must first select an appropriate structure. The question that we formulate about outcomes, then, must enable us to find a relevant memory that is organized in terms of a processing structure that is already active. It would be of little use if we queried memory for relevant experiences on which to base expectations if those experiences were stored in structures different from those we were examining at the time. The kinds of structures people imagine are the ones that organize outcomes in terms of goals.

To see what structure we could possibly have here, we need to examine what information we already have. First, we know an actor has taken something he wanted. Second, and most important, we believe that actor has evil intentions with respect to what he wants to do with what he now possesses. Having identified these two features, we claim to have found a high-level structure under which memories are organized (Seifert, Abelson and McKoon, 1986; Seifert, 1990).We call this structure a thematic organization packet, or TOP. (TOPs will be explained in detail in Chapter 8. Here I will simply note some of this particular TOP's properties.)

I shall call the TOP-level structure that is active here "Possession Goal; Evil Intent" or PG;EI for short. The first problem we have in using any knowledge structure is selecting it. In this case, we need to note goals and to speculate on the reasons for them. In the slumlord story, we are told those reasons. For Russia or Iraq, we would need to have precategorized these nations as actors with evil intentions. Once such a TOP has been found, we expect it to function much as would any high-level knowledge structure – as a source of predictions about what we can expect to happen within the context of that structure. Any TOP is a collection of information about what usually happens within a certain high-level context. It organizes a set of memories. In general, three kinds of information are stored with a given TOP. First is expectational information; TOPs provide a set of expectations about what may happen next under various circumstances within that TOP. Second is static information, knowledge of the state of the world that describes what is happening when that TOP is active. Third is relational information; this includes characterizations of the world that help us liken a TOP to other structures in memory. For example, the world *bully* naturally comes to mind in the TOP being discussed. This characterization may serve to link information similarly characterized but stored in different TOPs.

TOPs are searched in order to create a variety of expectations, including predictions about the outcome of the event being processed. We make a prediction about outcomes by supplying the relevant TOP with an index that gets us to notice a relevant memory organized by that TOP.

That memory gives us something with which we can make a prediction about an outcome. Here there is no failure of any kind in the processing of the input. What failure there might be is present in the memory one is reminded of; that is, our failure to plan adequately last time (in the Russian experience). Thus, the problem here is not one of error correction. Rather, an understander must use his knowledge of past experience to help him through a situation. He needs to assess a probable outcome because he is being called upon to make a decision of some type. Getting reminded of a relevant experience will help recall that process. Thus, outcome-driven reminding can be an active part of planning.

Outcomes and Reminding

The kind of reminding discussed in this chapter can be illustrated by two cases. Note that both are cross-contextual; their similarities are best expressed by common themes or patterns of goals, rather than by similar locations or scripts. These kinds of remindings are most relevant to the prediction of an outcome, and hence, to planning. In story I, I will focus on the use of predicting outcomes in understanding. In story J, I will focus on the use of predicting outcomes in planning.

I. Romeo and Juliet
When watching West Side Story, people are quite often reminded of Romeo and Juliet.

J. Munich and Afghanistan (and Kuwait)
When learning of the potential Iraqi invasion of Kuwait, people may, with good reason, be reminded of the prior Russian invasion of Afghanistan and of the appeasement process of the Munich accords.

These two examples of remindings have in common the failure of a predicted outcome, and signs of a similar failure were recognized as a strong possibility in the remindings at hand. In case I, we predict that Romeo and Juliet will live happily ever after due to her clever plan to take fake poison. In case J, we predict that giving in to the Nazis will let them get what they want and stop bothering us.

These cases provide a view of processing that has an understander continually searching for how it will all turn out in the end. We can't say the understander is just attempting to predict outcomes; we must also look at how he could actually do so. Once again, we must establish which high-level knowledge structure is being employed.

Consider case I, in which *West Side Story* reminds a viewer of *Romeo and Juliet*. Adopting the point of view that (1) we are constantly searching for outcomes and (2) outcomes are to be found by an index in a TOP, then in order for *West Side Story* to remind someone of *Romeo and Juliet*, the person, while trying to understand the story, must be using a memory structure that contains the *Romeo and Juliet* memory. Furthermore, this memory structure must be designed in some general, abstract form that might also come to contain the *West Side Story* memory after that similar event has been processed.

Thus we can ask,

1. What patterns are around to be noticed?
2. What TOP is used?
3. What indices are used in that TOP to find the outcome?

Here again a good way to approach these questions is to see what else might remind one of *Romeo and Juliet*. A number of key factors might contribute to a *Romeo and Juliet* reminding, including

1. young lovers
2. objections of parents
3. an attempt to get together surreptitiously
4. a false report of death
5. the false report causes a real death of one of the lovers

We can attempt to change some of these factors to test our intuitions about whether the reminding would still occur. For example, suppose the lovers were of the same sex. This might be considered a gay *Romeo and Juliet* story. Suppose the lovers were old and their children objected to the relationship. Or suppose, for young lovers, their respective ethnic groups objected (as in *West Side Story*). In fact, it seems reasonable to suppose for each of these permutations that we would still get the *Romeo and Juliet* reminding. We can conclude that neither gender, nor age, nor ethnicity is likely a relevant index to the TOP or a relevant part of the TOP for this story in memory.

Suppose we didn't have lovers, but business partners instead. Even then, if the rest of the story followed, *Romeo and Juliet* might still come to mind. Moving further down our list of factors, suppose there had been no attempt to get together; then there would be no story, so this is crucial. Similarly, suppose there was no false report of death. This seems crucial, but for the business partners, suppose this was transformed into a false report of a merger or bankruptcy. In that case, the *Romeo and Juliet* plot might still be there. The impossibility of righting things afterward seems rather important, though. The death, although it probably could be changed to some figurative death (like bankruptcy), also seems critical.

So what are we left with? We have two people trying to get together but being thwarted by outside opposition; eventually, there is a false report of a tragedy for one person that results in an actual tragedy for the other person. Let's call the TOP here "Mutual Goal Pursuit against Outside Opposition," or MG;OO for short. Two indices are "false report of tragedy" and "tragedy resulting from false report." Either of these indices can be used to find the *Romeo and Juliet* memory. Thus, the outcome could be predicted by "false report." Another index is the outcome, so it could also produce the reminding experience.

Now I will attempt to merge all this with the notions discussed in the last chapter. Roughly, the algorithm presented for failure-driven reminding was as follows:

Process according to knowledge structures.
Detect prediction failures.
Explain failure.
Create alternative account.
Access memory through belief.

In the cases I have been discussing, the TOPs selected were PG;EI and MG;OO. Comparing this to the failure-driven cases discussed in Chapter 3, one can see that the indices must be different. In those cases, explanations were created to account for expectation failures. Those explanations were the indices to memory. Here, as we shall see, the indexing mechanism works differently.

Once a TOP has been selected for processing, we begin to generate expectations. Expectations are generated by using appropriate indices to find specific episodes organized by that TOP. The indices are selected through a variety of techniques: by examining various features of the input story or by asking oneself general questions about the TOP, the answers to which can serve as indices. The trick in generating an index in the latter manner is to ask questions that have answers that have already been used as indices. One method for doing this is to attempt to solve the problem of the TOP. Since TOPs are collections of goal combinations in various circumstances, they have an associated problem. In PG;EI, the problem is how to react to the evil actor; in MG;OO, it is achieving the mutual goal. Imagining a particular solution can bring to mind specific episodes that tried that solution in the past.

In case I, once MG;OO has been selected as the relevant TOP, any number of indices that describe specific, unusual features of *West Side Story* will help to pull out the *Romeo and Juliet* episode from memory. One of these indices, for example, is false report of death of the co-planner. This gives us the actual memory; that is, the path to *Romeo and Juliet* is provided by that index. Thus the prediction here is that any story employing the MG;OO TOP and the false report of death index will remind you of *Romeo and Juliet*. The advantage of being reminded of *Romeo and Juliet* is that one can speculate, on the basis of that past episode, how the current episode being processed will turn out. In watching plays this may be of little import, but in real-life situations, knowing how a similar set of circumstances turned out can be extremely significant.

In case J, the TOP is PG;EI. It must be responded to. Expectations within PG;EI involve possible responses and the outcomes of those responses. For the case of *Romeo and Juliet*, we need do nothing other than observe events, because we are simply trying to understand a story line; but in case J, Carter wanted to take action and to have the American people approve. The understanding tasks are different in the two cases. In essence, we are trying in Case J to remind ourselves of the most relevant memory we possess to help us react to the situation. To do this, we must create indices that will lead us to the potential solution paths, so we can mentally try the solution and see which memories we are reminded of that involved that solution. This is the very nature of planning.

In case J, one possible plan, and therefore one possible index to PG;EI, is the null plan: Provide no opposition. Using this as in index in PG;EI will help retrieve the memory of the Nazis and Munich. The question, When an aggressor asked for more territory and no opposition was provided, what happened? would be answered by providing a prior episode in which the outcome was a series of escalating demands. From this memory we can then predict that there will be future failures whenever "provide no opposition" is the course chosen.

The moral here is that if you want to influence people's thinking indirectly, give them a situation that can be characterized by a TOP, and a possible index to that TOP. People will use that index to find a memory. If that memory contains negative consequences, people will then begin to believe that a course of action other than the one expressed by the index should be taken. The point of getting us to think about "provide no opposition" as a possible plan is to cause us to counterplan. "Provide no opposition fails," so perhaps something else will work.

After an index has yielded a bad effect, we try to create an alternative plan if the problem we are processing is our own. To do so, we must identify the causes of the failure in the original episode. For *Romeo and Juliet*, this is of little use for us to do as understanders, yet many people find themselves incapable of not doing so. We tend to try to create an alternative plan by negating one or more of the conditions in the failed plan. In case J, the obvious thing to do is to negate "provide no opposition" by making a plan that provides opposition. This new plan is equivalent to an explanation for the failure of the prior plan. Thus, for this kind of reminding, explanations are the last item produced since they are post hoc.

The most important thing we must do in outcome-driven reminding is to create a new belief or conclusion that will better enable future understanding. In case I, we must be able to create a belief like "You shouldn't let other people deter you from your goals." This is the conclusion most obviously drawn from the two dramas in case I, and it is the kind of creative generalization we seek to make. The creation of new structures from old ones that have failed is an important part of learning.

Drawing Conclusions

To predict outcomes, we must be able to draw conclusions from what has happened. One way to do this is to take two memories that we have found, by a reminding, to be related and to create from them a new rule that can be used in the understanding process. We want to learn from prior failures. We attempt to predict an outcome, and, coming upon a related memory, draw a conclusion that causes us to modify our behavior in order to avert the same problem we encountered last time.

We usually want to make a generalization from any reminding example that will help us next time around. Consider, then, the generalizations that might be drawn from the cases previously cited:

I. Be sure that your co-planner is informed of your plans.
J. When dealing with an aggressor who wants more, draw the line quickly.

In each case, what we want to do is to derive a rule that can be placed at an appropriate point in memory to aid us next time. To do this, we must isolate the reason for the outcome-related failure and index it in terms of that reason.

Simply stated then, I am proposing that in outcome-driven reminding (ODR) the task is to find a memory that will help in planning a reaction to a current problem. This kind of reminding is much more intentional than failure-driven reminding (FDR). In ODR, we are not only trying to understand why someone did what they did, we are also trying to modify plans for achieving certain goals.[1] Thus, though FDM is driven by expectations involving actions, ODR is driven by expectations involving plans and goals. The consequences for a system that learns from remindings are thus more profound in ODR because such remindings can effect generalizations that cause us to avoid possible dangers caused by bad planning.

Reminding is the key to our understanding. Finding a memory during processing forces us to modify our existing knowledge structures.[2] This modification takes the form of changing the expectations in the structures, or of creating new structures. Since structures and their expectations are forms of generalization in memory, this alteration process is a component part of an overall process of generalization.

In the remainder of this book, therefore, four significant issues will be addressed:

1. What structures are there in memory?
2. How are these structures altered to modify expectations and create new generalizations?
3. How can we find the right structures and memories held in those structures so that we can begin the process of expectation and reminding?
4. How does knowing all this about memory and learning help us teach better?

I will attempt to answer these questions in the following chapters. But some things can concluded at this juncture. First, we recognize that reminding is a ubiquitous phenomenon in memory. Often, a reminding is illustrative of previous processing in memory that has attempted

---

[1] The fact that we are trying to achieve certain goals greatly affects our ability to have remindings (Seifert, Abelson and McKoon, 1986).

[2] Ross (1996a, page 183).

to record failures of various kinds, together with the explanations of those failures. Such failures come from expectations we make about the way things are likely to happen, and from our desires for particular outcomes. These expectations are created at all levels of processing. People are constantly trying to figure out what will happen and what to do about it. They look for patterns and attempt to solidify those patterns by creating structures in their memories that encode various sets of expectations.

Second, reminding occurs in context and across contexts. When it occurs in context, we learn more detail about the context itself and we enlarge and store our knowledge base by making generalizations and later recalling expectations to those generalizations. When reminding occurs across contexts, we are able to use what we have observed in one domain to help us in another. Such leaps are the stuff of intelligence and insight. When we speak of an idea like *wisdom*, we mean the ability to draw conclusions from many arenas to help us come to new realizations about old phenomena.

Finally, since learning depends so strongly on cross-contextual reminding, it is reasonable to assume that education should focus on this as well. Teachers cannot provide analogies for their students; real learning requires coming to such conclusions on one's own. This cannot happen unless one is exposed to many things, but it would be an error to expose students to history without also having them attempt to explain it on their own. The necessity of presenting history in some sort of time line is thus obviated by the need to present complex historical issues from various time periods and then to allow students to come to their own conclusions about proper courses of action in these historical situations.

CHAPTER 5

Story-based Reminding

For thousands, maybe millions, of years people have been telling stories to each other. They have told stories around the campfire, they have traveled from town to town telling stories to relate the news of the day, they have told stories transmitted by electronic means to passive audiences incapable of doing anything but listening (and watching). Whatever the means, and whatever the venue, storytelling seems to play a major role in human interaction. We get reminded of stories and we use them in conversation to hold up our end of the conversation. In essence, conversation is a mutual remind-athon. Stories follow stories. In a group conversation we take turns in storytelling, as we each wait for our chance to say what we are reminded of.

In some sense, stories seem to be almost the opposite of scripts when viewed as a part of the functioning of memory. Stories are our personal take on what isn't scriptlike about the world; we don't tell a story unless it deviates from the norm in some interesting way. Stories embody our attempts to cope with complexity, whereas scripts obviate the need to think. No matter what the situation, people who have a script to apply need do little thinking; they just do what the script says and they can choose to ignore what doesn't fit. People have thousands of highly personal scripts used on a daily basis that others do not share. Every mundane aspect of life that requires little or no thought can be assumed to be a script. In fact, much of our early education revolves around learning the scripts that others expect us to follow. But, this can all be carried a bit too far. Situations that one person sees as following a script may seem quite open-ended to another person. The more scripts you know, the more situations in which you feel comfortable and capable of playing your role effectively. But, the more scripts you know, the more situations you will fail to wonder about, to be confused by, and to have to figure out on your own. Script-based understanding is a double-edged sword.

We tell stories in order to show what we believe to be true about the world. We derive what we believe from our experiences and, if we wish to persuade others, we tell the stories from which those beliefs were derived. If John explains to Bill his quandary about whether or not to marry Jane or Mary, and Bill responds simply, "Choose Mary," his reply would usually be seen as useless advice. If Bill responds, "Choose Mary because Mary is Irish, and Irish girls make good wives," he is being more helpful but not necessarily more convincing. But, if he responds with a story about a similar situation he was in, or had heard about, and recounts how things worked out, John is likely to be quite interested and willing to take the advice being offered.

Thinking involves indexing. In order to assimilate a story or experience (also referred to here as a *case*) into memory, we must attach it someplace in memory. Information without access to said information is not information at all. Memory, in order to be effective, must contain specific experiences, as well as indices to those experiences. The more information we are provided about a situation, the more places we can attach it to in memory and the more ways it can be compared to other cases in memory. Thus, a story is useful because it comes with many indices. These indices may be locations, beliefs, attitudes, quandaries, decisions, or conclusions. And, the more indices, the greater the number of comparisons to prior experiences and the greater the possibility of future retrieval – and, hence, greater learning.

People tell stories because they know that others like to hear them, although the reason people like to hear stories is not transparent to them. People need a context to help them relate what they have heard to what they already know. We understand events in terms of events we have already understood. When a decision-making heuristic, or rule of thumb, is presented to us without a context, we cannot decide the validity of the rule we have heard, nor do we know where to store it in our memories. Thus, what we are presented with is both difficult to evaluate and difficult to remember, making it virtually useless. People who fail to couch what they have to say in memorable stories will have their rules fall on deaf ears despite their best intentions and despite the best intentions of their listeners. A good teacher is not one who merely explains things correctly, but one who couches explanations in a memorable (i.e., an interesting) format.

Knowledge, then, is experiences and stories, and intelligence is the apt use of experience and of the creation and telling of stories. Memory is memory for stories, and the major processes of memory are the creation, storage, and retrieval of stories. The reminding is what makes all these processes work.

The process of reminding controls understanding and, therefore, conversation. Seen this way, conversations are really a series of remindings of already processed stories. The mind can be considered a collection of stories or experiences one has already had. A conversationalist is eager to tell one of his stories. He wants to tell a good one, a right one, but first he must be reminded of one he knows.

According to this view, it is almost as if we never say anything new; we just find what we have already said and say it again. But, we don't do this freely or randomly; rather, we look for the closest possible matches. But to do this, we must adopt a point of view that allows us to see a situation or experience as an instance of "something like that."

The story-based conception of talking presupposes that everything you might ever want to say has already been thought up. This is not as strange an idea as it seems. I am not suggesting that every sentence one will ever say is sitting in memory word for word. Rather, an adult has views of the world that are expressed by ideas he has thought up already and has probably expressed many times. But, because his views evolve, what he says once might not be identical to what he says the next time. But, the relation between the two statements will be strong and will occur to him as he begins to construct new thoughts. New ideas depend upon old ones.

Understanding Means Mapping Your Stories onto My Stories

For a listener, understanding means mapping the speaker's stories onto his own. One of the most interesting aspects of the way stories are used in memory is the effect they have on understanding. People attempt to construe new stories as old stories they have heard before, because absorbing new information is actually quite difficult to do. New ideas wander through our memories, causing us to revise beliefs, to make new generalizations, and to perform other unnatural acts (like thinking deeply).

A listener with many stories to tell pays enough attention to what you have said that he can relate the story in his repertoire that is most closely connected to what he has heard. This seemingly shallow understanding may be all we can really expect most of the time. This view may seem rather radical. After all, we do see and hear new things every day. To say that we never have to understand any brand new story may be overstating the case. And, of course, we do get presented with new stories – we just don't understand them as new stories. They may be new enough, but we nevertheless persist in seeing them as old stories. The fact that we get reminded of our own stories in response to hearing those of others means that our own stories were unusual in some way. If they had been ordinary cases, they would have been encoded in memory as scripts or some other structure, rather than as stories. Hearing similar stories causes a shift in memory; that is, we recognize the unusual cases to be both more understandable and more predictable because we now have a larger library of cases to recognize and interpret. Think about a person who knows only three stories and tells one of them no matter what story you tell him. The strong form of my hypothesis states that he must decide which of his three stories is most applicable in each situation. When he finds some way to relate a new story to one of his old ones, we can claim he has understood the new story as well as could be hoped.

The understanding process involves extracting elements from the input story that are precisely those elements used to label old stories in memory. Understanding is really the process of index extraction. This is an idiosyncratic process that depends upon which stories you have stored away and which indices you have used to label those stories. In some sense, then, no two people can really understand a story in the same way, because we can understand something only in terms of what we have already understood. Finding a familiar element causes us to activate the story that is labeled by that familiar element, and we understand the new story as if it were an exemplar of that old element. In this way, we find things to say to those who talk to us. These things differ considerably from person to person, thus accounting for the very different ways in which two people can understand the same story. Over time, the fact that we have interesting stories to tell may be of less significance than the fact the we can comprehend unusual events and accurately predict their outcomes.

People are constantly questioning themselves and each other to discover why someone has done something and what the consequences of that action are likely to be. We want to know *why*. Asking ourselves why something happened, or why someone did what he did, helps us create new indices on which to search for old stories that will help us process what we are attempting to understand. We learn when we encounter something that differs from what we already know by just enough to make it understandable, but not so much as to make it incomprehensible. In order to find out *how* we learn, we must find out how we know that we *nee*d to learn. In other words, we need to know how we discover anomalies. How do we know that something does not fit? Anomalies occur when the answers to questions are unknown. Then we seek to explain what was going on, and then we learn (Chi et al., 1989).[1]

Usually when someone does something, an observer tries to determine if that action *makes sense*. But, actions do not make sense absolutely. That is, we cannot determine whether actions make sense except by comparing them to other actions. In a world where everyone walks around with his thumb in his mouth, we don't need to explain why a given individual has his thumb in his mouth. In a world where almost no one does this, we must explain the action. Making sense (and therefore the idea of an anomaly in general) is clearly a relative thing – but relative to what? Relative to the stories we already know. We are satisfied, as observers of actions, when the stories we hear match our own. When the match is very similar, we tell our version of the story. When the match is hardly a match at all, when we have a contradictory story, we tell it. The middle cases are actually the most interesting – when we have no story to tell. What do we do then? We still look for one, by asking ourselves questions.

People do not consciously process information with the intent of finding out whether something is anomalous and needs explaining. In fact, quite the opposite is the case. An understander is trying to determine the place for an action he observes. To do this, he must find a place in memory that was expecting this new action. He may not find one, since not everything in life can be anticipated. A tension thus exists between the attempt to find a story that allows us to think no more, and the desire to see something as new and worth thinking about. So, a person unconsciously asks himself, "Do I know a story that relates to the incoming story, and is it one that will allow me to rest from mental processing or one that will cause me to have to think?"

Indexing Stories

Consider the following story:

K. Demolition and a bullfight
While watching the demolition of a building in Chicago, I was struck by how ineffectively the work was being done. The wreck-

---

[1] Also Read and Cesa (1991) and Graesser, Baggett and Williams (1996).

ing ball hit one of the concrete supports near its center again and again with little result. It was frustrating to watch the lack of progress.

This poorly executed demolition reminded me of the time I saw a bullfight in Spain. The matador kept dealing out blows to the bull with his sword with seemingly little effect. The failure to execute a "clean kill" made the whole affair grotesque.

The expectation failure that provides the index in the two parts of this story has something to do with the way in which the goals of the two observed agents, wrecking-ball operator and matador, are not being achieved. The failure also has to do with the failure of a prediction task, namely, the prediction that the column (and the bull) will fall. The index is formed from the anomaly of a prediction failure. Anomaly is at the heart of index formation for reminding. Any anomaly is set against the backdrop of relationships among the salient details of a story.

Anomalies serve as the trigger for memory access (Read and Cesa, 1991; Gick and McGarry, 1992; Johnson and Seifert, 1992). Finding an anomaly forces us to think about the anomaly, as well as about other stories we have not understood so well. A memory base exists of previous stories, which fall into two classes. The first class includes stories we feel we have understood; the second includes stories we found interesting but somewhat incomprehensible.

An understood story (i.e., a story that belongs to the first class of stories) is one for which we have many examples. One could claim that these stories represent our beliefs. A belief is defined here as a point of view we can illustrate with a number of good stories. Story A ("the steak and the haircut") fits into the second class of stories. The majority of obvious remindings are of this type; they rely on expectation failure, which derives from anomaly. The stories we are reminded of during expectation failure begin the process of belief formation.

In nonanomalous story reminding, we are reminded of an old story by a new one and feel compelled to tell the old story as a response. In a sense, our old story is the means for understanding the new story and so overpowers the new story that we remember little of it. In anomalous story reminding, we are reminded of an old story, and the experience of having that reminding feels somewhat peculiar. Rather than feeling compelled to tell our reminded story, we feel curious about the reminding, wondering how we happened to think about it. We might tell the story if it is appropriate to do so, but we still are left wondering what the connection is.

Let's look back at another example of an anomalous story reminding. The demolition/bullfight reminding (story K) may be interpreted in a variety of ways:

1. the frustrated observer (laborious destruction, botched kill)
2. the inept agent (crane operator, matador)
3. the blocked goal (destroy building, kill bull)
4. the noble object of destruction that holds up against all odds (pillar, bull)

Although all these interpretations are plausible, only one consistent and coherent rendering is responsible for the formation of an initial indexed probe of memory: The anomaly is in the theory of planning, which generates the expectations that a worker with a task to do will select an appropriate plan with the right resources (methods and tools) to execute the plan expeditiously. It is also the viewer's inference that the crane operator and the matador have selected the same causal model of planning, but have picked an inappropriate method for the plan. Seeing the futility of the crane operator's and matador's actions, in the presence of an aesthetic goal to see the job done cleanly, produces frustration or disappointment, a type of *behavior expectation failure.*

In general, an anomaly-based index is a system of interrelated goals, expectations, events, and explanations. The index needs to include causal information about events and about expected outcomes as contrasted to actual outcomes. It is the contrast between causal theories and causal realities that serves as the means for finding prior stories with the same anomalous character.

We might be tempted to imagine that we create questions for ourselves only when our curiosity is aroused by confusion about something we have observed, but we are often forced by social circumstances to create questions for ourselves to answer. When somebody says something to us, we are supposed to say something back. But what? Is there always something worth saying? Whether or not we have something important to say, given that we have to have something to say, and given that this happens to us all the time, we have developed various methods of coping with this situation. So, we ask ourselves questions. But the questions we ask ourselves about what others have told us cannot be dependent solely upon what we have heard. In a sense, since we are both asking and answering these questions, we need to know that we can answer a question before we ask it. That is, the questions we ask serve as memory calls, requests to get information from memory that will be of use in the formulation of a response to what we have heard.

In response to hearing a story, we want to know what questions to ask ourselves that would allow a story of our own to come to mind. We can start simply by considering the paradigmatic case in which the response to a story is a story in which one says, "The same thing happened to me." The call to memory that might retrieve a story where the same thing happened is obviously not likely to be *look for the same thing*. First, the same thing that happened is rarely the same thing literally. Second, the characterization of the initial story would have to be stored in memory within certain parameters. To put this another way, we can't look for *the same thing* without characterizing that thing, and that characterization immediately allows the possibility that *the same thing* will not be found.

Sameness, at the level being discussed, exists with respect to plans, the goals that drive those plans, and the themes that drive those goals. Thus, when someone tells you a story, you ask yourself, "Are there any events in my memory where I had a similar goal for a similar reason?" We can match new stories to old ones on the basis of identical goals. When confronted with new problems, people almost inevitably search their memories for similar problems they have already solved (Johnson and Seifert, 1992; Gholson et al., 1996). They are, in essence, recalling their own prior problem-solving stories.

When we understand a story, we relate it to something in our own lives. But to what? To see a story in a particular way means you have constructed an index that characterizes a "point" (often highly idiosyncratic) derived from the story. Usually the points derived from stories relate to goals, plans, beliefs, and lessons learned from the story. Here we are back to interestingness again. We don't focus on points that fail to relate to beliefs we already have – we look instead for ones that verify beliefs we already have. When a new story can be absorbed into our memories as a "natural fit" with other stories we already know, we feel we have understood the story.

Consider for a moment what it might mean for an understander to believe something and not be able to justify why he believes it. Certainly, inarticulate people have difficulty with that sort of thing. We use the ability to justify one's beliefs with evidence as a measure of intelligence and reasonableness. But how do intelligent people find the stories that explain why and what they believe? The mental mechanisms that are available must be ones that connect beliefs to stories.

The fact that we can do this is obvious. It follows, therefore, that beliefs are one possible index in memory. Construct a belief, and you should be able to find a story that exemplifies it.

An index is a juxtaposition of another person's beliefs (made evident by his statements or actions) and one's own beliefs. (We saw this in the *Romeo and Juliet* example, in which the belief conflict was the index.) Indices are not beliefs, but rather beliefs about beliefs. In other words, our reactions to the implicit beliefs of others cause us to consider what we believe about the same subject. Either we can directly access what we believe by finding our own belief and telling a story that exemplifies it, or we can use the belief expressed in the story as if it were one of our own and see what story we might have stored away in memory under that label. Alternatively, we can create a belief that is a juxtaposition of what we heard and what we might think about what we heard. This belief might already exist and thus we would find another story to tell, but if the belief is new, we must create a story that exemplifies it, or it will be lost.

Indices are phenomenally complicated and phenomenally important. We find what we want to say effortlessly and unconsciously. But, to do so, we must construct complex labels for events that describe their content, their import, their relation to what we know and what we believe, and much more. Effective indexing allows us to have stories to tell and enables us to learn from the juxtaposition of others' stories and the stories we are reminded of.

How does this kind of very subjective understanding work? The key point is that there is no one way to understand any story. When someone hears a story, he looks for beliefs that are being commented upon. Any story has many possible beliefs inherent in it. Someone listening to a story finds those beliefs by looking through the beliefs he already has. He is not as concerned with what he is hearing as he is with finding what he already knows that is relevant. Once we find a belief and connected story, no further processing, that is, no search for other beliefs, need be done. We rarely try to understand a story in more than one way. The mind cannot easily pursue multiple paths.

People as diverse as reading comprehension testers and artificial intelligence researchers agree that *understanding* is the incorporation of aspects of what one has understood into some permanent memory store. Learning something new is usually seen as incorporating something brand new into memory. My argument is that precious little of this kind of understanding actually takes place. We rarely really learn anything new at all. And measuring this kind of learning is foolhardy. It is likely to measure temporary phenomena, like whether someone has committed a random list to memory. Such lists have nowhere to live in memory, no memory structure to which they belong, so they fade rather quickly.

A more accurate measure of understanding is the one people use on a daily basis, namely a subjective evaluation of the story we get back in response to one of our own. People who have understood something can elaborate upon what they have understood with knowledge of their own, taken from their own previous experiences or from the experiences of others that they have absorbed. If their elaboration is a great deal like the story they were told, we feel they have understood. In this case, then, understanding means clever indexing. But, it should be clear, index extraction is a highly subjective process with no prescribed way of finding indices.

Learning Something New

The premise behind the conception of a dynamic memory is that we try to help ourselves in understanding by finding the most relevant information we have in our memory to use as a guide. But, when what is to be understood in a story is about beliefs, the kind of guidance we need changes. We don't need to know what will happen next or to assess someone's plan so we can counterplan against it. All we are trying to do is understand the stories we hear.

When the understanding process gets complicated, the primary mechanism we have available to guide our understanding, namely reminding, must work especially hard on rather scanty evidence to find something to get reminded of. The main fodder for reminding in such circumstances is beliefs. Our own beliefs cause our own personal stories to come to mind when those beliefs happen also to be indices in our own memories. But then a strange thing happens – we feel compelled to tell those stories. Once we have found our own story, we basically stop processing.

The reason for stopping is partially based upon our intentions in the first place. Since most of the time we are really just looking for something to say back in response, once we have found something, we have little reason to process further. But more important, what we have found usually relates to an arguable point, an idea subject to challenge, a belief about which we are uncertain. As learners, one of our goals is to gather evidence about the world so that we can formulate better beliefs, ones that will equip us better to deal with the real world. Once we have found a match between someone else's experience and our own, we are ready to begin thinking about the connections so that we can add or subtract beliefs from our own personal data base.

There is an unusual side effect to all this. We really cannot learn from other people's stories. In getting reminded of our own stories, ones that may be more poignant and more rich in detail than the ones we are hearing, we tend to get distracted into thinking more about what happened to us. The incoming story can get recalled in terms of the story of which we were reminded, but in the end, we rarely recall the stories of others easily. More often than not, other people's stories don't have the richness of detail and emotional impact that allows them to be stored in multiple ways in our memories. They do, on the other hand, provide enough details and emotions to allow them to be more easily stored than if the teller had simply told us his belief.

So we are left with an odd picture of understanding. Real communication is rather difficult to achieve. We do not easily remember what other people have said if they do not tell us in the form of a story. We can learn from the stories of others, but only if what we hear relates strongly to something we already know. We can learn from these stories to the extent that they cause us to rethink our own stories. But, mostly we learn from a reexamination of our own stories. We hear, in the stories of others, what we personally can relate to, by virtue of having heard or experienced, in some way, that story before. Understanding is an idiosyncratic affair. Our idiosyncrasies come from our stories.

Stories and Memory

Why, when something important happens to you, do you feel compelled to tell someone else about it? Even someone who is reticent to talk about himself can't help telling others about events significant to him. It's as if nothing has happened until an event is made explicit in language. Why do we tell stories? We often talk in order to tell about, comment upon, and analyze our own personal experiences.

Imagine, for example, that you have just returned from a vacation or that you meet someone who knows that you have recently been on a date that you were especially looking forward to. In either of these situations, when you are asked how it went, you can respond with a short pithy sentence or two, or you can begin to tell a story that captures the essential parts of the experience. Now imagine that another person asks you substantially the same question. How different is your second response likely to be from your first? Of course, the amount of time you have available to tell the story, or differences in intimacy with the person you tell it to, may affect the telling, but the likelihood is that, on a gross level, the subsequent stories you tell will leave out and emphasize the same things. The gist of the stories will be substantially the same.

The process of story creation, of condensing an experience into a story-size chunk that can be told in a reasonable amount of time, makes the story chunks smaller and smaller as details are forgotten (although they can get larger when fictional details are added). Normally, after much retelling of the story we have chosen to remember, we are left with only the details. In short, story creation is a memory process. As we tell a story, we are formulating the gist of the experience, which we can recall whenever we create a story describing that experience.

We need to tell someone else a story that describes our experience because the process of creating the story also creates the memory structure that will contain the gist of the story for the rest of our lives. Talking is remembering. It seems odd, at first, that this should be true. Certainly, psychologists have known for years that rehearsal helps memory. But telling a story isn't rehearsal, it is creation. The act of creating is a memorable experience in itself.

In order to remember an experience, then, we must tell it to someone. If we don't tell the story soon enough or often enough, or if we don't tell it at all, the experience cannot be coalesced into a gist. The component pieces of the story can mix with new information that continues to come in, and thus the pieces lose their coherency as a story. We cannot remember a great restaurant if we keep eating in ones quite like it day after day. Understanders need the time and the opportunity to reflect, otherwise the gist gets "lost in the details." This reflection can be in the form of telling stories to others or even just to ourselves. In other words, although parts of an experience may be remembered in terms of the memory structures that were activated – a restaurant may be recalled through cues involving food or a place or the particular company – the story itself does not exist as an entity in memory. Thus, without telling a story, we lose any generalization that might pertain to the whole of the experience. In the end, we tell stories in order to remember them.

100

Let's imagine a day in the life of a man living alone in a city. He works by himself and for himself. He sees and talks to no one about his particular experiences during the course of one day. He gets a haircut. He buys some groceries. He shops for new shoes. He fills out tax forms at home and watches some television. At work, he reads some material that has been sent to him, but he writes down nothing about that material. The next day he resumes a more normal life, interacting with people and talking about his experiences, but for some reason he never speaks to anyone about the day we have just described. What can he remember about that day? The answer to this is complex because we don't know two things. First, how unusual is this day for him? And, second, how much rehearsal has occurred? Let me explain why each of these questions matters.

What makes an event memorable is both its uniqueness (Berntsen, 1996) and its significance to you personally (Anderson and Conway, 1993).[2] For example, we easily remember the time we first do anything of significance. So, if this man has never spent a day alone or if he was deliberately trying out such a life style, he would probably remember the day. Or would he? At first glance, it seems probable that he would remember such a unique or significant day; therefore, how easily can we imagine the man's never telling anyone about it? If people are incapable of not telling others about significant events, then this man, too, feeling that the day was important, would be likely to mention it to someone.

This brings up the question of rehearsal. One phenomenon of memory is that people talk to themselves – not necessarily aloud, of course, but they do tell themselves stories and ask themselves questions about those stories, collecting disparate events into coherent wholes. So, let's imagine that although this man talked to no one about his day, he did talk to himself. What might he have said or wondered about? If rehearsal entails storytelling, he would have had to compose a story with some pertinent generalizations or observations drawn from the day. Moreover, he would have had to keep retelling himself that story in order to remember it.

What happens if he fails to tell anyone, including himself, about his day? Does he fail to recognize the grocery store where he shopped when he sees it again next week? Does he fill out his tax forms again? Must he reread the material that was sent to him at work? Of course

[2] Also Read and Cesa (1991).

not. Obviously, we can remember events that we have not discussed with anyone. But how? How are events like going to the grocery store remembered? Certainly such events never become stories, so they are not maintained in memory by repeated telling. How, then, are they maintained? The answer is that memory has two separate capacities, often referred to by psychologists as the semantic/episodic memory distinction. This distinction, however, misses the point.

Psychologists have long noted that memory must be organized hierarchically (Fivush 1984; Conway and Bekerian, 1987; Hue and Erickson, 1991), because certain information seems to be stored around general concepts that help us understand more subordinate concepts. So, for example, we know a flounder has gills simply because we know fish have gills and a flounder is a fish. Clearly, people must have information organized in this way at least to some extent, because they know a great deal more than they have ever actually experienced.

An episodic memory, on the other hand, is one in which we store actual events that have occurred in our own lives. So, visiting Grandma's house on Thanksgiving is an episode in memory. Such episodes don't seem to be organized hierarchically (even though they are sometimes in a general form and other times in a more specific form). Are *visits to Grandma on Thanksgiving* stored under *visits to relatives, holiday get-togethers,* or *wild parties I have attended?* Or, have so many *visits to Grandma on Thanksgiving* become a central category of its own? And, if so, what would the creation of such a category mean? Would it mean that the answer to what you ate that day was always turkey? It would if what you ate was always turkey, but the time you ate duck instead might also be remembered.

The distinction between semantic and episodic memory is a matter of some debate to psychologists, largely because the issues are not well defined. A neatly organized hierarchy of semantic concepts is easy to imagine, but the world is full of oddities and idiosyncratic events that fail to fit neatly into a preestablished hierarchy. For example, we may "know" from semantic memory that female horses have teats, but we may more readily access this fact from an episodic store if we witnessed our pet horse giving birth and then suckling its young.

A more useful distinction can be drawn between story-based memory on the one hand and a generalized event-based memory on the other. To understand this distinction, let's go back to the question of where our hero's grocery store, tax-form filing, and report-reading experiences are stored in his memory. We know that he can recall what he did in each instance; how is this ability to recall different than his ability to tell a story? Probably he cannot tell the story of his day, although he can recall certain aspects of it. This difference reflects itself in a kind of abstract idea of "place" in memory.

To "recall" the grocery store visit means to know he has been there. Had something interesting happened there, especially something that taught him something new, we can feel sure that he would remember it. But, how can we make this assertion when he probably won't be able to recall this day if he never talks about it to anyone? We seem to have a paradox here, but in fact, we do not.

When people have experiences in a grocery store, they update their knowledge of grocery stores. If this were not the case, people would never learn where the milk was, or how much things cost, or when to take out their check cashing card. When these things change, people change along with them. Sometimes it takes a few trials; they still look for the milk where it used to be, but eventually, changes in memory follow changes in reality. So, people learn from their experiences – but where does this learning take place in the mind?

People need a file of information about grocery stores that includes specific information about where their favorite grocery store keeps the milk and what it wants in order to cash a check. This file must also include general information about grocery stores apart from their favorite, so they can utilize expectations about their favorite store to help them in a new one. New experiences that teach us something worthwhile are added to our knowledge file.

What we are decidedly *not* doing, however, is updating our memories on what we might call a daily unit basis. That is, we are not making note that on October 16, we bought a quart of milk and six oranges. This sort of information does not help us learn anything about the world. People are intelligent rememberers. We remember an experience in order to add to a storehouse of knowledge that might be useful later on. This storehouse of knowledge is analogous to the psychologist's concept of semantic memory: We must have a way to store knowledge so that it can be used again next time, knowledge that teaches us about the world in general, knowledge that is rather similar from human being to human being. Although this notion that a part of memory should be devoted to such general knowledge seems inherently correct, the notion that such knowledge would not have at its core a seriously idiosyncratic component seems equally wrong. We may all know that a flounder is a fish and that a fish has gills, but we do not all know that our father used to eat flounder every Tuesday and, therefore, so did we, and we refuse to eat it ever again. Yet, this last fact is just as much a part of the definition of flounder for us as is the fact that a flounder has gills – maybe more so, since one fact is far more real to us than the other.

Any general storehouse of knowledge, then, is likely to depend very strongly upon the expectations about various objects and situations that have been gathered over a lifetime of experience. Thus, when a new experience occurs that speaks to what we already know about something, perhaps updating it, perhaps overriding it, we add that experience to our memories. Similarly, when we read something, the facts we garner from our reading go to particular places in memory, that is, to the structures we have that are repositories of information about those subjects. Through such structures, and through the sharing of smaller structures by larger structures, we build up generalizations about the world. Every time we use a particular body of knowledge in our interactions with the world, that knowledge gets altered by our experiences. We cannot fill out a tax form without using the prior experiences we have had in filling out tax forms as a guide to help us through the experience. But because that knowledge is being used as a guide, it changes. We add new information about tax forms, about the experience of filling them out, that overrides what we previously knew. When we are finished doing anything, therefore, our memories are altered by the experience. We don't know what we knew before, or what changed.

One consequence of this dynamic nature of memory is that because actual experiences are constantly being broken up into their component pieces and are being added to general event memory bit by bit in different places, no coherent whole remains. If we did not break up our daily experiences into their component parts, we would never learn anything cross contextually.

The process of updating our general knowledge base has an odd side effect. The construction of a memory that organizes information around generalized events destroys the coherence between the particular instantiation of those events. A single event of walking, therefore, becomes disconnected from its intended purpose of enabling one to go shopping at one particular time. So our hero doesn't know how he got to the grocery store on his weekly trip last Sunday. His only recourse is to make an educated guess: "I must have walked; it's not far, and I usually walk if it's a nice day, and it was June after all." In this way, people reconstruct stories whose details they have long since forgotten (Slackman and Nelson, 1984; Myles-Worsley, Cromer and Dodd, 1986).

Because of memory's need to effect a constant disconnection of previous events from those that follow, we feel a need to undo this process when something of significance occurs. We can stop the dynamic disconnection from taking place and can remember events in sequence by consciously giving our memories an event to remember that is a unit, specifically, a unit we have rehearsed, sometimes frequently. In this process, the role of stories in memory comes into play, and hence the concept of *story-based memory* arises.[3] Stories are a way of preserving the connectivity of events that would otherwise be disassociated over time. One reason we tell stories, therefore, is to help ourselves in remembering them.

For stories to be told without a great deal of effort, they must be stored away in a fashion that enables us to access them as a unit. If this were not the case, stories would have to be reconstructed each time they were told, a process that would become more and more difficult with time as a particular event faded from memory. Telling a story would require a great deal of work if we needed to collect all the events from memory and to reconstruct their interrelation. Further, stories would be quite different each time they were told, because reconstruction would not be the same each time. A different type of memory process, then, must be active here. Our hero who fails to tell stories from his isolated day will understand and remember what has happened to him in the sense that the facts will be available to him. But they will be available to him only when the various segments of his day are accessed for some reason, when someone asks him about his favorite grocery store, for example. What he will lose is the ability to tell a story about that particular day. The day will disappear as a unit from memory, as will various aspects of the day. What will be remembered will be in terms of what he knows about grocery stores, not a story in and of itself arising from the events of that day. To find that kind of story in his memory, he would have to have put it there consciously in the first place, by telling it either to someone or to himself. Similarly, if we want students to remember what they have done, they

---

[3] Kolodner (1993) on case-based reasoning.

must tell about it (at least, tell it to themselves if they can't share it with others). The more they have to think about what they tell, the more they will remember. Student learning depends upon student experience and the relating of that experience to others. The more interesting the experience, the more the students will want to tell it to others. Mandatory storytelling just doesn't work.

CHAPTER 6

The Kinds of Structures in Memory

Memory is a morass of complex structures, related by the episodes they point to and the temporal and causal connections between them. Learning means the augmentation and creation of such structures. Through experience, memories become useful containers of expectations about the world. But practice isn't the only thing needed to help people learn. Teaching becomes increasingly important as the level of abstraction required becomes more complex. Encouraging a student to see one experience as a variant of another is a key issue in teaching (Gholson et al., 1996; Bransford et al., 1989), as is encouraging the repetition of events that must be learned by practice. We learn through experience, reflection, and explanation, each of which helps us build the abstract memory structures we need.

The Nature of Understanding

Two people can have the same experience, yet encode it differently. They can see the same thing as confirmation of quite different beliefs, because we see in terms of what we have already experienced.[1] The structures we have available in memory are an embodiment of our experiences, and we understand new experiences in terms of our prior structures, which reflect how we have understood things in the past. Thus, it is critical to carefully reflect upon the nature of memory structures.

In Chapter 2, I discussed how a Burger King trip might remind someone of McDonald's. What kind of reminding is this? There are two possibilities. If McDonald's is encoded in memory as a failure of

---

[1] From an educational standpoint, this is one of the central motivations behind Piaget's notion of constructivism; we must teach students by working from their existing knowledge (Scardamalia and Bereiter, 1991; Bruer, 1993; Linn et al., 1994). Also Ross and Kennedy (1990), Seifert (1990), Kolodner (1993), and Gholson et al. (1996).

our normal expectations about restaurants, Burger King would constitute a similar failure, and reminding would occur because the same restaurant structure was accessed and the same failure was noted. On the other hand, McDonald's could be encoded in memory as an entity in its own right, apart from knowledge about restaurants in general. In that case, the natural processing of Burger King should lead to the same structure that encoded McDonald's. Use of a structure that has a unique referent (McDonald's) will also cause one to be reminded of that referent.

Understanding an input means finding the closest approximation in one's past experience to the input and coding the input in terms of the previous memory by means of an index that indicates the difference between the new input and the old memory (Hudson and Nelson, 1986; Hudson, Fivush and Kuebli, 1992). Understanding, then, implies using expectation failures driven by prototypical memories or by specific memories indexed under prototypical memories. Understanding is reminding (or recognizing, to take that word literally), and reminding is finding the correct memory structure to process an input. The major problem, then, in formulating a theory of understanding, is to find out what the requisite high-level memory structures might look like that are activated in reminding.

How Do High-Level Structures Get Built?

To discover how high-level structures are built, let us digress for a moment to the topic of how scripts or similar structures might come to exist in the human mind. Children, as we have noted in Schank and Abelson (1977) and as Nelson and Gruendel (1979) note, learn scripts from a very early age (Fivush, 1984; Slackman and Nelson, 1984; Adams and Worden, 1986; Ratner, Smith and Dion, 1986; Hull Smith et al., 1989; Bauer and Mandler, 1990; Farrar and Goodman, 1992). I hypothesize that the basic entity of human understanding is what I have termed the *personal script*, our private expectations about how things proceed in our own lives on a day-to-day or minute-to-minute basis. In the beginning, a child's world is organized solely in terms of personal scripts, that is, private expectations about getting a diaper changed or being fed. Such expectations abound for children, who can be quite vocal when their expectations are violated. The child who has gotten a piece of candy at every grocery store visit will complain wildly when he does not get it at the current grocery store. These expectations are not limited to such positively anticipated experiences, however. Trifles such as taking a different route to the same place or not being placed in the same seat as last time are very important to children and serve as reminders to us of the significance of personal scripts in children's lives.

As time goes on, children begin to notice that other human beings share some, but not all, of their expectations. When a child discovers, for example, that his personal restaurant script is also shared by other people, he can resort to a new method of storage for restaurant information. He can rely on a prototypical restaurant script with certain personal markings that store his own idiosyncratic points of view. He can begin to organize his experiences in terms that separate what is peculiar to his experience from what is shared by his culture. For example, adults know that getting in a car is not part of the restaurant script. However, this may be a very salient feature of a child's personal restaurant script. It is very important for a child to learn that the car experience must be separated from the restaurant experience so that he can recognize a restaurant without having gone there by car and so he can understand and talk about other people's restaurant experiences. Thus, the child must learn to reorganize his memory store according to cultural norms.

Adults do not abandon personal scripts as important organizational entities. We still expect the doorman to say good morning as he opens the door, or expect the children to demand to be played with immediately after dinner, or whatever sequences we are used to. We may no longer cry when these things do not happen, but we expect them nonetheless. These expectations pervade our lives just as they did when we were children.

We continue indefinitely to reorganize information we have stored (Ratcliff and McKoon, 1988; Wattenmaker, 1992; Ross, 1996b). New experiences are constantly being reorganized on the basis of similar experiences and cultural norms. The abstraction and generalization process for knowledge acquired through experience is thus a fundamental part of adult understanding. When you go to a dentist for the first time, everything in that experience is stored either as a single, isolated chunk, or in terms of experiences (with other dentists, perhaps) that seem similar. Repeated experiences with the same dentist or other dentists, and descriptions of others' experiences with dentists, serve to reorganize the original information in terms of what is peculiar to your dentist, dentists in general, yourself in dental offices, and so on. The reorganization process never stops. When similarities between dentists and doctors are seen, a further reorganization can be made in terms of health care professionals. When dentists' and lawyers' similarities are extracted, yet another memory organization point emerges. The key to understanding is this continual creation of new high-level structures where the essential similarities between different experiences are recorded (Seifert, Abelson and McKoon, 1986; McKoon, Ratcliff and Seifert, 1989).

According to this theoretical view of memory, one's concept of an event is simply the collocation of one's repeated encounters with that event. After only one trip to the dentist, the dentist who treated you is your prototypical dentist (there is no distinction in memory between a personal script and a prototypical representation of a dentist's visit based on only a single experience). Over time, your concept of a dentist evolves. Similar or identical parts of the various dentist experiences you have had are abstracted into structures representing the generalized prototype. New experiences are then stored in terms of their differences from the prototype (Hudson and Nelson, 1986; Hudson, Fivush and Kuebli, 1992).

Because memories are stored together in this way, we can draw inferences, or have expectations, in a new situation based on our access to prior relevant experiences in memory. This is why no two people will have the exact same encoding of a situation, though they may share some common expectations based on cultural norms – they each have their own personal experiences serving as a referent for all future similar episodes.

To begin a survey of different kinds of high-level structures, consider a possible story about a trip to the dentist. I will attempt to answer two questions with this example: What knowledge is used in processing the various parts of the story? and, What question does memory look like after the story has been processed? Since memory structures and processing structures are the same thing, it should be clear that any story has the potential for altering memory, especially if it differs from the prototypes that are being used to process it. In particular, any failures of expectations arising from those prototypes will in some way cause an alteration to memory.

Previously, Schank and Abelson (1977) said that the DENTIST script would handle a visit to the dentist. This script would contain a list of events normally found in visits to the dentist, connected together causally. In addition, tracks of such a script would represent the alternative sequences of events that could take place. Under this conception of a script, the script's primary role was as an orderer of scenes, each of which in turn served to order events within those scenes. Each action encoded in a script thus served as an expectation being made by memory about incoming input.

What of all this do I wish to keep in my present conception of things, and what do I believe to be missing? The first change I have been suggesting transforms the notion of a script from a passive data structure from which expectations are hung, to an active memory structure that changes in response to new input. The failure of expectations derived from a script will cause indices to be placed in the script at the failure points. When similar failures are noted, the memory indexed by them directs processing at the appropriate point. I have already discussed this to some extent and will have more to say about this self-organization process in Chapter 9. The key point here is that scripts are active memory structures.

What else is missing from the prior conception of scripts? As discussed in Chapter 1, a serious problem was demonstrated by the Bower, Black and Turner (1979) experiments, namely, the problem of determining the right level of information to be stored in scripts. It seems reasonable to suppose that what we know about dentists' waiting rooms is just what we know about waiting rooms in general and is not specific to dentists. Thus an event that occurs in a dentist's waiting room is more likely to be remembered as occurring in a waiting room than in a dentist's office. We can expect that what we know about waiting rooms in general may apply in a great many other circumstances.

The same thing is true of many of the other activities involved in a visit to a dentist. *Paying the bill* or *getting to the dentist's office* involves knowledge sources, and hence memories, that may not involve dentists at all. We use what we know about these two activities to help us understand a visit to the dentist – in fact, this very knowledge serves to form our expectations about what will go on during the visit – but there is no reason to assume that the memories and memory structures we use in these situations are stored in any way that connects them intimately to what we know about dentists. To drive to a dentist's office, we do not need to know anything about dentists except how to get to that particular dentist's office.

What I am suggesting, then, is that a lot of knowledge previously theorized to have been stored as part of the dentist script is, in reality, part of other memory structures used in understanding a story involving a dentist visit. Such a suggestion has three ramifications. First, it implies that scripts do not exist in the form previously proposed. Although it may be possible to collect all the expectations we have about a complex event into one complex structure, such a structure does not actually exist in memory. Instead, the expectations are distributed in smaller, shareable units. Second, if a diverse set of memory structures is used for processing a story about a visit to a dentist, and if memory structures are the same as processing structures, then it follows that a story about a visit to the dentist will get broken up by memory into several distinct pieces. That is, whatever happens in driving to the dentist's office, if it is of interest to memory, will be stored as a modification of what we know about driving, not dentists. Each event will be processed by, and stored in terms of, the structure that relates most closely to that event.

Such a scheme has the disadvantage of forcing us to use a reconstructive memory to help us recall events that have happened to us (although we may not be able to reconstruct everything) (Slackman and Nelson, 1984; Myles-Worsley, Cromer and Dodd, 1986; Farrar and Goodman, 1992). But this disadvantage is more than outweighed by the powerful advantage of enabling us to learn by generalizing from experiences by noticing commonalities. I shall discuss this trade-off more carefully in the remainder of this book.

The third important ramification is that there must be available some memory structures that connect other memory structures together. In order to reconstruct what has happened to us and to have the relevant structures available for processing when they are needed, memory structures must exist that tie other structures together in the proper order. Even though we have learned to disassociate memories about WAITING ROOM from those specific to DENTIST, we still need to know that dentist visits involve waiting rooms. Information about how memory structures are ordinarily linked in frequently occurring combinations is held in a *memory organization packet* or MOP.

It follows from what I have said so far that a MOP is both a memory structure and a processing structure. As a memory structure, a MOP has the role of providing a place to store new inputs. As a processing structure, a MOP has the role of providing expectations that enable the prediction of future inputs or the inference of implicit events on the basis of previously encountered, structurally similar events.[2] In short, a MOP is the high-level structure that processes new inputs by taking the aspects of those inputs that relate to that MOP and interpreting those aspects in terms of the past experiences most closely related to them. A MOP thus organizes related aspects of our experiences, such as the different scenes in a dentist's office visit.

Some Detail

I said in Chapter 1 that scenes hold memories. Scenes are general structures that describe how and where a particular set of actions takes place. WAITING ROOM or AIRPORT RENT-A-CAR COUNTER are possible scenes. Scripts (in the new formulation of them) embody specific predictions connected to the more general scene that dominates them. Thus, an individual might have a DOCTOR JONES' WAITING ROOM script that differs in some way from the more general WAITING ROOM scene. Scenes, therefore, can point to scripts that embody specific aspects of those scenes. Scripts can also hold memories that are organized around expectation failures within that script. According to this theoretical view, a script is bounded by the scene that contains it. Thus, scripts do not cross scene boundaries.

MOPs differ from scenes and scripts in the amount of knowledge they cover and the generality of that knowledge. A script must be limited to a sequence of actions that take place in one physical setting. Similarly, a scene is setting bounded. But a MOP can contain information that covers many settings. Furthermore, a MOP has a purpose that is not readily inferable from each of the scenes or scripts that it contains. Because of this, memory confusions can take place when we forget which MOP a particular scene-based memory was connected to. This is like remembering what you did without remembering exactly why you were doing it.

It is important to consider how MOPs function in the understanding process. The primary job of a MOP in processing new inputs is to provide relevant memory structures that will in turn provide expectations necessary to understanding what is being received. Thus MOPs are responsible for filling in implicit information about what events must have happened but were not explicitly remembered.

At least two MOPs are relevant to the processing, memory, and understanding of what a visit to a dentist's office entails; they are

---

[2] See Seifert, Abelson and McKoon (1986) and McKoon, Ratcliff and Seifert (1989) for evidence of such structures in memory.

M–PROFESSIONAL OFFICE VISIT and M–CONTRACT. Each of these MOPs organizes scenes and scripts relevant to the processing of any story involving a visit to a dentist. WAITING ROOM, for example, is one of the scenes in M–PROFESSIONAL OFFICE VISIT (henceforth M–POV).

The primary function of M–POV is to provide the correct sequencing of the scenes that provide the appropriate expectations for use in processing. In order to create the proper set of expectations, we must recognize which MOPs are applicable. How do we do this? Consider the following story:

L. Waiting for the dentist
I went to the dentist's yesterday. While I was reading a magazine, I noticed that a patient who arrived after me was being taken ahead of me. The dentist will probably still overcharge me!

Previously, in the script-based theory, I would have said that the first line of this story called in a comprehensive dentist script. I am currently postulating that no such entity should exist in memory as a pre-stored chunk. A memory that used a high-level structure such as *dentist visit* would not be able to take advantage of similarities across experiences. Thus it would not learn in any truly interesting way. We must be able to remember an experience by retrieving the memories of the pieces that composed that experience.

In processing the first sentence of this story, we must call in the relevant MOPs, insofar as we can determine them, and begin to set up expectations to help in processing the rest of the story. This is done as follows: The phrase "went to the dentist" refers to *dentist*, which is something about which we have information. *Dentist* is a token in memory. Every token in memory has information attached to it telling us where to look for further information. Attached to the dentist token is, among other things, information about the MOPs that a dentist, in the role as a professional health care provider, is likely to participate in.

The information attached to the dentist token relevant to this example is a combination of MOPs and information about the conditions in the world that tell us when those MOPs are likely to be active. This includes parsing information about which words or concepts in the context *dentist* may help to tell us which MOP may be active. In this case, "go to dentist" activated the MOP that refers to going to a dentist's office for professional dental services. This activates M–POV, which has information attached to it concerning which other MOPs might also be active when M–POV is active. In addition to what we know about visits to a professional's office, we also know quite a bit about why the actors in the various scenes of that MOP do what they do. Knowing this allows us to predict further actions not explicitly part of M–POV. For example, it is in no sense a requisite part of M–POV for people to pay for the service they get. (Services could be free, as dental care is in various countries.) Included as part of M–POV in our storyteller's experience, then, is information that the MOP M–CONTRACT is also activated when M–POV is activated. That is, this person knows that an implicit contract has been made by patient and dentist, that a bill will be sent as a result of this contract, that the patient will be sued if payment isn't made, and so on.

A MOP serves to organize a set of scenes and scripts commonly associated in memory with a goal. Thus, M–POV organizes what we know about what ordinarily takes place in a visit to a professional's office. It would not have in it anything specific to the higher-level goals involved in such a visit. But M–HEALTH PROTECTION, which does include such information, is also activated by "go to dentist." As we shall see later on, MOPs tend to come in threes. The three active in a dentist visit are M–HEALTH PROTECTION, M–CONTRACT, and M–POV. These correspond to personal, societal, and physical MOPs respectively.

A scene defines a setting, an instrumental goal, and actions that take place in that setting in service of that goal. These actions are defined in terms of specific and generalized memories relating to that setting and goal. For example, *ordering in a restaurant* or *getting your baggage in an airport* are scenes. As long as there is an identifiable physical setting and a goal being pursued with that setting, we have a scene. A script, which I will now refer to as a scriptlet, to make its reduced status clear, is a sequence of actions that take place within a scene. Many scriptlets can encode the various possibilities for the realization of a scene. That is, a scriptlet instantiates or colors a scene. Scenes contain general information; scriptlets provide the specifics. This will be explained more carefully in Chapter 7.

Let us look in detail at the structure of two of the MOPs, M–POV and M-CONTRACT. M–POV has the following structure (the entities between the plus signs are the structures organized by the MOP):

[get there] + WAITING ROOM + GET SERVICE + PAY +
    [get back]

M–CONTRACT consists of
[get contact] + NEGOTIATE + AGREE + DELIVER + PAY

The most important aspect of the structures organized by a MOP is that the structures should be general enough to be used by other MOPs. For example, the PAY scene is used by a great many MOPs in addition to M–POV. If you lost your wallet, you might attempt to figure out where you had it last. You might remember putting it down near a cash register while paying. The problem then would be to differentiate one PAY event from another. The fact that this is difficult indicates that PAY is a shared structure.

There is another way in which sharing memory structures can cause memory confusion. An event that takes place in WAITING ROOM will be stored in WAITING ROOM and thus will be linked to M–POV. But M–POV can be linked to a variety of different situations (dentists, accountants, lawyers, etc.) that use M–POV. Thus, an event that takes place in a WAITING ROOM may easily become disassociated from the particular waiting room that was used.

We are constantly reconstructing episodic memories using generic MOP information. As we repeatedly have similar experiences, distinguishing between the details of a particular episode and the generic details provided by the MOP becomes increasingly difficult (Adams and Worden, 1986; McKoon, Ratcliff and Seifert, 1989; Farrar and Goodman, 1992). But the disadvantage of sharing memory structures (i.e., it creates possibilities for memory confusion) is outweighed by the advantage gained in allowing generalizations. At the cost of being unable, on occasion, to remember which waiting room a certain event occurred in, or where a certain instance of paying took place, we gain the advantage of having all the knowledge we have acquired from all our professional office visits, or from all the situations in which we have had to pay for something, available to us to deal with a new situation.

At the point when M–POV has been accessed in understanding, we are ready to add new events to the memory structures that M–POV organizes. Further, we can use M–POV to fill in implicit information between steps in a chain of events by assuming that intermediate scenes, not explicitly stated, actually took place and should be processed. As I have said, the sentence "I went to the dentist's yesterday" gets us to look at what we know about dentists. Some of what we know is the MOPs that are activated by a visit to a dentist. This allows

```
┌─────────────────────────────────────────────────────────────┐
│ M–HEALTH PROTECTION                                           │
│                                                               │
│                          M–POV                                │
│                                                               │
│                                       M–CONTRACT              │
│                                                               │
│                                                               │
│ Detect + Find + Make + [Get + Enter + Waiting + Inner + Pay + │
│                                                               │
│ Exit + [Go Problem Fixer Appt. There] Room Office Back]       │
└─────────────────────────────────────────────────────────────┘
```

Figure 6.1

us to predict, in general, what sequence of events will follow. When the sentence "While I was reading a magazine, I noticed that a patient who arrived after me was being taken ahead of me" is encountered, it can be interpreted in terms of knowledge stored in M–POV and WAITING ROOMS. What we have here is an expectation failure from the script-let of *customer queuing* that is organized by WAITING ROOM. We can understand that there is a potential problem here because of our failed expectation for what normally happens in WAITING ROOM. This expectation was activated by M–POV, which activated WAITING ROOM, which activated $CUSTOMER QUEUING, which held the actual expectation.

The final sentence, "The dentist will probably still overcharge me!" refers to the PAY scene of M–CONTRACT. What we have in a *dentist visit* are three MOPs, in terms of which memories will be stored, with each MOP connecting to the various scenes that contain the expecta-tions necessary for processing (Figure 6.1). Seen temporally, each scene follows the next, so the end product looks very much like a scriptlet. But, we have no reason to believe that any structure that represents such a linear combination of scenes ever exists in memory as one whole piece at one time.

Other MOPs may also be relevant here. For example, a trip of sorts is involved in this visit, so there is a TRIP MOP. Similarly, there are MOPs active for the dentist's motivations and for other higher-level issues.

Some Perspective

What general characteristics do MOPs, scenes, and scriptlets share? Any structure in memory that can be used as a container both of mem-

117

ories and of information relevant to processing new inputs must contain the following:

- a prototype
- a set of expectations organized in terms of the prototype
- a set of memories organized in terms of the previously failed expectations of the prototype
- a characteristic goal

A MOP organizes such structures. A scene is a general description of a setting and activities in pursuit of a goal relevant to that setting. A scriptlet is a particular instantiation of a scene. Ordinarily, there are many scriptlets attached to one scene.

Given these definitions, let us now consider how the memory and understanding process might work. An episode does not enter memory as a unit. Various knowledge sources are used in the processing of any episode. During that processing, those knowledge sources are changed by the information in the episode. What we know about a subject is altered by new information about that subject; any episode we process provides such new information. Since a new episode carries information of many different types, this implies that the initial episode has been somehow *broken up*, with its various pieces being assigned different locations in memory depending on the knowledge used to process them.

According to this view then, memory would seem to have a set of knowledge structures, each of which contains pieces of various episodes. However, it seems unlikely that this is exactly the case. Under some circumstances, when an episode breaks into pieces, each piece is useless in retrieving the other pieces of that episode. At other times, an entire episode is retrievable through a piece of that episode.

This difference is related to the problem of reconstructive memory. Consider an argument that one has with one's spouse in a car. Is it possible to retrieve the purpose or destination of the trip, or what happened prior to entry into the car? The answer depends upon the reconstructability of the episode, given a scene from that episode. An episode is reconstructable if there are events or objects present in a scene from that episode that in some sense depend on prior or subsequent scenes. Such dependence can occur for three reasons. The dependence may occur because a particular element present in the given scene directly correlates with a specific element in a prior or subsequent scene. Or, it may occur because general information is available by which the prior and subsequent scenes can be *figured out*. A third possibility is that it might occur because the particular memory was not broken up but rather stored as a complete episode, such as in the case of an extreme expectation failure.

In the last case, we have an instance of the use of MOPs. MOPs provide, among other things, the temporal precedences among scenes in a standard situation. For example, we know that an airplane trip involves arrival at the airport, followed by checking in, followed by waiting in the waiting area, and so on. This information is all part of M–AIRPLANE TRIP.

We can use this information to reconstruct episodes based on the memory of some portion of them. That is, given a scene, we can, by examining a MOP that the scene might belong to, infer what other scenes must also have occurred. When any memory structure is considered as a possible holder of a memory we are seeking, we can search that structure by using indices that were found in the initial scene. I am claiming, then, that most episodes are broken apart in terms of the structures employed in understanding them (during processing), stored in terms of those same structures in memory, and are reconstructable by various search techniques. Episodes that follow the norm are remembered not as wholes, but as pieces (although sometimes those pieces can be very large if there is a great deal of confusion about what exactly went wrong).

An Example

Consider the problem of recalling the details of a particular visit to a city you've frequently visited. No one structure in memory contains all the details of this trip. But there is likely to be a node in memory that contains some of the details of the trip directly and that can be used to reconstruct much of the trip. The following things seem to be true:

1. Some details of the trip may be recalled apart from the purpose of the trip.
2. The purpose of the trip may be recalled apart from details of the trip that were not connected with that purpose.
3. Incidents that occurred on the trip that had nothing to do in principle with the trip (e.g., reading a certain book) may be recalled completely apart from the trip.

4. Scenes normally associated with trips can used to reconstruct memories of this specific trip, but many of their details will be missing.

5. The trip may be recalled through some conclusion or generalization drawn from it at an appropriate time (i.e., "That reminds me of the time I took a trip and had no expectations for it and everything worked out perfectly").

6. The trip may be recalled through some malfunction in the ordinary flow of the trip.

7. The trip may be recalled by any of its scenes being brought to mind.

8. Scenes that were part of one trip may get confused with similar scenes that were part of other trips.

9. Results or effects of the trip may serve as cues for recalling different scenes of the trip.

Other issues could be stated here as well, but these will do for now. Anything that can be remembered in its own right, apart from the trip itself, is a candidate for consideration as a structure in memory. Thus, since the purpose of the trip (e.g., a meeting) can be recalled apart from the trip itself, that purpose is a structure. Similarly, if the airplane ride can be recalled apart from the trip, there must be a separate structure for it. Additionally, since some structures clearly package other structures in a way that allows reconstruction, there must be such structures available in memory as well.

Thus, we would expect structures such as M–ATTEND MEETING, M–TRIP, M–AIRPLANE, M–RENT-A-CAR, M–HOTEL to exist. Some of these structures point to others. M–TRIP would include M–AIRPLANE, M–HOTEL, and M–RENT-A-CAR, for example. Within these MOPs would be various scenes, such as *check into the hotel* or *coffee break at meeting*. Some of these scenes are retrievable through others and some are retrievable only directly. Thus, it might be possible to reconstruct which hotel one stayed in and therefore the *check out* scene by recalling information about the physical surroundings in the *discussion* scene in M–ATTEND MEETING. On the other hand, it is rather unlikely, unless something peculiar occurred there, that the *rent-a-car bus* scene would be easily recalled by anything other than direct search. To recall such a scene, it is almost always necessary to get to the scene via the MOP it is a part of. So to answer the question, What was the seat configuration in the rent-a-car bus? it is necessary to go from M–TRIP to M–RENT-A-CAR and then to the right scene. Such information can be found only by finding the one scene that stores those low-level details.

Other MOPs, and therefore other scenes, can be related to such a trip, of course. For example, one might also use the structures M–ROMANCE, M–BUSINESS DEAL, or M–PARTY. Further, the juxtaposition of various MOPs and goals associated with those MOPs might cause one to place certain aspects of a particular trip in special structures.

The point is that many things can go on in one's life at one time. A trip to attend a meeting can have an unexpected business deal, a romance, or a travel screw-up as part of it. These would tend to get disassociated from the original experience because of "mushing" in scenes and reconstruction from scenes, but they do not get forgotten – they are merely placed in different structures. Each of these things would be remembered in its own structure, disassociated from the particular trip, and involved with others of its kind (i.e., romances with other romances, business deals with other business deals).

The connection in memory between these items can come in either of two ways. One possibility is that since they were a part of the flow of events, their place in time can be retrieved in the reconstruction process. This assumes the view that reconstruction in memory means going through a scene, finding which MOP or MOPs it was part of, and then searching other scenes organized by that MOP with indices derived from the original scene. The other possibility is that a TOP has been created for them. Remember that a TOP is a high-level structure in memory that stores information independent from any particular domain. TOPs represent generalizations or conclusions having to do with abstractions from actual events (Barsalou and Ross, 1986; Seifert, Abelson and McKoon, 1986; Seifert, 1990). The plot of *Romeo and Juliet* would be stored in terms of a TOP about mutual goal pursuit. Similarly, a belief that *happenstance business deals result from trips whose main purpose is a meeting of another sort* might be stored in terms of some *fortuitous circumstances* TOP. (TOPs will be discussed in greater detail in Chapter 8.)

Learning means the augmentation and creation of memory structures. We can learn M–POV in three ways: by learning the MOP itself, by learning the scenes, or by learning the scriptlets. Since learning requires practice, it is easier to learn scriptlets than MOPs because they are easier to practice. So, to learn a scriptlet one must practice it. Teaching scriptlets is simple and straightforward. No discussion, theory, or abstraction is warranted. Simply do it. Or, allow the learner to do it with coaching as needed.

Scenes are somewhat more difficult to learn than scriptlets. They are abstractions. We need to see the paying scene in a restaurant as being substantially the same thing as the one in the grocery store or the doctor's office, even though they may look different and may employ different scriptlets. Paying is paying, and understanding this means thinking about it at a level of abstraction that is not necessarily obvious.

This problem becomes more acute with respect to MOPs. These are entirely abstract entities. A contract is an abstraction and entering into one is not always explicit or straightforward. When we enter a restaurant, we know that we have entered into an implied contract as soon as we order, but a child does not know this. Often, MOPs must be explained.

As noted, teaching becomes more important as the level of abstraction required becomes less obvious to the learner. Abstraction is very hard to do on one's own but is critical to being able to see the world in interesting ways (Chi, Feltovich and Glaser, 1981; Reimann and Chi, 1989). Without abstraction, every event is a unit unto itself, life has no regularities, and all expectations are of a rather dull and specific sort. It is generalization across experiences that makes the memory, so to speak. This is where teachers can help in what otherwise is a fairly automatic and nonconscious process. Explanations are critical in the generalization process and sometimes we just cannot provide our own; we need a teacher to help us.

CHAPTER 7

Memory Organization Packets

MOPs Defined

A MOP consists of a set of scenes directed toward the achieve-ment of a goal. A MOP always has one major scene whose goal is the essence or purpose of the events organized by the MOP.

Since memories are found in scenes, a very important part of mem-ory organization is our ability to travel from scene to scene. A MOP is an organizer of scenes. Finding the appropriate MOP, in memory search, enables one to answer the question, What would come next? when the answer is another scene. That is, MOPs provide information about how various scenes are connected to one another. Finding a MOP is not a conscious process. We don't sit around saying to our-selves, "I wonder what MOP would work well here?" But, we do seek to know where we are, what's going on, and what method there is to the madness we have just encountered. This means knowing what scene we are in and what scene is coming next.

Most of the MOPs I have discussed so far have been *physical MOPs*. They can contain scenes that seem societal in nature, but what is actu-ally happening is that one scene is being governed by two MOPs. Thus, for example, both M–CONTRACT, which is a *societal MOP*, and M–AIRPLANE, which is a *physical* MOP, share a PAY scene. *Paying* can be seen as both a physical event and a societal event. The *physical* PAY scene from AIRPLANE may exist and contain memories if you bought your ticket at the airport. If you bought your ticket by asking your sec-retary to order it from a travel agent, the scene is a *societal* PAY scene; that is, it is not physically bounded, because there are no physical memories contained within it. The social PAY scene is always activated by the physical PAY scene, but the opposite is not the case. Thus, M–CONTRACT is in place every time you take an airplane trip. The different MOPs provide expectations in each case. Events confirming those expectations will be remembered in terms of both active scenes.

Personal MOPs are idiosyncratic sets of scenes that can include both personal scenes and either physical or societal scenes. To some extent, all MOPs are idiosyncratic; they may have no relation to how someone else might behave. Any planned behavior that is entirely self-motivated and self-initiated, without regard to how others may make plans for similar goals, would certainly be encoded in a personal MOP. Alternatively, some personal MOPs can be a variation on a more standard MOP, in which some personal scenes are added to, or replace, one or more standard physical or societal scenes. These might relate to one's own particular way of getting what one wants.

All MOPs come from goals (Trzebinski and Richards, 1986; Seifert, 1990). We are in a restaurant because we are hungry, in a plane because we want to get somewhere. Personal MOPs are also goal driven, but they tend to be used in pursuit of goals of a higher level (more complex than just getting fed, for instance) than the others. For very high level goals, even personal MOPs sometimes become relatively standardized. The goal of health preservation, for example, would relate to a personal MOP for dealing with this goal that might be quite a bit like everyone else's method. The important point in personal MOPs is how they are related to high-level goals, because people tend to be more idiosyncratic in pursuing those high-level goals not determined by society norms than in pursuing mundane ones.

Since nearly every episode has physical, societal, and personal aspects to it, any episode is likely to have at least three different MOPs that are useful in processing what happens in the episode. These same three MOPs will also be used for storing the memories that result from that processing. When a person visits a doctor, the visit can be understood, stored, and later recalled, in terms of its physical aspects – driving, waiting, being examined, leaving, and so on. It can also be understood in terms of its societal aspects, in this case an implicit agreement to pay for services rendered. In addition, the visit can be understood in terms of the various personal goals that were being operated on by the participants in the events. In the patient's case, this is M–HEALTH PRESERVATION. In the doctor's, M–JOB controls the action.

A three-part division is relevant for processing any input event. I am suggesting that, for every input, the following questions must be asked:

What transpired physically?
Where did those events take place?

What societal conventions were employed?
What impact did the events have on the social position of the participants?

How are participants affected?
What personal goals were achieved by the events?

Each pair of questions corresponds to the scenes (and the MOPs that encode them) that are used in processing an event. Thus, a MOP is an orderer of scenes and does not explicity contain memories of particular episodes. To better see how MOPs function, therefore, it is necessary to have a good grasp of what a scene is. A simple definition of a scene is

> a memory structure that groups together actions that have a shared goal and that occurred at the same time. A scene provides a sequence of general actions. Specific memories are stored in scenes, indexed with respect to how they differ from the general action in the scene. Specific memories are actually stored as attachments to particular *scriptlets* that reside in those scenes.

Scenes organize specific memories in terms of their relationship to the general structure of that scene. Scriptlets represent common instantiations of a scene. Thus, a scene consists of a generally defined sequence of actions, whereas a scriptlet represents particular realizations of the generalizations in a scene. Specific memories can be organized under scriptlets, in terms of expectation, since a scriptlet is no more than a scene that has been colored (particularly instantiated) in a given way. So, for example, M–CONTRACT is a MOP that contains the PAY scene. The PAY scene can be instantiated by the *$credit card* scriptlet, and the various expectation failures that occur might include "over the limit" or "they only take cash or checks" or "at Sam's restaurant they won't take American Express."

Physical scenes represent a kind of snapshot of one's surroundings at a given time. Memories grouped in physical scenes provide information about what happened and how things looked. But not everything we know and care about is physical. Ordering of memories can occur even when the memories are made up of information that is not physical in its basis. Thus, for example, we can know something about how an event can manifest itself societally. This is the essence of M–CONTRACT, the MOP mentioned earlier as a part of a doctor visit. In other words, M–CONTRACT organizes some scenes that are not physically bounded. Entities such as AGREE, or DELIVER, while behaving very much like scenes in a physical MOP, also have no specific physical instantiation.

Processing with MOPs

When we begin to specify which MOPs will be used in processing a specific story, these questions arise: What can be a MOP? How many MOPs are there likely to be in a system?

Storing all the knowledge one has about X in one chunk prohibits generalization between experiences with X and related ones with Y and Z. With MOPs, the issue of which structures can be in a system becomes a question of how general a high-level knowledge structure can be in its storage of information. If we store things generally, then useful generalization can occur across contexts, allowing us to learn from experiences across contexts. But, if we store information *too* generally, we will fail to develop specialized knowledge that illustrates expertise. Expertise is nice of course, but it can overload a system if too much is available at one time. Thus it is the performance of the system as a whole that provides the constraint on which MOPs can be operative.

There can be no correct answer to what content a MOP can have, and therefore to what is and is not a MOP. After all, people cannot be right or wrong in their use of knowledge structures. Any mental entity that provides expectations for outcomes and events can be a knowledge structure in memory. But when mental structures are ordered in a particular way, then a MOP exists. In other words, MOPs and mental structures are viewpoints imposed by an observer on the world. A person can (perhaps tentatively) believe that the world has a certain structure. This belief will cause expectations to arise about what will happen next. Memories will be indexed in terms of failures obtained from those expectations (Adams and Worden, 1986; Hudson and Nelson, 1986; Read and Cesa, 1991; Gick and McGarry, 1992; Hudson, Fivush and Kuebli, 1992). Prototypes will be developed that indicate which entities are expected. In other words, memory creates its own organization.

Having said this, I can begin to discuss which particular structures and MOPs might be present in a typical observer of the world. Whatever claims I make about which MOPs and which structures are necessary for processing a particular story are not immutable. It helps, since the world is not entirely chaotic, to have structures and MOPs in one's memory that relate to the rest of the world's collective view of the world. But no one person's view is the same as any other person's view. The more we know about a subject, the more we must change our view of it and the more our MOPs and structures for processing information about that subject differ from the rest of the world's collective view of that subject.

Consider the processing of the beginning of a hypothetical news story that describes a diplomatic visit for the purpose of negotiations:

M. Secretary Albright's trip to Israel
U.S. Secretary of State Madeline Albright has gone on a trip to Israel to negotiate with Israeli Prime Minister Benjamin Netanyahu. She is hoping to convince him to trade land for peace.

We must be prepared to use what we already know about Mrs. Albright, negotiations, plane trips, the Middle East, and so on, to understand this story. In this sense of *understand*, understanding has two main parts: We must be able to infer things we are not told directly, and we must be able to fit what we are told and what we have inferred into an overall picture of what is going on. In other words, we must update what we know. To do each of these things, we must be prepared to process what we have not yet seen. This helps us eliminate ambiguities and enables us to pay more processing attention to the unexpected, where it is needed most.

If, in addition to the two main parts of understanding just outlined, we consider the issue of the expectations, we see that understanding will consist of the creation of expectations, inference of implicit information, and memory modification (learning). Any memory structures proposed for handling a simple story about Mrs. Albright's trip to Israel must be useful for these tasks. To put this more concretely, whatever we might want to know about this trip must have a place to go in memory once we know it. Further, whatever implicit information we wish to glean from what we hear must have been present explicitly in a memory structure that was accessed during processing. We are asking, therefore, What information and memories do we need? In what memory structures are they to be found? How do we access them at just the right time?

A meeting for the purposes of negotiation in which each participant is trying to defend the interests of his country would require the activation of all three kinds of MOPs (physical, societal, and personal) by each participant in processing the interaction. For instance, when Mrs. Albright stands up at a critical moment in negotiating, it could be seen as a physical act (she got up to go somewhere), a societal act (she wanted to indicate her disgust with the proposals; she wanted to indicate that the United States is not easily pushed around), or a personal act (she felt like she couldn't take it any more; she had to go to the bathroom). Different MOPs provide various expectations here, so these interpretations can be made at any given point. From a physical point of view, certain things happened on the trip. For instance, whatever else this story is, it is also a story about an airplane trip. In order to have that knowledge available for use, we must have recognized this fact. An event that takes place in an airplane can be recalled by remembering the physical aspects of the situation. Understanding that an airplane was used for transportation may or may not turn out to be important in understanding what went on. Further, we can expect that anything we are told about the airplane part of the trip would use memories from M–AIRPLANE to help us in understanding it, because expectation failures from M–AIRPLANE would be stored there. Events that occurred in the airplane, say an important discussion with an aide, would likely be stored some place in memory other than M–AIRPLANE. In that case, M–AIRPLANE would simply be background, not of great use for retrieval.

MOPs and Scripts

I have alluded several times in the course of defining MOPs to the relationship between MOPs and the version of scripts as presented in Schank and Abelson (1977). I have done so because I believe the question of how MOPs and the earlier version of scripts relate is both an obvious and an important one. Before I leave the subject of MOPs (temporarily), I would like to examine this issue once more in detail.

If MOPs are things like M–AIRPLANE and M–STATE DINNER, what is really different from scripts? Have we just replaced $ with M? One of my initial motivations for revamping the theory of high-level knowledge structures was to account for the possibility of recognition confusions in memory (see Chapter 2). I was looking for psychologically valid high-level structures that could be used for both processing and storage. I wanted appropriate remindings to be accounted for by whatever structures I proposed.

So, to return to the question at hand, what is the difference between $AIRPLANE and M–AIRPLANE? This question is really a more general one about the difference between MOPs and scripts. A MOP is an ordered set of scenes; a script is an ordered set of scenes. But the definition of *scene* is different in each case.

For a MOP, a scene is a structure that can be shared by a great many other MOPs. This matters a great deal because our memories often get confused by surroundings. We remember where we were or what we were specifically doing but lose the larger context of our actions. The MOPs are the context, scenes are the immediate surroundings, and scriptlets are the details. Each of these has an important role in memory. In the old conception of a script, a scene was particular to a given script and was not accessible without that script. In the new conception, what I now call scriptlets are scene specific. No scriptlet transcends the boundaries of a scene.

To make this specific, let us actually look at M–AIRPLANE and $AIRPLANE. $AIRPLANE was more or less a list of all the events of an entire airplane trip, including making the reservation, getting to the airport, checking in, riding in the plane, and eating the meal. In SAM and FRUMP, these would all be stored in a single complex structure, complete with optional tracks, under the name $AIRPLANE.

However, such a structure is useless for generalization or reminding across and within contexts. For this, we need structures that are far more general than a detailed list of events, however complex. For example, getting someplace by car and making reservations by telephone are two scenes that would most likely be part of $AIRPLANE but that could not possibly be part of M–AIRPLANE. The reason for this is that one could easily confuse one trip in a car to visit a friend who lives near the airport with a trip to the airport to catch a flight. Similarly, one could easily confuse a phone conversation making airline reservations with one making hotel reservations.

The problem with the old conception of scripts was that too much of what could be defined generally, and of what is likely to be stored in a general fashion in memory, was defined specifically as a part of a particular scriptlet. When one takes away from $AIRPLANE everything that could have been defined generally, only things specific to $AIRPLANE, (e.g., getting on the plane, being seated, being instructed about oxygen masks) are left. These are what I now call scriptlets. M–AIRPLANE as a MOP organizes a set of scenes. One of these scenes is CHECK IN. But, CHECK IN is a scene that is shared by a great many

MOPs (M–DOCTOR VISIT and M–HOTEL might also use CHECK IN). So, various specializations of CHECK IN exist that supply detailed knowledge that colors the generality of that scene. Thus, $AIRPLANE CHECK IN is a scriptlet that is attached to CHECK IN and that gets used, in conjunction with the generalizations available from CHECK IN itself, when M–AIRPLANE is active. This leaves us with a rather impoverished airplane scriptlet, but with a much more powerful memory organization.

Each of the scenes used by M–AIRPLANE is constructed as generally as possible. However, the idiosyncratic history of a given person's memory makes its presence felt here. For example, one of the scenes of M–AIRPLANE is WAITING AREA. It is reasonable to ask, Is this the same as the scene called WAITING ROOM in M–POV? The answer to such a question depends upon the experiences a person has had and the generalizations he has formulated. It is perfectly plausible to imagine that a person who has previously been to both a doctor's and a lawyer's office and has constructed a scene called WAITING ROOM might, upon his first encounter at an airport, see the waiting area as a version of WAITING ROOM. And, then again, he might not.

My point is that the possibility for such generalizations, for interpreting a new experience in terms of what our memory believes to be the most relevant old one, must exist (Kolodner, 1993; also diSessa, 1982; Scardamalia and Bereiter, 1991; Gick and McGarry, 1992; Bruer 1993; Linn et al., 1994; and Gholson et al., 1996). In order for us to make generalizations, scenes must be memory structures in their own right, distinct from the structures with which they are used in processing. Scripts were too restrictive in this regard.

Given the theoretical structure of a memory with MOPs, scenes, scriptlets, and other structures, one might assume there is a set of immutable entities with no flexibility. The most interesting facet of human memory is our ability to take an input and find the most relevant memory we have to help process it. This is done by a reliance on indices derived from expectation failures (Adams and Worden, 1986; Hudson and Nelson, 1986; Read and Cesa, 1991; Hudson, Fivush and Kuebli, 1992). In essence, failure is the root of change. Thus, memory adapts successfully by failing often. A practical problem for a theorist is that since the memory structures I propose are so changeable, the theorist will have trouble making definite statements about their specifics.

Thus, the issue of what can be either a scene or a MOP must await a description of the processes by which memory alters its existing structures. There is no right answer to what can be a scene or a MOP. The actual entities used by a memory vary according to the inputs that have been processed and the generalizations that have been made.

What I can do here is discuss the nature of structures that are likely to be active in one situation. Returning to the question of what is needed to process story M about Mrs. Albright, recall that for any input about a person, we must ask physical, societal, and personal questions in order to activate the requisite MOPs. For this story, the physical MOPs needed include M–AIRPLANE, M–HOTEL, M–MEET-ING, and M–STATE DINNER.

Listing all the scenes these MOPs organize would be rather point-less, but it is nevertheless important to get a feel for their level of gen-erality. For example, the physical scene CHECK–IN is used by both M–AIRPLANE and M–HOTEL. This, of course, can create confusions in recall, but, as I have said, such confusions are the price we pay for learning by generalization. Both M–MEETING and M–AIRPLANE contain a scene for [get to place]. This scene is likely to be DRIVE. Similarly, each of these MOPs has the potential scene GREETING that takes place when DRIVE is concluded. The fact that GREETING is optional and frequently absent will nevertheless not ameliorate poten-tial confusions, such as trying to recall where an odd thing that hap-pened while you were being introduced to somebody actually occurred.

Some societal MOPs likely to be active for story M are M–NEGO-TIATE, M–MEETING, M–DISCUSSION, M–CONTRACT, M–DIPLO-MACY, and M–SOCIAL OCCASION. This is not intended to be an exhaustive list for this story. I am simply trying to give the flavor of the kinds of structures that might need to be employed here. Note that many of the MOPs listed are not concerned exclusively with a diplo-matic trip. For example, M–NEGOTIATE can also be used to under-stand a story about a labor relations expert whose job is to negotiate between labor and management. Is it reasonable that such structures be similar or possibly identical? Is there some reason to have wars and strikes grouped similarly in memory? In a case in which the memory is that of a negotiator with expertise in one area, if he were called upon to function in the other area, he would of course rely upon his exper-tise in the first domain to help him in the second. As he became profi-cient in the second area, he might learn to refine his conceptions of the two related experiences by noting expectation failures and eventually constructing different structures for each.

The strategy is to use all the relevant MOPs we can find, at the right level of generality, demarcate their various interwoven scenes, and then color those scenes with scriptlets when such knowledge is available. Thus, if we know that M–TRIP and M–VIP VISIT are both applicable, we can determine that after the plane lands there may be a red carpet (the red carpet ceremony is a scene, and many scriptlets may take place in that scene, such as *using a microphone* or *bowing to a Japanese diplomat*) and a speech at the airport. We know that [get to place] will likely be filled by a limousine provided by one of the governments involved, and so on.

Thus, determining what is likely to happen next in a situation is a matter of first determining which MOPs might be active. Then we must decide which type of description of the episode we are interested in. Do we want to know what will happen next at a physical or at a societal level? Usually we wish to know both. Then we must attempt to mix the MOPs we have collected to create specific expectations relevant to the given situation. After an input appears, we must determine which MOPs it relates to and how that input should affect those MOPs. (The MOPs that were used do not remain unaffected by their use in processing. Every input has the potential for changing the MOPs active in processing it if an expectation violation is detected.)

The last set of MOPs active in this story are personal; many of them are potentially active at any given point: M–DIPLOMAT, M–STATUS, M–ACT IN ROLE, M–PATRIOTISM, M–DO GOOD JOB, M–SUCCESS, and M-CONVINCE PERSON. Which MOPs are actually used depends upon the personal goals and habits of the particular participants. In order to understand what someone is doing, we must attempt to assess why they are doing it. Further, doing something requires knowing how to go about it. Personal MOPs serve to codify one's experiences in achieving one's personal growth. One problem here is that, whereas in the case of physical and societal MOPs we were assessing structures that we can reasonably assume are common to many people, personal MOPs present a different situation.

There are a great many different personal world views, and thus, when we are trying to understand someone's personal MOP, we must usually guess. For that reason, I will not spend too much time on personal MOPs. Speculating on why Mrs. Albright does what she does may be too difficult. In a sense, we cannot fully understand somebody until we know what their personal MOPs are. For most people, we never do learn what they are.

As people who attempt to understand the world around us, we spend a great deal of time trying to understand the conceptions of the world that other people have. As noted, this is actually quite difficult to do, but we try nevertheless, because we want to be able to accurately predict what actions the people with whom we associate are likely to take. In some sense, a good teacher is someone who understands the MOPs of his students to the extent that he can induce failure so that those MOPs can be modified. Knowing what someone expects is the beginning of our understanding how to change that person's expectations.

Teaching MOPs

We don't actually teach MOPs directly. On the other hand, students do learn them. The question is, how?

MOPs are all about experiential learning, so we would not learn how to assimilate facts by studying how MOPs are formed and how they change over time. But when it comes to actual doing, it is MOPs that contain the relevant experiences from which one can generalize. So, when we talk about student learning, we need to talk about student doing.

Unfortunately there isn't a lot of student doing in school. Of course, students write papers, perform calculations, make presentations, and such, but they don't actually "do" anything in a non–student sense. What I mean is that if you were going to learn a language, for example, there is typically a great difference between what is learned in school and what is learned in life. In school, a language student learns grammar and vocabulary, and reads and writes. In advanced courses, a student might talk with other students in the language he is learning. But, it is an entirely different situation if the student finds himself in a foreign country where that language is spoken and he would like to order food, or close a business deal, or pick up a woman in a bar. The linguistic expressions associated with such activities are part of the experience itself. We learn how to close a business deal by learning the business deal MOP, and any variations and embellishments to that MOP must come the way we learn anything else, through failure, explanation, and the acquisition of cases. In essence, what we know about a situation becomes second nature after we experience it a lot.

So, when one finds oneself in France working on a business deal and one is invited to lunch, one learns that business is not to be discussed at that lunch. This is really no different than learning how to order in a restaurant in France and learning what linguistic expressions work to help get what you want. Language learned outside of the context (and thus outside of the MOP) in which it is be employed is unlikely to be recalled in a timely way in a given situation, because the information contained in the MOP is what drives the processing at that point.

If this is true of language learning, it is equally true of learning anything else. Learning skills out of the context of their intended use typically leads to "inert" (i.e., useless) knowledge (diSessa, 1982; Reif and Larkin, 1991; Bruer, 1993; Lampert, 1995). In school, we don't typically teach "doing" subjects. Foreign language is a "doing" subject, but we tend to teach it in a memorization, fact recitation, descriptive way. For less obviously "doing" subjects, it should come as no surprise that school teaches analysis rather than behavior. Bransford et al. (1989) write that often students "can think *about* the model, but they tend not to 'think in terms of the model.'" In other words, what they've learned is pretty much useless if they actually want to *do* anything *with* the model. Thus, when one learns one's own language in school, one learns about gerunds and dangling participles instead of simply practicing speaking and writing and being corrected. When one learns about history, one hears stories and reasons instead of doing history.

What exactly would *doing history* mean? The MOPs learned in history courses as they currently exist are about historical analysis, memorization, or argumentation. When we are asked to state five reasons for the Civil War, we are building and using MOPs about how to make such an argument. M–SEARCH FOR REASON or M–SHOW CAUSE (to the extent that these are actually MOPs) are not actually real-world MOPs; they are useful mostly in school. They give the students experience in being students. Although this may prepare students for being students or even professors, it is unlikely to prepare them for much else (Wiley and Voss, 1996).

On the other hand, if we put students in a decision-making situation, they can learn how to make decisions, and this certainly seems valuable in the real world. For example, in a simulation, a student could play the role of a member of Lincoln's cabinet. He might have to prepare economic cost/benefit arguments about whether the war should be pursued. Thus, he might build and learn M–CONVINCE, M–CONTRACT, and M–GATHER DATA, or other such MOPs that would all be in service of M–DECIDE. Actually experiencing the process of making a decision allows one to augment one's own decision-making capacity with more experiences, even if the experiences are historical and derived from simulations. Things learned in context remain in memory indexed under that context. Since the contexts are MOPs, the level of generalization would be not about the Civil War but about decision making, and getting people to buy into your point of view, and other processes that are part of daily life. And, since such processes are a part of daily life, they get practiced and our skill in executing them constantly improves. So, rather than forget the facts we learned about the Civil War a few weeks after learning them, we can, through a "living" of the Civil War, incorporate our experience into our constantly expanding daily repertoire of MOPs.

In a way, MOPs are living things. Dynamic memory absorbs new information like a sponge when that information is relevant to what someone is working on daily. School must translate what it wants to teach into an augmentation of real life, or else what is contained within school will be quickly forgotten.

A big problem for schools, as opposed to real life, is emotion. We can learn from real experiences or from really poignant stories. But really poignant storytelling is pretty much a one-on-one affair, and we hear only what we are emotionally ready to hear. A good teaching situation is one in which the student has been put in a position in which he is receptive to new information. Failure to achieve one's goals often will facilitate this receptivity. A student might better be able to understand the Civil War by analogy to family issues, for example. This could be especially true for a student from a family whose members don't talk to each other because they disagree about something so fundamental that they really hate each other. The emotional impact of this family dynamic may well increase this student's comprehension of the war. In a deep sense, education isn't about knowledge or getting students to know what has happened. It is about getting them to *feel* what has happened. This is not so easy to do. Education, as it is in schools today, is emotionless. This is a huge problem.

Reality is the best teacher, but simply telling someone about something won't do. Emotion, and experiencing for yourself, are the key. But, schools are unlikely to adopt a "reality proposal" such as sending students studying the Civil War on long marches through muddy fields, or having students live together as a way to understand the challenges of marriage, so the next best thing is simulation. Simulates can be done either with or without computers. Simulations provide the opportunity to do things that couldn't be done in any other way. Simulated marriage on a computer really is a possibility (and is more likely to be adopted by schools than a course calling for students to live together).

But suppose you actually did put two 14-year-olds together to "be married" for a week. Some things might happen that would not be great and also possibly not what you wanted. Suppose they fell in love and never wanted to part. That isn't exactly what you were trying to teach. Nevertheless, it would an emotional experience and one from which a great deal of learning would take place. I am not actually proposing this, of course. I am just suggesting that MOPs are acquired through real emotional situations. I have always believed that kids learn more from summer camp than they learn from school. At camp they get caught up in all kinds of emotional experiences – summer love, or a baseball team, or a color war. They're psychologically invested in getting along with the other kids in the bunk, and with finding a girlfriend, and so on. All of this is more important in terms of their development as adults than learning about the Pythagorean theorem in a math class.

If one assumes that MOP creation is what learning is all about, then it is clear that the schools are backwards. They don't allow students to *do* things. As schools are currently constituted, with "learn by telling" and emotionless experiences, they are a waste of time. From a parent's point of view, it is more important for the children to go to summer camp, or join a college fraternity, or join the army – activities that involve actual *doing*.

CHAPTER 8

Thematic Organization Packets

Much of our ability to understand, and to be creative and novel in our understanding, is due to our ability to see connections and to draw parallels between events. Of course, when the parallels drawn are between one episode of eating in a restaurant and a similar episode, our work doesn't seem creative, even though it results in a new idiosyncratic mental structure. Drawing parallels between events in one arena and those in a very different context seems more creative. We can recognize that what we have learned to do in one situation may apply in another.

When a person acts stupidly in one situation and suffers the consequences, we expect him to learn from his experiences. We find it hard to understand why he would repeat the same behavior in a new, but similar, circumstance. The kind of learning from experience we expect of people comes from our belief that they can and do recognize similarities in situations.

I used this argument in previous chapters as a justification for structures like MOPs. But even MOPs are too specific. As noted in Chapter 4, we often get reminded across situations that have only very little in common on the surface. Thus, there must be structures that capture similarities between situations that occur in different domains and, furthermore, these structures must be able to capture similarities that are far deeper than those on the surface. If we know something about an abstract situation apart from any specific context, that information must reside somewhere in memory.

The key to reminding, memory organization, and generalization is the ability to create new structures that coordinate or emphasize the abstract significance of a combination of episodes. I call structures that represent this abstract, domain-independent information *thematic organization packets,* or TOPs. TOPs are responsible for our ability to

1. be reminded of a story that illustrates a point;
2. come up with adages such as "A stitch in time saves nine" or "Neither a borrower nor a lender be" at an appropriate point;

3. recognize an old story in new trappings;
4. notice co-occurrences of seemingly disparate events and draw conclusions from their co-occurrence;
5. *know* how something will turn out because the steps leading to it have been *seen* before;
6. learn information from one situation that will apply in another;
7. predict an outcome for a newly encountered situation; and
8. explain why something happened the way it did.

How do people recognize that a TOP is relevant at any given point? We cannot just create entities ad infinitum, without some belief that these entities can be found in memory at just the right time in processing. For example, it makes sense to believe that there must be some high-level structure in memory that corresponds to the notion of imperialism. The arguments for this are straightforward: People know things about imperialism; they can recognize from a sequence of actions that it is taking place; and they have a set of beliefs about what should be done about it. However, all of this does not argue that there is a TOP devoted to *international* imperialism. Instead, the concept of imperialism in its broadest version should be embodied in a TOP structure. If a tighter definition of imperialism (as in international affairs) is used as a TOP, the ability to apply information learned about imperialism to analogous situations will be lost. Ideally, information about political imperialism between countries would be found within a broader TOP, indexed by attributes involving countries or land possession. This TOP can be used to explain particular situations.

One of the most obvious facts about any high-level memory structure is that for a given high-level structure to be found, it must bear some relationship to the entities that a processing system is already looking for. Thus, TOPs must conform in some way to things we are already looking for while trying to understanding something. Consider the notion of escalating *demands*. Such a TOP could have been proposed to handle the Munich/Afghanistan example (story J) presented in Chapter 4. But would we ever find it? To do so would require that we be tracking demands while processing the story. However, unless we believe that demands are *always* tracked during understanding, it is hard to explain why we would be tracking them here unless we already knew that demands were relevant to the TOP we were trying to find. Thus, to propose a TOP that is indexed by concepts that we were not already tracking during normal understanding would be circular.

The same is true of *imperialism*. If we knew we had to look for imperialism, then we could find it; but knowing we have to look for it is the crux of the problem. A structure representing a more general option than imperialism is of more use and is also easier to call up during processing.

How do we recognize that a high-level structure such as a TOP is relevant at any given point? This is the frame selection problem, which has (or should have) concerned everyone investigating systems that attempt to understand the world around them (Minsky, 1975; Bain, 1986; Koton, 1989). How do we know we are in a restaurant or a hotel, or recognize imperialism when we see evidence of it? Restaurant, hotel, and imperialism are mental structures, but they also have physical components. When physical components are blatantly obvious, there is no problem in knowing where you are in mental space. Seeing a big sign that says "Hotel" will pretty well activate the mental structure needed for operating in a hotel. But what are the signs pointing out "imperialism"? One of the paradoxes that make the frame selection problem a real issue is that sometimes one has to be looking for the appropriate frame without knowing that one is looking for it. We find these structures because we have previously linked them to things we know about.

The solution to this problem depends upon the fact that high-level structures in memory are indexed in terms of notions that are already being tracked. With respect to TOPs, this translates into a formulation in terms of goals, plans, themes, and other entities that must be tracked during the normal understanding process.

The two TOPs presented in Chapter 4 fit in with this view of the nature of TOPs (PG;EI [POSSESSION GOAL; EVIL INTENT] and MG;OO [MUTUAL GOAL PURSUIT AGAINST OUTSIDE OPPOSITION]). We are constantly looking for goals, using a sort of giant road map of goal and plan relationships. When we see that someone has a goal, we head down the road indicated by that goal. Hearing more about that goal (e.g., if we hear about a plan, a complicating circumstance, a result) will point us to a particular set of minor roads off the major road indicated by the initial goal conditions. At the end of one of the minor roads is a TOP, the collection of all memories that previously used that road, ones that had the same goals and conditions. Since there are likely to be a great many memories stored in a TOP, various indices are needed within it to find particular memories. Thus, TOPs are convenient collections of memories involving goals and plans, stored in terms of a sufficiently abstract vocabulary to be useful across domains. In order for cross-contextual reminding to occur, it should be sufficient for one situation to elicit another in memory if the two situations share initial goals, planning, or other conditions, and one or more distinguishing features.

Once a relevant TOP is found, and reminding occurs, TOPs (like all memory structures) can be altered by noting unsuccessful outcomes. Within a TOP, modifications to plans can be placed so as to alter future decisions about courses of action appropriate to achieve the goal that is the basis of the TOP.

The Range of TOPs

For any reminding that crosses contexts, we can expect to find two experiences that share (a) a goal type, (b) some planning or other conditions, and (c) one or more identical, low-level features. The first two make up the TOP; the third serves as an index or as indices within it. (The same TOP may be triggered by any number of different low-level features. Low-level feature sharing is not a necessary component of reminding, however. The sharing of low-level features is simply an added advantage that raises the likelihood of the occurrence of reminding.) Such an analysis holds up with respect to the examples of cross-contextual reminding discussed in Chapter 4. The indices are these:

REMINDING	GOAL	CONDITIONS	FEATURES
Romeo and Juliet / *West Side Story*	Mutual goal pursuit	Outside opposition	Young lovers; false report of death
Munich / Afghanistan	Possession goal	Evil intent	Countries; invasions

As another example of how this method works, consider the example from Norman and Schank (1982):

N. The ostrich and the sunbather
We were walking on the cliffs about one hundred feet over the beach. As we passed a relatively deserted section of the beach, we looked down and saw a man sunbathing, lying naked on the ledge. He was peering out over the beach, looking quite content.

N said, "Look at that person. I'll bet he's thinking he is hiding from everyone, but he doesn't realize that people above can see him quite distinctly. He reminds me of an ostrich. Ostrich? Why does it remind me of an ostrich?"

Analyzed according to the method just given, this example would have the following indices:

REMINDING	GOAL	CONDITIONS	FEATURES
Sunbather/	Goal	Planner	Sand;
ostrich	blocked	unaware	hiding

It can be seen from these examples that TOPs are goal based. Memories are indexed off of TOPs by whatever features happen to be peculiar to those memories. These features are quite often very low level, but they can be high level as well, such as plans. Thus, these features can range from common themes to simple things like *sand*. Usually, as we have seen, more than one such identical feature is required for one memory to elicit another. Actually, considering that the goal type and conditions would also be identical in a TOP-based reminding, there really is a great deal of commonality between any two memories with identical features that are stored in a TOP. These memories share gross characteristics in terms of their goal relationships and conditions, and very particular characteristics that uniquely define those actual memories.

One must ask at this point about the range of possible TOPs. Can every possible combination of goal and conditions form a TOP? The answer to this is basically yes. The most common real-world correlates of TOPs are common proverbs that concern planning. These are always about goals and about the problems that come up in the plan to achieve those goals. One of my favorite proverbs is "A pig with two owners will soon starve." The goal is simple enough, namely keeping the pig alive. The error in the normal plan, the assumption that feeding is someone else's responsibility, creates the proverb. Once an issue like this comes up, it can cause a TOP to be created to account for this situation and its variants.

Memory is self-organizing. Any category that is useful for structuring memories will be used once the opportunity to create it appears. Any TOP that contains too many memories or too few memories will be discriminated or abandoned as is deemed appropriate by the memory itself. It follows that any organization of human memory is likely to be highly idiosyncratic. No one person can be expected to have a memory organization exactly like someone else's, except for those culturally common memory organizers (like proverbs) that are provided to a person by others. Indeed, what we consider to be individual differences in intelligence may be no more than differences in the ability to make abstractions that create memory organizations that allow insights unavailable to those who have failed to make such abstractions.

But this does not mean that we cannot make a stab at differentiating between possible TOPs. The task is to find the right level of abstract description that is useful across domains. We are looking for the principles behind memory organization. TOPs that reflect those principles, although they might reorganize themselves, would still maintain their basic commonalities despite particular experiences.

Other TOP Uses

One of the most important uses for TOPs is in conversation. Consider the following argument between an Israeli and an Arab:

O. The Israeli and the Arab
Israeli: Why don't the Arabs recognize the existence of Israel?
Arab: Why doesn't Israel conform to UN Resolution 242?
Israeli: Because the resolution says that every state in the
        region must have the right to exist within secure and
        recognized borders; we would like to have secure
        borders first.
Arab: But what about the rights of the Palestinians to secure
        a homeland?

This conversation illustrates another of the uses of TOPs. In conversations, we do more than simply answer questions that have been asked of us. We also think about what we have been asked. In doing so, we formulate an answer that puts forth our point of view. We make especially sure to do this when we are in an argument or an academic discussion. In order to put forth a point of view while not totally disregarding the question we have been asked, we must find relevant information in our memories that relates that topic to our point of view on the subject. If this is done in a very specific way, that is, if the topic of the first sentence of the Israeli/Arab argument is narrowly construed to be the recognition of Israel, then the requisite generality needed for the kind of answers being discussed would be lost. TOPs are needed here so that specific inputs can be processed by general structures that contain memories relating to those inputs in an interesting way. Formulating a good response to an assertion often requires one to draw analogies from other contexts.

I am not arguing here that TOPs contain the rules for generating a response. Rather, I am suggesting that the rules used by a speaker need relevant memories to operate on. Further, I am suggesting that conversations like example O depend heavily on a sort of *intentional reminding*. That is, an understander seeks, in his processing of a new input in a conversation, to be reminded of a memory that relates to what he has just heard and that provides evidence for the point of view he wishes to defend (Hammond, Seifert and Gray, 1991). Although TOPs are not the mechanism for generating a response in conversation, they are the mechanism for generating remindings that may be used in that conversation.

In order for the Arab in the argument (example O) to be able to respond as he does in the second sentence, he must analyze the first sentence in the following way: First he must formulate an initial, straightforward response to the input; this initial response is something like "Why should we do something for you?" To formulate this response, he had to look up Israel in his memory and find that it was his enemy, and then look up recognition, find out what it is and that it is what Israel wants. At this point, a TOP is easily found, because the notion of enemy leads rather directly to that of a competition goal.

The next problem for the Arab is to identify the conditions of the goal type that was found, so that a TOP can be utilized; many options are available for this. He can look for solution conditions or result conditions. (These will be discussed at length in the next section.) Let us assume he decides to consider solution conditions. That is, he has in essence asked himself, "What can be done about a competition goal?" He knows that one possibility is compromise. He selects that path and thus finds the TOP: Competition Goal; Compromise Solution (CG;CS).

Notice that a TOP such as CG;CS is of great generality, but that it nevertheless pertains to this situation. Memories stored there will include prior known compromises, problems with compromises, and so on. The understander thus has a wide range of memories available to him at this point. To come up with an actual response, he must provide his own indices.

In the prior examples of processing with TOPs in the form of remindings, those indices were already provided (e.g., getting reminded of *Romeo and Juliet* while watching *West Side Story*). The problem was for the understander to follow what had been said until the relevant memory was reached. The input itself informed the understander of what the TOPs and the indices in the TOPs were going to be.

Here, in a heated conversation, this is not the case. It is not in the Israeli's interest to provide the Arab with a good response, so he does not point to where a good one can be found. Nor does a good understanding of what the speaker has said require a complex analysis, because some responses are really just knee-jerk reactions. But a good response that is in the Arab's interest does require such effort.

Thus, TOPs are used here in a manner different from that discussed in the reminding examples. Because of this, a new problem for the understander is the selection of good indices. These should reflect both the situation described in the input and the intentions of the understander with respect to the formulation of a new response. In the example, the first index would likely be *Middle East problem*. This is not absolutely necessary, however. It is certainly possible to go to a different level of conversation by discussing an analogous conflict in history that also happens to be stored in CG;CS.

The second index depends on the Arab's intentions. To formulate the response given, the Arab would have had to use the index *Arab's demands*. Characteristics of a TOP are used to index that TOP. Thus, in a CG;CS, the compromise the Arab wanted would be a good index for him to use. The memory about Resolution 242 that is found in this way, together with the intention to assert the Arab's needs (and some knowledge about how questions can be used in arguments), is sufficient to produce the response. The Israeli's response is more or less an answer to the question the Arab asked. It uses the same TOP (CG;CS), with the indices of *Israel's needs* and *Resolution 242*.

The Israeli's response brings up the topic of secure borders. Here again, CG;CS is necessary for understanding what the Israeli has said and for formulating the response. The indices this time are *secure borders* and, again, *Arab needs*. These indices allow the Palestinians' need for borders to be found in the Arab's memory.

More Reminding

The primary issue with respect to TOPs is their usefulness as memory structures and hence as processing structures. Although MOPs are specific to a given domain, TOPs encode domain-independent knowledge. TOPs contain information that will apply in many different domains. Clearly we have such domain-independent knowledge or we wouldn't be able to transfer knowledge from one experience to another (Seifert, Abelson and McKoon, 1986; Gick and McGarry, 1992; Gholson et al., 1996). The question is whether memories are stored in terms of such structures. Note here that I am not suggesting that any memory is stored only in terms of TOPs. As I suggested in Chapter 7, MOPs can contain knowledge pertinent to negotiations and treaties. But there are also TOPs active in such situations that are useful for bringing in memories involving other domains of knowledge that may have relevance in the current situation. Thus, CG;CS might well be an active TOP in a negotiation story.

Now consider two reminding experiences.

P. Dining with dieters

X was about to go out for lunch with Y. Y specifically asked X to go to a restaurant that served pizza, because Y was on a diet and would be able to order one slice of pizza at this restaurant. X agreed. When they got there, Y ordered two slices. This reminded X of the time that he went out to dinner with Z. X wanted to go to a Mexican restaurant; Z was on a diet, so she wanted fish. She suggested a Mexican restaurant that served fish. X didn't like this restaurant but he agreed. When they got there, Z ordered salad (which she could have gotten at any Mexican restaurant).

Q. Unreliable students

When W heard the stories about the restaurants, she was reminded of making an appointment with a student at the only time the student could make it. This time was very inopportune for W but she agreed. At the agreed upon time, the student failed to show up.

These stories both use the TOP of COMPETITION GOAL; COMPROMISE SOLUTION (CG;CS). The indices in story P are *diet, restaurant, feeling had,* and the characterization *reneged on promise.* In story Q we have CG;CS and the *reneged on promise* and *feeling had* indices. Stories P and Q and the Middle East crisis share nothing in common in the way of context, yet they rely upon the same structure in memory for storage and learning. The consequence of this is not that one episode is likely to remind someone of the other (the indices would be different), but that information about how to deal with people in such situations can be applied across contexts.

Various types of learning might take place in these situations. One might expect that the next time, X will be less likely to agree to a compromise with a person who is dieting when it comes to choosing restaurants. That is the lowest-level conclusion possible here. Across contexts, if X were one of the Arab or Israeli negotiators, it is possible he would be more skeptical of deals in those domains. It may not seem logical to apply what happened to you in a restaurant to a decision about an international negotiation, but people make such domain-crossing conclusions all the time and learn from them.

Other Types of TOPs

Consider the following story:

R. Supply and demand
X was talking about how there was no marijuana around for a month or two. Then, all of a sudden, everyone was able to get as much as they wanted. But the price had gone up twenty-five percent. This reminded X of the oil situation the previous year. People waited in lines because of a shortage that cleared up as soon as the price had risen a significant amount.

I propose POSSESSION GOAL; COMMODITY UNAVAILABLE (PG;CU) as the active TOP here. Many possible plans are available for processing this. Schank and Abelson (1977) discussed the plan D–CONTROL, which contained seven planboxes for getting what you wanted. Some of these were ASK, BARGAIN, THREATEN, and OVERPOWER. Now I am suggesting that, just as is the case with scripts, plans are simultaneously memory and processing structures. Thus, the particular methods we use can serve to organize memories, as do scripts. But, it seems clear that a structure such as POSSESSION GOAL; ASK is much too general, because too many experiences would be categorized under it. (Let me emphasize again that no structure I propose is *right*. Any memory structure can be used until it contains too much or too little. Then it must be abandoned. Any dynamic, self-organizing memory must have the ability to create and abandon structures as seen fit. I can only suggest here what the principles of such an organization might be.)

The organization I propose for story R is based on the significant conditions that affect planning for the possession goal. COMMODITY UNAVAILABLE alters the notion of the kind of planning that must be done. That is, knowing that a commodity is unavailable, we do not go through the litany of, Should I ask for it?, Should I bargain for it? and so on. Rather, we plan according to the situation.

This particular story has only a peripheral relationship with planning, as the planning knowledge is learned during the experience. The next time a commodity becomes unavailable, we would expect X to think, "I'll just wait for a while. It will be available soon at a higher price." The lack of validity of this rule in a world different from the one in which X lives is irrelevant.

The indices in case R are *becomes available later, higher price,* and perhaps *controlled by unethical people.* We would also expect that the conclusion drawn from case R (i.e., unethical people who control the commodity will put it back on the market when they've raised the price) will also serve as an index to the TOP PG;CU after case R has been processed.

More than one TOP can be active at a given time. We have knowledge about the situations in which goals occur, as well as information specific to the pursuit of any particular goal. Thus, someone can be in a goal completion situation for a possession goal. In that case, TOPs of both types will carry relevant expectations and memories. Because this is true, it can be seen that the conditions in each TOP must be dependent upon the nature of the goal being characterized. That is, each condition must depend on whatever unique quality the goal part of the TOP contains. That uniqueness is what specifies the TOP's condition.

So far then, I have proposed a set of high-level memory structures that relate to different aspects of what is going on in a situation. In general, we want to be able to apply two kinds of memories to help us understand any new inputs at this level. First, we want to apply knowledge that has nothing to do with the particular goal we are tracking. Such information is about goals pursued in that situation in general, regardless of what the actual goal is. Second, we want to apply memories that are about the kind of goal we are tracking. Such information, which we would like to have available to us when necessary, is about specific goal types.

For example, *The ostrich and the sunbather* (story N) is possibly reached by two TOPs. Information about ostriches can be categorized using a *hiding* index inside PRESERVATION GOAL; APPARENTLY SUCCESSFUL PLAN. However, the sunbather was not likely to have been pursuing a preservation goal. The reminding, however, could have occurred because of the TOP the two memories share: GOAL BLOCKED; PLANNER UNAWARE.

It is important to understand that memories must be multiply indexed in this fashion. (I say multiply because there are many other possibilities here. The ostrich information can be found with respect to our knowledge about ostriches, zoos, hiding, and various MOPs that an ostrich might participate in, if any.) Multiple indexing is one source of intelligence and of our ability to learn. This implies a multiple categorization of an input event, which, though difficult, is a key issue in understanding.

TOPs as Explanations

As previously noted, one of the most common places to find TOPs is in proverbs. Proverbs represent a kind of cultural wisdom obtained over the years. We learn proverbs as a way of not having to form our own TOPs. They are, in fact, TOPs that we are taught.

Consider the following:

S. Proverbial advice
A friend was telling me about a job opportunity she was trying to arrange for herself. She had asked the people where she worked to arrange something for her in a new city where she was going to live temporarily. They seemed amenable to this idea, even considering it a good opportunity for them. But, the senior people who made such decisions were all away until the end of the summer and my friend was leaving before that. One day she heard that the only remaining senior person had been joking with another employee about her job opportunity in a way that made it seem that he thought it was a very good idea to arrange some work for her with the company. My friend

asked my advice; I told her to go see him right away. "Make hay while the sun shines," I said.

I began to think about the advice I had given, specifically about the literal meaning of what I had said. Having grown up in a city, I had no idea about why one should make hay in the sunshine, although I could make some guesses about it. I also wondered about how this phrase came to be in my, or anybody else's, vocabulary. Somehow, some good old farm wisdom had worked its way down into the everyday vocabulary of an urban professor. Moreover, I knew that this phrase was going to be readily understandable by my friend. But the key point here is not where this proverb came from, or why I happen to know it, or how it was understood. The real issue is, How did I know to say it at that moment?

A proverb is a kind of completed TOP and comes with an explanation for the complex behavior contained within it. We are constantly searching for explanations. Making them up for ourselves is actually quite difficult. Fortunately, our culture teaches us some of them, so that when we face an issue, there is cultural wisdom available in the form of proverbs to help us explain to ourselves what is happening to us.

What exactly does one do in order to retrieve and apply an explanation TOP such as a proverb? In the situation described (story S), I was analyzing what my friend had said in terms of her goals and plans to achieve those goals, and integrating that analysis with my knowledge of how people in various situations are likely to behave and with my beliefs about which plans work best in various situations. I decided that my friend had to take her opportunity when it arrived, and that as long as the man in charge was thinking about her favorably, it would be a good time to ask. This much is fairly obvious. The issue is, What happened next? The next thing I had to do was express my advice, and, suddenly, this proverb occurred to me and I said it. (There is an issue here of which came first, the proverb or the decision. One cannot always tell with such remindings whether the decision drives the reminding or vice versa.) The main point is that TOPs are about the knowledge we use in such situations. Whether we feel reminded or not, we reach a point in memory where relevant knowledge is contained and we use that knowledge in our thinking, for storing memories, and for getting smarter about the issues that organize themselves inside the TOP.

In order to use an explanation TOP, one must first be reminded of it. Proverbs that embody culturally shared explanation TOPs are applied by reminding, but somehow this form of reminding does not feel exactly like the remindings discussed earlier. One doesn't exactly feel reminded of the proverb. It is more like the proverb comes to mind. Also, one is aware, when *this* proverb comes to mind, that the reminding is not unique to oneself. It is reasonable to assume that the person you are talking to knows the proverb and will readily appreciate the wisdom in it.

This is *culturally shared reminding* (CSR), a type of precompiled reminding of which one expects to be reminded in situations in which it might be useful. This is in contrast to expectation failure–based remindings, when one is, in some sense, surprised to discover an old memory still lurking about. In expectation failure–based reminding, a failure of an expectation about what is going to happen next causes the memory of another event, one involving a similar expectation failure, to be called to mind, if the explanation of the expectation failure in both cases is identical (Read and Cesa, 1991; Gick and McGarry, 1992). Explanation TOPs don't contain expectation failures; they contain solutions instead.

In other words, when the problem is to figure out why a wrong expectation was generated by memory, the solution is to keep around potential explanations of why the expectation failed, so that if, in the future, the same thing occurs, memory can be updated. Reminding, in this case, entails holding past mistakes at the ready so that learning can occur. The key problem, as always, is indexing. How can these memories be found later? The answer, I suggest, is that we index them with the explanation that was concocted as the potential resolution of the failure. In CSR reminding, the problem is not learning, but planning. We are not trying to recover from a wrong expectation. Rather, we are trying to plan effectively. But in planning, as in any other mental activity, the object is to find old experiences and use them to guide planning of new ones. The best plan is one that one has been used effectively before.

The trick in planning, therefore, is to get reminded well; if you are reminded of an effective plan, you can use it. But, as always, getting reminded means having a well-organized memory, one that is indexed by means that enable retrieval. In planning, therefore, one wants to find a specific relevant experience. This is often the point of human conversation. One person tells another a problem, and the other, having gotten reminded, will relate his most germane experience to the first. And what if he doesn't have a germane experience? The next best thing is precompiled, culturally shared experience. That is, we can give advice in terms of tried and true wisdom that may not be from our own personal experience but is generally agreed upon to be wise. Often such advice is quite cliched and subject to funny looks. Nevertheless, such things do come to mind. The question for us is, how?

The indexing scheme that the mind employs must be strongly connected with the parameters that define a CSR type proverb in the first place. Therefore, once I had determined that I thought that my friend should ask for what she wanted right away, I was able to find the proverb to express my opinion. When I analyzed her situation in terms of the characteristics that happen to be expressed by the proverb, the analysis had to have been in the form of unique identifiers that would be associated with that proverb. These identifiers were relevant indices that I had extracted from her story. I claim that they are exactly the same as the indices the mind would have to use in order to be able to use such proverbs at a given point. And, more importantly, because correctly using proverbs isn't my goal, these indices would be the very same abstract characterizations in terms of which the mind stores TOPs and in terms of which new inputs would be analyzed.

The indices contained in proverbs relate to everyday goal and plan problems that are quite universal across cultures. Thus, they are likely to be the indices naturally used by the mind. To put this another way, everyone is concerned with the issues proverbs address, and the human mind naturally organizes information around such universal features of living. Culturally shared remindings are thus a form of TOP. Either we can attempt to explain something in brand new terms, or we can use a TOP and tweak it, in order to make life simpler. The same is true with reminding. Either we can get reminded of a particular individual event that was stored in terms of an expectation failure, or we can get reminded of a culturally shared experience with its associated proverb. In the former case, the work we do is much harder and the possibility for a creative solution is therefore much greater. In the latter case, the answer about what to do is much simpler (just follow the advice of the proverb), but the possibility of producing anything creative is much smaller. Thus, for the general question, What should I do? the answer is either consider a case that is quite like the first as an example to guide you (expectation failure–based reminding), or follow the generally accepted wisdom on the subject (culturally shared reminding).

151

Real learning depends upon the constant creation and testing of
TOPs of various sorts. We need to understand the world around us
and so we must constantly make generalizations, using reminding and
explanation to help us do so (Read and Cesa, 1991; Ross, 1996a). Our
attempts to explain what we don't understand are attempts to make
generalizations about various aspects of the world. We don't seek only
to know why a given person does what he does, although we may
accept an explanation that pertains only to him if that's the best we can
do. We want also to know how this new rule we have just learned can
apply to other, similar situations. We seek to generalize the behavior of
others in such a way as to create rules that will hold in circumstances
other than those we have just encountered.

Examining our successes and failures helps us improve. If we do
this examination ourselves, we can utilize only what we already know,
so we must be reminded. What we know comes in two forms: personally constructed TOPs and TOPs we were taught. Those we are taught
come mostly from our parents or from other figures who lend us their
wisdom when we are confused. Ideally, we would like teachers to be
able to provide TOPs as well. To do this, they must be available at the
time of need, which means at the time when a student is searching for
an explanation.

If we wish to account for failures, then when we do fail, we must
explain our failures in a way that helps us modify the aspect of our
behavior that was in error. Finding just which aspect is most significant can be a serious problem, however. We must come up with explanations that correctly cover the range of behaviors that interest us. Our
explanations must be inclusive and instructive. They must include
more behavior than that which we just saw, and they must instruct us
on how to behave in future situations of a like kind. Establishing
which kinds of situations constitute like kinds is one of the main problems of generalization.

We do not get reminded every time we attempt to explain something. Not all explanations are so significant as to cause a reminding.
However, we would like to learn something significant from our
efforts at explanation if we can.

The explanation process involves the following steps:

1. Get confused.
2. Find the goal that was thwarted.

3. Question why what was expected to happen didn't happen.
4. Find the TOP that contains an explanation that answers the question in (3).
5. Take the explanation and establish whether it can be generalized beyond the current case by reminding.
6. If reminding is found, find the breadth of the generalization to be formed.
7. Reorganize memory using the new generalized rule.

Reminding, if it occurs, is one method by which the generalization of an explanation can be justified and through which the new explanation can be used at a high level to reorganize some rule in memory. As an example of this, consider the following:

T. Signs
I was walking along the beach in Puerto Rico and noticed signs saying that it was unsafe to swim, yet everyone was swimming and it was clearly safe. I explained this to myself – after seeing a second sign of a different sort, warning about the dangers of walking in a given place – by assuming that the hotel that put up these signs was just trying to cover itself legally in case of an accident. At this point, that is, after the explanation, I was reminded of signs in Connecticut that say "Road legally closed" when the road is in full use. I had previously explained these signs to myself in the same way.

Here is an example of reminding as verification. First an anomaly is discovered. Next an explanation is concocted. When the reminding occurs, it serves to convince the mind that the concocted explanation is reliable. It also gives potential for scoping the generalization that will be formed from the explanation. Here we see that both a state (Connecticut) and an institution (a hotel) can make the same rules for the same reason. Thus our new rule has to be generalized at a level high enough to cover *institutions that could have liability under certain circumstances*. The trick is to not overgeneralize. We learn from these examples that some signs should be ignored. But which signs and under which circumstances? We want to learn to ignore signs some of the time, but not all of the time.

Is there a TOP for stop signs? No. But there is a TOP for *warnings to limit liability*, and it can be accessed through any sign if we consider the sign to have such a warning as its purpose. The issue is how we see things. The right way of analyzing a situation gives us the right TOP to help us bring previous experiences to the fore to help out. Any reminding that occurs has the advantage of bringing to the conscious two examples that have been analyzed similarly but not consciously. Thus, we can make generalizations by looking at two experiences that have already been determined to have some important aspect in common.

People have powerful models of the world. Through these models, which are based on the accumulated set of experiences a person has had, new experiences are interpreted. When the new experiences a person perceives fit nicely into the framework of expectations that have been derived from experience, the person has little problem understanding. However, a new experience is often anomalous in some way and doesn't correspond to what we expect. In that case, we must reevaluate what is going on and attempt to explain why we were wrong in our expectations. We must do this or we will fail to grow as a result of our experiences. Learning requires expectation failure and the explanation of expectation failure. But, expectation failure is not a simple process. When we have only a few expectations and they turn out to be incorrect, finding which one failed is not that complex a process. In the real world, however, at any given moment we have a tremendously large number of expectations. TOPs are a very important way of organizing them.

CHAPTER 9

Generalization and Memory

Developing Structures

People have widely differing experiences and must deal with a variety situations in the world. To keep track of these things, each person must create and maintain his own memory and processing structures. No one single set or configuration of structures can be used to explain the diversity of understanding and skills that we see in the world. It seems quite unlikely, then, that any particular structures are innate, though the ability to form and manipulate such structures may very well be.

No two people are likely to have identical structures except when those structures reflect the physical nature of the world or when those two people must function in identical societal arrangements. Even then, our individual experiences alter our view of the world to such an extent that we can still expect major differences. Each person's mental structures will contain distinct personal experiences and different expectations. Thus, we can expect people to have rather idiosyncratic TOPs, MOPs, scenes, and scriptlets. How do these structures get built in the first place? How do existing structures get altered once they have been built? How do new structures get created out of a reorganization of old structures?

To build our own memory structures, we must be able to recognize that a current experience is in some way similar to one that has occurred previously and we must be able to focus on the important aspects of both episodes and eliminate from consideration those aspects of the current situation that are irrelevant to the retrieved memory. Recognizing that a situation is the same, in some significant ways, as the one we encountered and stored previously is the key to our initial attempts at learning. Let's start with how we learn scenes.

Expectations are primarily scene connected for a small child. But what typifies a scene for a child of about six months of age? Children appear to develop scriptlets even at that young age (Hull Smith et al., 1989). A small child has only a limited number of different physical locations that he is likely to be in. But since a scene is made up of more than just physical location, being in the crib and crying is probably a different scene for a child from being in the crib and playing with a toy, and a child is likely to have expectations about the first situation that do not apply in the latter. A scene is a combination of physical aspects and goals.

The features that determine a scene are varied. Although they include physical information of the sort available to a child, they also include goals, intentions, and social dynamics that are likely to be unknown to him. Thus, at the simplest level, a scene is physically determined. When a child learns to identify certain patterns of actions that recur as personal scriptlets, he does so in terms of the physical scene that surrounds those actions. As we will see, however, this physical awareness alone will be inadequate for the processing of much of what a child experiences.

At the same time that a child is building scriptlets, he is also beginning to build MOPs. If a scene is physically bounded, and a scriptlet is limited by that boundary, then any other actions that regularly co-occur with a scene, but in a different physical location, must be stored in terms of a different, but connected, scene. The connecting of scenes together is the role of MOPs. Thus, at the same time that a child begins to develop personal scriptlets, he must also be developing scenes and MOPs. These three kinds of high-level knowledge structures are developed in parallel.

Dealing with Expectation Failure

The dominating factor in building and altering memory structures is expectation failure. In order to discover what the options are when an expectation fails, let's imagine some memory events that might well occur in the life of a small child.

A. Expectation Modification

When a child has eaten only hamburgers in restaurants, one can presume he would have an expectation that he gets hamburgers when he eats in restaurants. Upon having a hot dog in a restaurant, he would have to modify his expectation. The child must learn which parts of his expectations are firm and which parts must be given enough flexibility to withstand changes. At first, he creates an ORDER scene for himself that he may not have had before; this scene has in it one $ORDER scriptlet. Initially, he may not know how the hamburger came to be there. He may cry when his expectations are violated. But, in time, he gets the idea that there is a choice point and, eventually, he will insert his will at that point. This is how ORDER gets created and modified.

B. Scriptlet Alteration

In an adult, scriptlets are scene specific and rather rigid, with very little variability in them. The child's task, therefore, in his quest to supply himself with a set of adult scriptlets, is to attempt to separate out the invariant elements in what he observes and to place them in one unit as a mental structure. To do this, he may need help. He may learn that he has to put his napkin on his lap, for example, by having been told to do it or by having it done for him so many times that eventually he does it without thinking. This is how scriptlets get created and, once created, they rarely change.

C. Indexing Expectation Failures

Now we get to the heart of the matter. Scriptlets must be organized in such a way that they carry information particular to the circumstances they describe. At the same time, we want general information to be available to help. In the situation I have described, an ordering scriptlet should contain restaurant-specific information. At the same time, the ORDER scene should contain information about ordering in general that will be available for use at appropriate parts of the scriptlet.

Scriplets become scenes over time. The endless hamburger ordering that is all the time the same, and thus a scriptlet, is rocked by a massive expectation failure (the hot dog). At first there is hysteria, but later, generalization and variables. People who never get beyond the scriptlet stage eat the same thing in the same restaurant every time. Others begin to see variation, and thus scene creation, as an interesting thing rather than something to get hysterical about.

The generalization problem doesn't end here. Each restaurant differs from another. Some people will generalize across restaurants and see additional variables to be added to the ORDER scene, variables that vary according to restaurant type and according to specific restaurants. Others order filet of sole in every restaurant they enter.

Consider a child in his crib with a wet diaper. Imagine that this child is always played with in his crib after his diaper is changed.

There is no particular reason for the child to realize that the structures for DIAPER CHANGING and PLAYING IN THE CRIB are unrelated. In fact, in his world they are most certainly related. But, the child will eventually experience diaper changing in a different environment. Further, he will experience PLAYING IN THE CRIB without DIAPER CHANGING. We would like our child to be able to apply what he has learned from a diaper change outside the crib to one inside the crib. Similarly, if he has learned a game in the crib, it would be nice if he could ask for it in another circumstance. To do this, he must separate these two events from each other, and he must also separate them from their physical locations. In short, he must create a MOP.

Consider another example. At a certain age, a child may go in a car only to travel to restaurants, and he may always go to restaurants in a car. For an adult, CAR and RESTAURANT should be two quite different and unrelated structures. CAR is a scene that may have a number of scripts related to it. RESTAURANT is actually a MOP, M–RESTAU-RANT, that consists of many different scenes (such as ORDER and EAT) connected to each other in a variety of ways. The child, in noting the independence of these entities, must create a structure to connect them. But because M–RESTAURANT is a MOP, what he must construct is something that can take M–RESTAURANT as one of its pieces. The problem here is to create mental structures that contain other mental structures. Thus, the child must be able to make the scene CAR into a variable in a larger structure, so that a car is seen as one of many modes of possible transportation to places he wants to go. There are two important lessons he needs to learn: You can take a car to places besides restaurants, and you can take other forms of transportation to a restaurant. Each of these involves constant refinement of M–RESTAURANT. This process is quite complex.

It follows from what I have been saying about creating MOPs that every scene is a variable in that MOP. Thus, ORDER, EAT, and so on are independent structures that are simply colocated by the MOP. This has to be true because we can separate out EAT from the restaurant experience and discover that some of what we learn in that situation applies even when we are not in a restaurant. If you discover that a certain kind of fish disagrees with you, then, even though recalling that fact should bring to mind the restaurant scene in which the discovery took place, it would be foolish to suggest that you would fail to remember this experience when eating in someone's home. Similar arguments pertain to something learned when ordering in a restaurant that might apply when ordering in a store; knowledge relevant to persuading the clerk to get you what you want might well have come from a restaurant experience.

I argued earlier that when an expectation fails, an index is created at that point in the memory structure with a link to the memory of the experience that caused the failure (Adams and Worden, 1986; Hudson and Nelson, 1986; Read and Cesa, 1991; Hudson, Fivush and Kuebli, 1992). The index, I argued, was either an explanation of the failure itself or a significant aspect of the failure experience. Now consider a four-year-old child in a restaurant. Viewed as a physical entity only, restaurant ordering looks only like restaurant ordering. Therefore the set of expectations built up by the child's ordering in a restaurant would be restaurant specific. But imagine that one of these expectations fails. For example, suppose the child demands of the waitress, "Get me the ketchup!" and the waitress gets mad and leaves. Ideally, the child will mark this failure in the ORDER scene and attempt to explain it. We want him to mark this ORDER scene failure so that it can apply beyond the immediate restaurant context.

Now consider a different expectation failure. In this hypothetical example, the child orders a hamburger and it comes back burnt. This is a different sort of failure. In both examples, the child failed to get what he wanted. But the explanations are radically different in the two cases. In particular, the explanations differ in their implications for how behavior must be modified in the future. Future behavior modification is the essence of the problem. If the child learns effectively from both of these situations, we would expect him to be more polite as a result of the first failure and, in response to the second, perhaps ask his parents not to go to that restaurant again, or not to order hamburgers again. (Or, more practically, he might learn from this experience to specify his desires more precisely when ordering particular types of food such as hamburgers.)

The child can learn from this experience in other ways as well. For example, he could attribute the bad luck in ordering to the kind of person being dealt with. So, instead of modifying his ORDER scene, he could create a scene called DEALING WITH PEOPLE OF A CERTAIN ETHNICITY. He could then attribute his problems to a stereotype of some sort and could see being patronizing, or having to speak slowly, or specifying what he wants in detail, as the solution. He would then have generalized this experience to an arena apart from restaurants, which might include a variety of service-related scenes or personal scenes. Our initial reaction to such behavior is to condemn it, but stereotypes of this sort are very important for learning. For example, suppose the waitress didn't speak English very well. In that case, learning to deal with this situation and learning to generalize the learned behavior to other similar situations would be quite important.

Where will new knowledge reside? In the case of the child being rude, the knowledge of how to talk politely to waitresses could readily be incorporated into the particular scriptlet $restaurant–order. But if it were, the child would not be able to apply what he had learned from this experience to ordering in situations that did not involve restaurants. This is the kind of expectation failure that results in modifying the scene ORDER rather than a particular scriptlet in ORDER. ORDER is part of the MOP M–RESTAURANT, which is a physical MOP. The scriptlet $restaurant–order is indexed under ORDER and is responsible for detailing the physical behavior of the waitress and the customer (coming to the table, reading the menu, etc.). For an adult, ORDER also fills a placeholder in the related MOP M–CONTRACT (which has been implicitly activated by the placeholder in M–RESTAURANT) for specifying the details of the negotiation for delivery. The failure should be marked in ORDER, rather than in these other MOPs or in scriptlets that relate to ORDER.

Thus, higher-level learning and generalization take place by our indexing a given expectation failure in terms of the TOPs, MOPs, scenes, and scriptlets that were active whenever the expectation failure occurred. Not all expectation failures have such global ramifications. I shall now consider this issue in more detail.

Explaining Expectation Failure

When an expectation generated by an existing knowledge structure fails, the failure is marked with a pointer from the expectation to the memory that exemplifies the failure of that expectation (Adams and Worden, 1986; Hudson and Nelson, 1986; Read and Cesa, 1991; Hudson, Fivush and Kuebli, 1992). As I've said, this is why reminding occurs. The pointer optimally carries with it an explanation of the failure, so that the person can know under what future circumstances he should use this information and recall that information in a format that is most useful, for example, as a reminding.

To make this more concrete, consider the Legal Seafood case from Chapter 2. After processing an episode at Legal Seafood, we would want to have detected and indexed a MOP-based expectation failure. Why is this a MOP-based failure and how does a system know what structure to alter? The MOP M–RESTAURANT indicates the order of occurrence of scenes in a sequence. One way, then, that a MOP can fail is by predicting an ordering of scenes that turns out to be wrong. In Legal Seafood, the PAYING scene comes immediately after the ordering scene. Thus M–RESTAURANT would be marked, at least initially, with an index after ORDER that PAY came next in this particular instance. But, simply marking M–RESTAURANT is not enough.

The main question generated by any expectation failure is, What alteration of the structure responsible for that expectation must be made? In general, we can look at this as a two-step problem. First, we must identify the conditions that obtained when the failure occurred. Second, we must decide whether the failure in question is indicative of a failure in the knowledge structure itself or of just a failure of a specific expectation in that structure. The first step involves the determination of how a current context differs from situations in which the failed expectation was valid. The second step involves the determination of what aspect of a structure should be altered to accommodate the current failure.

This final alteration of structure may take one of three forms: (a) alteration of a specific expectation within the structure; (b) abandonment and replacement of the entire structure; or (c) reorganization of the placement of the structure. In terms of the restaurant example, these three possibilities work out to be as follows:

a) M–RESTAURANT could be altered by attaching to one of its expectations a pointer to an episode where that expectation failed.

b) M–RESTAURANT could be abandoned as a failed MOP. One or more new MOPs would then be constructed to replace it, for example, M–FAST FOOD or M–FINE DINING.

c) M–RESTAURANT would be unaltered except in terms of the conditions under which it was called up in the first place. Those conditions would be altered to point to a new MOP under the conditions that obtained in the episode that caused the failure, and to point to M–RESTAURANT otherwise. This is subtly different from case (b), because here entities such as M–FAST FOOD and M–FINE DINING might be created, but M–RESTAURANT would not be replaced. (It could also be the case that the new MOP might not get activated right away, because we might not "recognize" the conditions we're in. We might still operate under the old MOP until the point that it fails, and then the old MOP would point to a new MOP rather than to a reminding.)

These three possibilities – alteration, replacement, and reorganization – are, in general, possibilities that occur any time an expectation fails. How do we choose from among them?

In the case of a first-time failure that does not produce a reminding, we take the event that surrounds the failure, decide which expectation is responsible for the failure, and index the failure under the expectation to blame. This is what enables reminding. Reminding, in one of its most common forms, illustrates the use of the storage of an episode in terms of a failed expectation (Read and Cesa, 1991; Gick and McGarry, 1992). The storage is made as a way of holding off the decision on whether to alter existing MOPs pending further experiences of the same sort.

In cases where the failure reminds us of a similar failure, we must create a new structure to handle what are now seen not as failures, but as repeated and possibly normal aspects of a situation. This new structure will itself have expectations that now anticipate events once seen as failures. The question in this case, then, is whether to replace the old structure altogether, or to simply reorganize memory to accommodate the use of both the old and new structures. The answer to this question depends upon the confidence associated with the original structure, and confidence depends, for the most part, upon frequency of use. In cases in which the old structure has never been used without an incidence of failure, or has never been used at all, we would tend to replace it. In the case of a frequently used structure, however, we would reorganize our memory to incorporate both the old and new structures and to include a means to get to the correct one at the correct time.

Recall the visitor to Burger King and McDonald's. A first encounter with Burger King, for a person whose knowledge structures contain only the standard M–RESTAURANT, would produce expectation failures in the sequential order of the scenes ORDER, SEATING, and PAY. When multiple failures like this occur, it is a good bet that the MOP being used was of little value. Thus, in a situation of multiple failure, a new MOP must be constructed. This construction is complex since it involves reworking the existing MOP to create the new one. This is done by altering the MOP first, and the scenes second, as follows: In Burger King, as in Legal Seafood, PAY comes right after ORDER (we might even expect a reminding here if Legal Seafood had been experienced first). There is an additional problem with respect to M–RESTAURANT in that the SEATING scene follows PAY and ORDER. There are also some scriptlet expectation failures. For example, *$restaurant–order* is not usually done while standing.

The first thing that must be done is to construct a new MOP. (Assuming M–RESTAURANT has a high confidence attached to it in memory, we may decide to reorganize rather than replace.) To construct a new MOP, we start with the scenes of the old MOP and reorder them according to the new episode. This is easy in the case of what we will temporarily call M–BURGER KING. But, although the scenes may be the same, the scriptlets are different. A scene describes what takes place in general. And, in general, what takes place in a regular restaurant and in a fast food restaurant is the same. But the specifics are different. Therefore, we do not want to use the scriptlets associated with M–RESTAURANT; we want to construct new ones. Actually, since the new scriptlet is identical to a first Burger King episode, the real problem is to alter the scenes.

At this point we have a new MOP, M–BURGER KING, containing the scenes ENTER + ORDER + PAY + SEATING, with very specific scripts attached to each. Two problems remain: We must encode the scripts correctly in the scene, and we must make M–BURGER KING more abstract so that it is a MOP that is more likely to be of great use, namely M–FAST FOOD. These two problems are related.

The scene alteration problem depends, after all, on how a scene is constructed in the first place. ORDER, as I have said, is a scene used by a great many MOPs. Some of these might include M–RESTAURANT, M–SHOPPING, M–PROVIDE SERVICE, M–OFFICE, M–TELEPHONE BUYING, and M–TRAVEL AGENT. For the scene ORDER to be used by this diverse set of MOPs, it must be written in as general a way as possible. ORDER is both a physical and a societal scene. That is, it expresses both the generalizations that are valid when someone is physically ordering something and those that pertain to the relationship between the participants in an ORDERing situation. At first glance, such a scene may seem much too general and, in fact, it probably would not actually be used "as is" in any given situation. But it doesn't have to be. The role of a scriptlet attached to a scene is to color the scene with the particulars of that context. In other words, a scriptlet is a copy of a scene with particulars filled in. For a scriptlet to be used, a copy of the scene is made that alters the scene in appropriate ways, leaving intact the parts that fit perfectly.

Here is the advantage of this scheme: Knowledge about ordering in general, which has been acquired from experiences ordering in restaurants, will be known to apply to other contexts because the piece that was acquired will have been copied unchanged from the scene. The only way such knowledge can apply across the board to all ordering is if it relates to a non–restaurant specific portion of the scriptlet. In other words, expectation failures that are scriptlet specific are stored in terms of the scriptlet itself. But expectation failures that are due to expectations derived unchanged from a scene are stored in terms of the original scene.

What happens when a child's rude demand, "Get me some ketchup!" goes unfilled in the restaurant? First, there is expectation failure (probably this is the case for both the child and the waitress, but we'll focus on the child's expectation failure). The episode is indexed off of *$restaurant–order* but, because this scriptlet has been copied directly from the ORDER scene, its index is moved up to the scene level. When the same failure occurs in an auto parts store, or in a fast food restaurant, or in any other scriptlet that copies the scriptlet directly from ORDER, a reminding occurs. Any second instance causes a reevaluation of the failed expectation. This reevaluation in turn results in an attempt to explain the failure.

In the case of the child's rude demand, the explanation is that service staff like to be spoken to politely. Finding such explanations is an extremely complex process, and explanations are not always easily discoverable. We may need to be told; we may never find out. But when we do find an explanation, it enables us to modify ORDER accordingly. This allows every MOP that uses ORDER to have that fix incorporated into it without doing a thing. The new, altered ORDER is simply used by any MOP that previously used the old ORDER. In other words, the child should now remember to speak politely to anyone who is in a serving role.

If *$restaurant–order* were connected directly to M–RESTAURANT, and *$auto parts–order* were connected directly to M–STORE, then failures would not be generalized optimally. If only the scriptlets, which have a very local scoping, are affected, the scenes, which are used throughout the memory, would not be able to carry the knowledge learned from one context to another. That is, unless ORDER were affected, no general learning would take place.

Consider the Burger King example again. The problem in constructing M–BURGER KING is to take each scene that that MOP uses and to treat each action that occurs within it in terms of its deviation from the baseline scene. Thus, *$Burger King–order* is built by noting how the actions observed in the first experience with Burger King differ from the ORDER scene.

The next step is to change M–BURGER KING into the more general M–FAST FOOD. To do this, it is necessary to index M–BURGER KING in terms of M–RESTAURANT. The reason for this is that a patron entering McDonald's for the first time should be reminded of Burger King. The patron should know to use M–BURGER KING rather than M–RESTAURANT, and to develop the specific M–BURGER KING into the more useful M–FAST FOOD by generalizing the roles and circumstances in which it can be used. How can this be accomplished? One way is to index M–BURGER KING in M–RESTAURANT at the point of failed expectation relevant to Burger King. This would mean noting that the ordering of the scene was different in a particular way. A marker, then, would have to be placed in M–RESTAURANT at the point of the past expectation failure. This marker would itself direct the attention of the processor both to the episode in which the failure occurred and to M–BURGER KING itself.

After this rerouting of processing has occurred a few times in the same way (because the individual has now been to more than one kind of fast food restaurant), the reminding ceases to occur. At that point, M–BURGER KING has been transformed into a MOP with entry conditions of its own, that is, into one that can be called in for use without its even being seen as a deviant type of restaurant. To put this more generally, a new MOP is grown at the point where its conditions for use have been detected, so it can be called up independently from the MOP in which it originated as an expectation failure. Thus, after a few trials, M–RESTAURANT and M–FAST FOOD are independent MOPs.

Teaching MOPs

Real learning means building and altering one's MOPs and TOPs. Teaching therefore must be about putting students in situations in which this building and alteration is enabled. It follows that role playing drives learning because role playing is a form of learning by doing. From a teaching perspective, this is not a new idea. For instance, a form of role playing is often used in corporate training situations today. Unfortunately the roles are not always played by professionals, and they're not always played with experts around. But the idea is fundamentally sound. If the roles are played by people who know how to play them, then learning *can* take place, because real MOPs will be built by the student. The real issue is getting a student to reason on his own about the problems that have occurred in a scenario in which he is playing a role. This cannot be taught explicitly. We can't tell students how to reason, but we can cause them to want to reason. To make this happen, we must create simulations of situations that entail the MOPs and TOPs we want students to add to their repertoire. We must understand and appreciate that every student is not going to get the same lesson. In real life, and in simulated experience, everyone is not on the same page at the same time.

Some teaching methods follow from what I have been saying:

Teaching method #1: Let students explore by designing, constructing, and building something themselves. The intent is not that they learn how to construct a particular object. The value is in their beginning to acquire various planning MOPs, physical MOPs, and other structures that they might not have had when they started. New experiences bring new MOPs.[1]

Teaching method #2: Failure-driven learning is enabled by one's playing a realistic role. We need to have people fail, so we need to put them in a real role (or a simulation of that role if the real role is not safe or practical). The role should be of interest to the people, of course. Many roles enable convincing and argumentation, contracts, or ordering – and these are the general stuff of MOP building in life.

Teaching method #3: To teach facts, allow them to be picked up unintentionally in the service of a goal. Facts should not be taught explicitly but should be taught in the service of things people are trying to find out (diSessa, 1982; Bransford et al., 1989; Bruer, 1993); otherwise, the facts may not be remembered. To the extent that they are remembered, they will be placed in a memory structure that has been built for the express purpose of containing them. Thus, they will not be recalled in another context where they might be needed. To put this another way, facts learned for school purposes are remembered when those school

---

[1] Much of the educational literature on constructivism (Harel and Papert, 1991; Scardamalia and Bereiter, 1991; Jackson et al., 1994; Kafai and Resnick, 1996;) provides strong evidence of the educational merits of having students design and build things themselves.

purposes occur again; they do not transfer over to real-life situations (diSessa, 1982; Bransford et al., 1989; Reif and Larkin, 1991; Lampert, 1995).

Teaching method #4: Create "learning-by-doing" situations by use of simulation. Put people into the most realistic situations possible. Make a school store. Organize a team to build a house. Run a mock United Nations. These things are often seen as extracurricular in school. But children learn more from such experiences than they do from the actual curriculum. In a rational world, these experiences would be the curriculum. The true value of having other students in the classroom is the potential this gives for interactions. Children need to learn about how to get along with others – how to express their desires or to accomplish their goals. This can be accomplished in school by use of complex simulations of real-world situations.

Teaching method #5: Experts need to be available on an as-needed basis. Make use of the stories of experts or teachers, and keep in mind that good teachers teach if, and only if, students want to know. Don't miss a good opportunity for learning; make the experts available at all times. Technology-based learning can be extremely helpful for this because domain experts and other kinds of teachers can record their knowledge in a medium that can be played, and replayed, at any time. If the lesson is used, it will be remembered. A student needs a place to index a new teaching story. This indexing is made easy when the student has failed and a good story is provided at the ideal time as an explanation that can be immediately utilized.[2]

Teaching method #6: Last, but not least, please make it fun. Learning is supposed to be fun. Have you ever watched little kids, before the age of six, before they go to school? They learn everything, they're eager, they love it, they can't wait. They look forward to school, too, that first day. By the second day they're not so sure anymore. Unfortunately, most learning environments don't take motivation very seriously,[3] which in turn takes the enjoyment out of the experience.

---

[2] Centered around the subject of learning in the workplace is a significant literature on the need for "just-in-time" learning (Watkins and Marsick, 1993; Brinkerhoff and Gill, 1994).

What we are really trying to do is to teach people to think. To do this, you need to cause expectations to fail, to tell stories, and to induce goals. Students emerging from this kind of teaching environment may not be able to state explicitly what has been learned, any more than they can accurately describe Burger King, but articulation of added factual knowledge is not what education ought to be about. A successful student in a well-designed course should have learned how to perform. Education should be about performance, not competence.

Some Educational Software

At the Institute for the Learning Sciences, we've developed quite a bit of software that reflects these teaching methods. In order to give a sense of the kinds of environments we can use to develop MOPs and TOPs in students, I will describe some of this software developed both for students in schools and in the workplace.

In conjunction with the U.S. Environmental Protection Agency (EPA) we developed a computer-based learning environment called *Community Partnering for Environmental Results*. The goal was to build a simulation-based system that can be used by employees of the EPA to practice and refine public outreach and community relations skills.

The student is placed in the role of EPA coordinator, facing challenges that mirror those that would arise in real life. The student must take action to address those challenges. The student must field telephone calls, run meetings, seek input, and manage community relations (including relations with state and local agencies) for various simulated EPA initiatives or projects. The EPA coordinator played by the student works for the fictional community of Evans Bay. Via news videos and background documents and reports, the student is introduced to some of the environmental issues in the town. He is asked to conduct a "Question and Answer" meeting to identify the public's concerns. This entails interacting with simulated audience members who, through the use of blue-screen video technology, appear to be speaking directly to the student, heightening the realism of the simulated meeting. The scenario is designed to make the meeting very challenging; some members of the audience can be quite unpleasant. Moreover, a response that makes one audience member happy may

---

[3]Ames's 1990 study, for instance, found that most teacher training programs do not adequately address the issue of motivation.

cause another to become upset. If the student exhibits a lack of preparation, insensitivity to the public's feelings, poor judgment, or other common problems, the audience becomes even more hostile.

This is, of course, how one learns the mental structures necessary for handling a public meeting, or getting buy-in from hostile constituents, or making deals. The student learns much more than simply the problems facing EPA workers.

The Advise Project encompasses two main components: the creation of several teaching applications and a software authoring tool that can be used to quickly build additional applications. The goal is to teach a particular subject matter while helping students learn to reason and to make arguments about complex issues by requiring them to wrestle with difficult policy-making decisions. This type of high-level reasoning requires students to reason from past cases, evaluate the reliability of expert opinions, and make decisions based on incomplete information. To learn these skills, the student plays the role of advisor to an important decision-maker who faces a crisis situation. The student is given the mission of evaluating several courses of action designed to solve the crisis and then preparing a report that details the evidence for and against each option.

In one such learning environment, "Crisis in Krasnovia," the student plays a top advisor to the President of the United States, who asks the student to review and evaluate possible U.S. responses to the situation in Krasnovia, a fictional country based on the former Yugoslavia. The student can call on a panel of advisors to help with his evaluation. These advisors – whose policy preferences run the gamut from military intervention to diplomacy – offer their opinions buttressed with evidence from a video database that includes interviews with real experts in history and foreign policy, as well as information and footage about past foreign policy problems that seem relevant to the case at hand. The student evaluates available options by asking questions of the advisors and consulting with the experts in the system's video database. Finally, he constructs a report to the president that outlines his conclusions and offers supporting evidence from the video database. As he goes through this process, advisors in the system may chime in to offer opinions about the evidence he is selecting. Once the student has finished, he submits his report to the president, who critiques it based on how thoroughly the student has documented his opinions, how consistent the report is, and how well it articulates the administration's foreign policy goals.

How can a student learn history? One way is to live it (virtually, that is). Deciding whether to bomb a country that does not behave in our interests relates to the discussions we had earlier about the TOPs relating to imperialism. The only way to build such TOPs is to confront students with the need to make these decisions themselves. "Crisis in Krasnovia" provides just such opportunities.

The role of nutrition has been recognized to be significant in a wide range of medical problems and treatments. Yet very few medical professionals receive much, if any, education on nutritional concepts. The MOPs and TOPs needed to be a nutritionist cannot really be learned in any way other than by playing the role of a nutritionist. To address this need, the *Nutrition Project* seeks to provide essential nutrition education through a system in which students play the role of a physician asked to assess the nutritional needs of three pregnant women in very different states of health and to make appropriate nutritional recommendations. To conduct the assessment, the student may interview the patient, review a nutritional questionnaire completed by the patient, and request anthropometric data and laboratory tests. To support his investigation, he may also consult a database of video clips, text, and graphics, all containing expert knowledge about the domain. The student's task is to assess the patients' nutritional risk factors, if any, and report his conclusions and recommendations. He also must decide whether to refer a patient to a dietitian for further consultation.

Designed for an undergraduate course in art history at Northwestern University, *Is It a Rembrandt?* teaches about the painting techniques of Rembrandt, his significance as an artist, and the process of authenticating paintings, by asking the student to decide the authenticity of three paintings attributed to Rembrandt. Playing the role of an art investigator, the student is introduced to and uses the methods employed by scholars to determine authenticity: examining features of a painting such as subject, composition, and palette; reviewing conservation records; and performing scientific tests such as X-ray analysis, dendrochronology, autoradiography, and pigment analysis. The student eventually submits a conclusion on the authenticity of the paintings in a report to the museum's curator.

The teachers from the art department with which we collaborated on this project thought the issue they wanted to teach was simply determining the attribution of a painting. But, what is really being taught is decision making and reasoning from evidence. In many teaching situations like this one, the experts think they are teaching the facts of their discipline when often what they are really teaching is MOPs that have utility in a variety of situations in life.

We developed another learning environment called *Emerging Economies*, for business school students at Nothwestern's Kellogg School seeking to master the intricacies of doing business in an emerging economy. Emerging economies are those in countries around the world that seem poised for explosive growth (e.g., China, Brazil, some areas in Eastern Europe, and countries in South Asia). They are the places where every business that wants to grow wants to be. The problem is that business success in these unevenly developed, dynamic, highly charged, and culturally distant markets is by no means assured. Without prior experience to lean upon, it is all too easy to make a fatal misstep, and people with experience in these markets are in short supply.

In this system, the student's task is to advise a fictional company's CEO on how best to take the company into an emerging economy. In this role of consultant, the student must learn from experts about how other companies have fared in these markets and must draw conclusions from the experts' experiences. This process is made possible by the system's collection of experts available in the form of digitized video interview clips. The student learns to analyze the results of these experiences and is thus able to prepare his recommendation report for the fictional CEO.

We built a learning environment, called *Invitation to a Revolution*, to teach students about the social dynamics leading up to the French Revolution. This is accomplished through a role-playing simulation in which students engage in conversations with a variety of representative characters from the time of the French Revolution. The purpose of these conversations (and the student's goal) is to convince the fictional characters to join the new National Assembly intending to peacefully reform the government of France. The student learns about the fissures in French society at the time and the issues and grievances that impelled change. Background information on the issues of the day, which offer insight into how the various characters might respond to different proposals, is presented.

This is what I mean by simulated "learning by doing." If you can't do the real thing, computer simulations of this kind serve to help students build and modify the same mental structures that would be altered had they done the real thing.

CHAPTER 10

Learning by Doing

All real learning involves learning by doing. But, do we know what we are learning when we learn by doing? At first glance, learning seems to be a conscious process. We tell people things, they hear them, and they learn them – consciousness, pure and simple. The idea that we learn by being told is pervasive in discussions of learning (Strauss and Shilony, 1994). Nevertheless, most of what we know of any importance in our daily lives is actually nonconscious. Furthermore, it seems fairly obvious that we don't learn nonconscious stuff consciously. The distinction between nonconscious and conscious learning is thus an important one to explore.

Most conceptions of knowledge involve an approach that implies that we know what we know. Following this is the idea that we can teach that knowledge by simply telling people what we want them to know (diSessa, 1982; Bruer, 1993; Bransford et al., 1989). To some extent this is true. For instance, we learn multiplication tables by memorizing them. But memorization doesn't provide much knowledge that is of real value. Proponents of learning by doing (as opposed to learning by being told) have long lamented the school system's lack of understanding regarding the idea that people learn by doing as their primary way of learning. For example, John Dewey remarked in 1916:[1]

Why is it, in spite of the fact that teaching by pouring in, learning by passive absorption, are universally condemned, that they are still so entrenched in practice? That education is not an affair of "telling" and being told, but an active constructive process, is a principle almost as generally violated in practice as conceded in theory. Is not this deplorable situation due to the fact that the doc-

[1] In *Democracy and Education*, 1966, p. 38.

trine is itself merely told?...But its enactment in practice requires that the school environment be equipped with agencies for doing ... to an extent rarely attained.

What Dewey did not realize, indeed what most school systems do not realize, is that what learning by doing teaches is different than what learning by being told tries to teach. Learning by doing teaches nonconscious knowledge, whereas learning by being told teaches conscious knowledge. An important question is, Which of these is most important? Before I answer that question, however, we must inquire as to what nonconscious knowledge looks like and what it is we learn when we learn by doing.

The cognitive basis of learning by doing has not been fully understood by many educators or psychologists, and mostly they have been unwilling to agree to the implementation of practices based on these notions in the classroom. Part of the reason for this is that they can't say exactly what it is that learning by doing teaches (although we certainly know it isn't primarily facts, the darlings of the "drill them and test them" school of educational thought). The theory of dynamic memory can help with this by providing insight into the advantages gained by learning by doing.

As long as we believe that knowledge is the stuff of which we are conscious, then we must, in principle, teach knowledge of which we are cognizant. On the other hand, if we recognize that the knowledge critical to living in the world is in fact nonconscious, then when we teach we need to be addressing the nonconscious mind. It seems at first glance that this is a tall order, that we don't know how to do it. But the fact is, we do it all the time. Nonconscious learning is the most common form of learning; it just isn't all that common in school. It is in the MOPs and TOPs we acquire, and continue to develop, through our daily experiences just living in the world.

How do we acquire MOPs and TOPs? The answer to this is very simple – we learn them, by practicing them over and over. We can learn them through expectation failure, explaining the failure to ourselves, and then altering the appropriate MOP. In short, we learn them without trying to, without memorizing anything, simply by doing them. This is the unconscious learning process in action. This is our dynamic memory.

The first time we do something, we are highly dependent upon finding some prior experience that will help us understand the current situation. Reminding is the process by which case-based reasoning (e.g., reasoning by relying upon cases of experiences we have previously stored in memory, rather than reasoning by applying rules) takes place. (There will be more on case-based reasoning in Chapter 12.)

When we attempt to understand anything, we do so, quite unconsciously, by attempting to find something in our memories that looks sufficiently like it so that it will be helpful in processing. The reminding process allows us to learn by causing us to constantly compare new experiences to old ones, enabling us to make generalizations from the conjunction of the two experiences. The reminding process is not always conscious, however, so we are not always aware that we have made a generalization or have revised an expectation.

One of two things happens during this nonconscious comparison process. Our minds recognize either that the new experience is significantly different from the one we have compared it to, or that it is really very much like it. (I will ignore gray, "in between" cases here.) When a new experience is found to be different from our prior closest memory, we must create a new case for it. For instance, we can use our prior knowledge of trains to help us out on our first airplane ride, but we soon realize that though the comparison may have been helpful for initial processing, airplanes are really cases of their own and, eventually, we treat them as a new thing entirely.

Our nonconscious processor may not know to do this initially. How can one's mind know, on the basis of just one airplane ride, not to treat it as a specialization of train travel? But, by our tenth airplane ride, we will have long since forgotten that comparison. Instead, in trying to compare airplane rides to each other, we will have created an airplane script that predicts what airplane rides are like in general, including the information that one should not expect much of the meal. This is, of course, the other aspect of the comparison process. Finding a new experience to be a lot like an old experience allows our mind to build a script (Fivush, 1984; Hudson and Nelson, 1986; Hudson, Fivush and Kuebli, 1992). As we build scripts, we begin to lose our memories of the specific details of the experiences on which they are based. Details of episodes that share a common script gradually disappear from memory and, when we try to recall them, we are likely to replace those details with generic script content (Hudson and Nelson, 1986; Farrar and Goodman, 1990; Farrar and Goodman, 1992).

So, either we use new cases as new material to add to our library of cases, or we use new cases to help build up our detailed script knowledge. We can of course decide that our new case is of no interest whatsoever because it is exactly what we have experienced many times before. In that instance, hardly any learning occurs at all.

Learning can take place in any memory structure. Memory structures are, by their very nature, meant to be alterable (McKoon and Ratcliff, 1992; Wattenmaker, 1992; Ross, 1996b). However, recall from the discussion in the previous chapter that when we learn about something that takes place in a restaurant, we need to know whether what we are learning is about restaurants per se, and thus we must alter the restaurant MOP, or about some aspect of restaurants that has significance beyond restaurants, such as "paying." In the latter case, we need to alter what we know about a scene, or something that just happened to occur in a restaurant and has nothing to do with the MOP or scene in which it occurred. We also must alter what we know about some more abstract MOP (such as embarrassment or romance) that might have been operating at the same time in the same place.

Why We Learn by Doing

The object of learning in learn by doing is the acquisition of scriptlets. The skills we refer to when we ask about people's abilities almost always refer to scriptlets. Let me explain.

Our abilities are bound up in scriptlets. When we say we know how to do something, we are often referring to one or more scriptlets we have acquired over the years. These are often quite unconscious. We cannot easily describe what we know to someone who doesn't have the right scriptlet. Scriptlets often consist of very low level skills we have practiced many times over the years. But this practice almost never takes place for its own sake; we practice scriptlets solely because we are repeatedly pursuing the same goal. We never use a scriptlet except in service of a goal (except of course in school, where there is the backward notion that rote practice of decontextualized skills will actually be of practical value).

Two good examples of a scriptlet are "setting up a VCR for taping" and "sending electronic mail." In the twenty-five years that electronic mail has existed, I have had to use probably ten different systems. Although I was told how to use each one, I rarely remembered what was said long enough to try it out. I could use one when someone watched over my shoulder, but then I would forget by the next try. My actual *learning* of the systems came through repeated practice, and repeated trial and error – that is, I learned to use e-mail by actually using it. I am quite adept at the two systems I now use, although I probably don't know all the features of either. I have no interest in how these systems work, but I am interested in sending and receiving e-mail. This goal caused me to try the systems until I got good at them. These trials were held in the course of use, not as outside practice. This was a case of motivated learning by doing.

Perhaps a more everyday example is using a VCR. I had one of the very first models of VCRs and over time I have owned many different machines. They each have different ways of setting up a recording, yet I can operate all of them. I find them annoying to use, but I like to record and watch movies, so I have learned to use them. Yet, if I am away from any of them for very long, I tend to forget how they operate. Scriptlets tend to decay in memory if they are not used. Fortunately I know some generic information about how VCRs work and this helps me relearn the scriptlet I need. Again, you could say that I have skills (in this case, recording on my VCRs), and that I have learned those skills by doing.

I am mentioning all this for a simple reason. We want students to know the exceptional cases from which they can learn and make judgments on their own about new situations. And, we want students to know how to do things, to have sets of skills. But, when we talk about the "skills" we want students to have, we often get confused by what we mean by the term, talking about what we want students to know (e.g., math skills), or how we want students to comport themselves (e.g., personal interaction skills), and not about what we want them to be able to do (diSessa, 1982; Bransford et al., 1989; Reif and Larkin, 1991; Strauss and Shilony, 1994).

Students need to acquire scriptlets so that they can perform the actions contained therein. Students will easily acquire scriptlets acquired in the natural course of the pursuit of a goal that is of interest to them. Goals play a critical role in how we store and retrieve memories (Dweck, 1986; Seifert, Abelson and McKoon, 1986; Hudson, 1988; Bruer, 1993). This is what "learn by doing" is all about.

How to Do It: Skills as Scriptlets

Schools and their curricula are in desperate need of redesign. We must begin to help students acquire experiences naturally, the way they might outside of school. We must allow students to acquire cases, MOPs and TOPs, and scriptlets; to get reminded; and to construct their own explanations when their expectations fail. We must put students in situations where they have expectations and then allow them to construct stories about what happened and why (Chi et al., 1989). There are clear links in memory between expectations, expectation failures, and our explanations for the failures. Further, all three serve as critical cues for remindings (Read and Cesa, 1991). In short, we must let students do things in a realistic context that relates to things they will actually do later on in life (diSessa, 1982; Bransford et al., 1989; Bruer, 1993; Lampert, 1995; Wiley and Voss, 1996).

Any curriculum redesign process must therefore begin with an understanding of what skills we want students to learn. These skills must then be put into some natural situation around which a scenario can be constructed. The scenarios need not be of one form; they could be partially instructor led, or entirely student directed. They can take as long as the designers want, perhaps presenting a lesson to be learned in a single day or, alternatively, requiring several weeks of students' work. The scenarios and accompanying case libraries (the stories of experts that are used when students fail) might be paper based, or video based, or they might be built directly into software. In any case, human experts (live, on tape, or in text) ought to be available for the teaching of skills on an as-needed basis.

Skills ought to be taught by the method most appropriate for their acquisition. The hard part is assessing what a skill *is* and what it is *not*. For this reason, seeing skills as scriptlets is quite helpful. Broadly speaking, there are three classes of scriptlets: cognitive, perceptual, and physical.

I have been talking so far about cognitive scriptlets. These naturally have a physical component (if they didn't, nothing would ever happen). Thus the VCR scriptlet is mostly a prescription about what to do in a cognitive sense, the physical aspect being no more than button pushing. Similarly, the e-mail scriptlet involves only mouse clicks and keyboard strokes at the physical level.

Purely physical scriptlets do occur – typing and button pushing on a remote control device being two of them, for example. More interesting ones are bicycle riding, brake pedal pushing on a car, and brushing one's teeth.

Perceptual scriptlets involve the recognition of things, such as recognizing individual people, noticing dangerous situations, or the perceptual part of hitting a baseball.[2]

When we say that someone has a skill in the sense of skill that is appropriate here, we mean he has a scriptlet that might involve a primary cognitive scriptlet and some physical and perceptual ones as well. This distinction is not that important here, and I shall just use the term *scriptlet* to refer to a mental entity that might actually involve a mix of all three types of scriptlets. Thus the following general descriptions apply: A *cognitive scriptlet* refers to knowledge about use. This knowledge is usually consciously available. That is, a person in possession of that knowledge can talk about it. If the sentence "John knows how to use X" makes sense for a given X, then X is a cognitive scriptlet.

A *physical scriptlet* refers to knowledge about operations. This knowledge is not usually consciously available. That is, a person in possession of a physical scriptlet may not be able to talk about it. If the sentence "John knows how to operate an X" makes sense for a given X, then X is a physical scriptlet.

A *perceptual scriptlet* refers to knowledge about observations. This knowledge is not usually consciously available. A person in possession of a perceptual scriptlet may not be able to talk about it. If the sentence "John knows how to recognize an X" makes sense for a given X, then X is a perceptual scriptlet.

What I am referring to here is what is commonly meant by *skills*. The problem with this word, and why I feel the need to avoid it, is that the word has no clear definition. We can say, for example, that someone is skilled at mathematics, or is a skilled negotiator, or has mastered basic language skills, or is skilled at cooking. When we talk about skills, we are often referring to what we believe a person "knows how to do." Unfortunately, this can mean just about anything at all. Any human action or capability can be referred as a skill, so the word offers us very little to go with if we want to teach skills. We are left in the position of saying that we want to teach just about anything.

What exactly is the problem here? Why shouldn't memorizing a list of biological terminology be a skill, for example? It could be a skill, of course, since one could require it of students, some would be better than others, and we could say that they were more skilled in biology

---

[2] In another example of what are essentially perceptual scriptlets, Bransford et al. (1989) describe a study of psychologists who can recognize mental illnesses in patients but cannot articulate how they recognize these illnesses.

and give them a better score on an exam than those who were less skilled. But, looked at in terms of scriptlets, we can see that the skill involved is actually a cognitive scriptlet involving memorization. If we wanted to teach this scriptlet, we would have to teach someone how to memorize, so that they would become good at memorization rather than at biology.

One problem with the word *skill* is that we can say, "John knows how to do mathematics" or "John knows how to do biology" and still feel comfortable that we are talking about skills because we are talking about knowing how to do something. The illusion is that mathematics or biology is a kind of thing one can learn to do. We might expect our employees to know how to do systems installation or to manage other employees, for example. But, although these may seem like skills, in each case they are really collections of a large number of scriptlets. This becomes clear when one thinks about teaching someone to do any of these things.

You can't teach someone to do biology, but you can teach them to dissect a frog (a physical scriptlet), or relate diet components to biological functions (a cognitive scriptlet), or interpret chemical equations (a perceptual scriptlet). In fact, even these scriptlets are likely to be made up of many smaller scriptlets (such as knife handling). Similarly, you can't teach someone to do mathematics, but you can teach them addition, and even eventually how to prove a theorem in plane geometry, thereby changing a cognitive scriptlet into a perceptual one over time.

In business, this means we have to stop thinking about teaching management techniques or communication methods. Why? Because these are not scriptlets. They tend to be taught the way high school biology is taught, as facts to be memorized, which, as I have said, is relevant to teach only if memorization is the scriptlet you want students to master. But, if we want students to get good at managing or communicating, we have to do something else.

It is important to understand the difference between a skill that is teachable and a skill set that is not teachable by itself. Whatever doing biology or managing employees might be, these things cannot be only one skill. They are collections of various, possibly quite unrelated, scriptlets. (For example, doing biology might entail using a knife properly and using a microscope properly. These skills are related only in the sense that they sometimes co-occur.) If we confuse scriptlets to be learned with convenient headings that we have learned to describe as skill sets, the courses we design will lose their focus.

Recognizing the skill set to which a scriptlet naturally belongs is critical to curriculum redesign. If one did need to learn some type of calculation to learn to do biology, for example, two very different ways to approach this problem exist. We could, as most schools do today, separate the skill sets in traditional ways, requiring a course in mathematics prior to biology, for example. The first problem with this method is that by grouping these skills separately we risk losing the student's interest. By making a biology student take chemistry or calculus, we risk killing off a budding biologist by making him focus on subjects that may not interest him and at which he may not have much talent. A second risk is that much of what else is taught in such prerequisites may not be at all germane to the needs of the biology student. Most of what is taught in school simply does not address students' later needs (Bransford et al., 1989; Reif and Larkin, 1991; Lampert, 1995). What makes up a coherent course in mathematics is likely to be determined by someone who has an agenda other than helping the biology student be a good biologist. As a consequence of this, the aspects of mathematics of most interest to a biologist might be little dwelt upon by the mathematician. In fact, a biologist is likely to be the real expert when it comes to the mathematics he uses on a daily basis. The mathematician is more likely to understand, and therefore to teach, the theory behind the necessary mathematics rather than the practice of such mathematics.

This problem is even more apparent in the relationship between academic psychology and human resource management. Many people believe undergraduate psychology majors are good prospects for being human resources specialists. But if they are, it can only be because of their inherent interest in the subject, not because of what is taught in psychology courses. In the popular image, psychology majors have learned about how to get along with people and understand human relations. In reality, psychology majors have learned how to be miniature academic psychologists. They have learned how to run an experiment, how to do the relevant statistical analyses, and how to appreciate the various subspecialties in academic psychology, none of which has much to do with how to understand, or to get along with, people better (Wiley and Voss, 1996).

What should be done is to break down traditional academic lines, to teach cross curricularly with a focus on what we want students to actually be able to do in the real world, and to teach skills, or scriptlets, relevant to this activity on an as-needed basis. Doing this allows for the creation of goal-based scenarios that entail the learning of many different and often unrelated scriptlets in the pursuit of a common goal. To put this another way, a scriptlet is something that fits into the following situation:

a1: I need John to do X.
b1: John doesn't know how to do X.
a2: Well, then teach him how to do X.
b2: That's easier said than done; learning to do X requires experience.

Part of the point here is that, in business especially, one wouldn't have this dialogue if X were "human resource management." In that case, a1 and b1 would make little sense. X might be "to fire somebody," however, in which case such a dialogue might make sense. Further, it also makes sense that one can't learn to fire somebody except by firing somebody. This is the best way to spot a scriptlet. The only way to learn a scriptlet is to practice it. What this suggests, of course, is that the best way to teach a scriptlet is in practice situations. If one wanted to teach "firing someone," practice scenarios would be constructed in which such talents could be learned and experiences could be gained before one tried it out for real.

Looked at in this way, biology is not a scriptlet, but properly dissecting a frog is. Physics is not a scriptlet, but performing a calculation needed in a physics experiment is. Managing people is not a scriptlet, but making sure that a job is done on time and within a budget is. Writing a letter is a set of scriptlets. Computer programming is composed of many scriptlets (learning how to do a loop, for example, is a scriptlet, as is writing that loop in FORTRAN). Reading a financial report involves a multiplicity of scriptlets. Playing a musical instrument involves multiple scriptlets. In short, if one has to learn to do something, and it is relatively easy for an expert to tell whether or not one has done it properly, then we are talking about a scriptlet or a natural grouping of scriptlets. Confusion arises when we talk about major job classifications (or major academic domains) as if they are skills, when in fact they comprise numerous scriptlets that are often quite difficult to define.

When we attempt to determine where needed scriptlets lie, we may well discover that this is a difficult task not only because of the normal English language usage of the term *skill*, but also because of the way in which courses have traditionally been taught. We are quite used to

181

courses in biology, economics, history, or psychology. Since the content of these courses is rarely looked at from a scriptlet-related point of view, the definition of these courses is usually quite scriptlet independent (Strauss and Shilony, 1994).

Unfortunately, courses often involve a number of issues that have nothing to do with scriptlets at all. First, courses almost always involve grades. This often means tests with quantifiable measures, which means measures of vocabulary rather than measures of actual achievements. Sometimes, tests will test scriptlets. This frequently happens in mathematics, for example, but even then the test typically doesn't include a meaningful call for the use of these scriptlets. Most of the time, tests are oriented toward just getting a student to reiterate the teacher's point of view, which is not a scriptlet at all – except in a kind of perverted view of the term.

Second, courses tend to try to make the student into a kind of mini-scholar of the field in question. Teachers are afraid that their students will have been in an English literature course and not have read Dickens, or have been in a philosophy course and not know Plato, or in an economics course and not know Malthus. Thus, most courses have a serious bent toward the history of a particular field. This comes at the expense of time spent on scriptlets (thus, how to actually do anything is ignored) and, more importantly, tends to shift the focus toward scholarship.[3] This shift toward scholarship means courses will have a heavy emphasis on facts. (The "literacy lists of the field" are big here.) So, knowing what a particular scholar said and being able to reconcile his view with particular conditions or with the views of an opposing scholar become the meat of such courses and of the tests that provide the grades for such courses.

The emphasis becomes one of *reading about* a subject and being able to argue in a scholarly way about that subject, rather than learning how to actually do anything in that subject's domain of practice. Thus philosophy courses don't ask the students to "do philosophy" but ask them to read about those who have done philosophy. In the case of philosophy this may not seem so bad. There have been great philosophers, the world does not change all that much in the really important issues, and an argument could be made that all the important things having been said already. Even so, the scriptlets of philosophy, which

---

[3] Reif and Larkin (1991); diSessa (1982) found that many physics students learn physics formulae but don't know how to use physics in their day-to-day lives.

I take to be original reasoned thought and argument, are only periph-erally taught if they are taught at all.

Matters become much worse when the courses under discussion are in fields where the great thoughts have clearly not all been thought and where much remains to be learned. Economics and psychology come to mind here. Students are asked to read the great works in these fields, but not to do much of anything expect spit back what they have read. The argument is that they should be learning to "do economics" or to "do psychology," but it is not at all clear what this might mean. The fact that this is not clear is part of the problem.

Of course, one can be cynical about such fields and say they con-tain no scriptlets to be taught. But people engaged in such work do employ a number of scriptlets, although they are often associated with other subject areas, such as statistics. Nevertheless, just because prac-titioners can do good work in their field is no reason to suppose that they understand how they do what they do well enough to be able to teach the scriptlets that they have. And, even if they did know how to teach those scriptlets, it would still be reasonable to ask if they are worth learning for the student who only wants to take one or two courses in psychology or economics. After all, wouldn't the students be better off with a survey of work in the field without our attempting to teach them scriptlets that take a very long time to learn and that they may never use?

This then is the essence of the conflict: In education in general, there is a choice between a survey of past works in a field and learn-ing how to be a practitioner in that field. My position is simple. Survey courses tend to teach to the test, emphasize the point of view of the instructor, leave students years later with very little memory of what they learned in order to pass the test, and are generally a waste of time.

Scriptlets, on the other hand, are testable in simple ways, are not biased toward the teacher's point of view, remain with students for a very long time, and provide a framework into which the work of the great masters of that skill can best be appreciated. Further, and this is the main point, mastery of scriptlets builds confidence and is much more easily motivated in school, and the process tends to get students to think about what they are doing (Trzebinski and Richards, 1986; Seifert, 1990).

As an example, consider musical education. My position here is that musical education ought to begin with learning to play an instrument and that, after the many scriptlets relevant to an instrument have been learned, students will be better able to appreciate the work of musicians who have gone before them. By the same reasoning, if we want students to understand music theory, they should have to create some music first.

This may not seem like such a radical idea, since many music schools do exactly this. But such a point is often devalued as we get to higher education, where music scholars are often clearly differentiated from musicians and it is the former who teach the courses. Further, high school courses, and even some elementary school courses, often perpetuate the biases of university-level music professors, thus creating non–learn-by-doing courses in a subject area where the set of scriptlets is as easily definable as is ever possible.

Many elementary schools are smarter than this and teach kids to play musical instruments anyway. The same is not true, unfortunately, in subjects considered more central to a child's education. We don't let children just do physics (diSessa, 1982). In fact, we hardly even know what that means. We do let students do math, because we know what that means, but we lose track of why we are doing it. I suspect schools really like to teach scriptlets when the scriptlets can be identified. They are easy to measure and thus fit well into our test-oriented society.

But what happens when a scriptlet is hard to identify? We know we want students to be able to read and understand, but it isn't all that easy to know when students actually have the requisite scriptlets to do that, especially when the material they are reading doesn't interest them. But, it is easy to tell if a student can solve a quadratic equation (it is a cognitive scriptlet), so schools emphasize mathematics. The point is that although identifying relevant scriptlets is indeed difficult, one should be wary of teaching any scriptlet just because it is, in fact, something easy to teach. We need to teach *relevant* scriptlets. This means knowing what one can do with that scriptlet. It is a good idea, therefore, to know what scriptlets one needs for what real purpose before one goes about designing a curriculum.

The Idea of Curriculum

Schools are full of curricula – that is, agreed upon sets of courses that constitute what the designers of curricula feel their students must learn in order to be deemed "qualified" in a given subject. The curriculum for French covers certain aspects of French language, culture, and history, as deemed appropriate by the designers of that curriculum. The mathematics curriculum covers certain material in the third grade, certain parts of geometry in high school, and so on. When colleges say they require four years of mathematics, they mean that they require study in certain particular aspects of mathematics, to be studied over the course of a certain number of years, with certain tests at the end. There is some variation in these curricula from school to school, of course, but not all that much, especially when standardized tests loom at the end.

The idea of a curriculum is that a school has the right, indeed the obligation, to say what should be learned about a given subject. And therein lies the rub. There is a serious problem with the idea of a curriculum.

It follows from the arguments stated thus far that a curriculum ought to be no more than a collection of scriptlets to be acquired. That is, if real knowledge comes from doing, and if scriptlets are what are acquired in doing, then any curriculum, course, or teaching program should be no more than, and no less than, a set of exercises that allow students to acquire scriptlets in the natural way scriptlets are acquired, that is, by practice. Of course, there is the issue of motivation. No one will learn a scriptlet, much less practice one, unless there is real motivation to drive what may be real work (Dweck, 1986; Ames, 1990). Take, for example, the scriptlets mentioned earlier: programming a VCR and sending e-mail. These are not intrinsically rewarding activities; we learn them because we want the results they bring. A course designer must recognize that it is these results that serve as the real motivation to acquire these scriptlets.

Under this light, the idea of curriculum becomes very clear. Scriptlets enable people to do things. To motivate a student to learn a scriptlet, one of three things needs to be true: the student must find the result of the scriptlet to be intrinsically rewarding; the scriptlet must be part of a package of scriptlets that is intrinsically rewarding; or the scriptlet must be an example of what I shall term *in order to* learning.

Not every scriptlet is intrinsically rewarding to learn. Sending e-mail and programming VCRs are intrinsically rewarding because one wants to achieve the result that comes from doing them correctly. Other intrinsically rewarding scriptlets might be "making toast," "making a phone call," or "hitting a golf ball." But, on the whole, we learn scriptlets because they are part of a larger package or because they are useful in order to do something else.

Many scriptlets can be grouped together to accomplish a goal. No one of them would naturally stand alone. The classic restaurant script that I later reclassified as a restaurant MOP is, for instance, a collection of scriptlets that includes ordering, paying, and so on. Driving a car is a collection of scriptlets that includes starting the engine, braking, and changing lanes. Playing baseball is a collection of scriptlets that includes fielding a ground ball to your left, hitting the curve ball, or sliding into a base. Not one of these things is ever done for its own sake. Nevertheless, they all take practice, and one can learn to do them so that one is quite skilled at various subtleties that might arise. (Although practice is very important, I am not recommending practice outside of a realistic need and context. All too often, schools have students practice skills before they actually "do" anything, thereby eliminating both motivation and context.)

In discussing examples of memory structures, I have referred in this book to the ORDER and PAY scenes and I've said that MOPs package these scenes. One should not confuse scenes with scriptlets, although it is quite easy to do so. Remember that I am using the term *scriptlet* in order to avoid using the wider term *skill*. By scriptlet I do indeed mean one aspect of the word skill – the aspect that is relevant when thinking about the difference between scenes and scriptlets. There is a restaurant paying scene that has within it a paying scriptlet that might be no more than the skill of knowing how to fill in a credit card slip properly. The scene has other properties (such as the presence of the waitress and the use of a little plastic tray) that have nothing to do with the scriptlet at all. The scriptlet refers to the practices, or to the set of actions, one learns as a part of one's role within a scene.

We do not often refer to scriptlets by themselves. Although we might say that we know how to make toast or change a tire or program a VCR, it is less common to say that we know how to start a car or pay a restaurant check. Nevertheless, these are all one category of scriptlet. The second category of scriptlet, the one we never brag about, is part of the packaged scriptlets we learn simply because they are part of a package. The package itself is worth bragging about, not the component scriptlets. So, one can say that one is good at playing baseball or that one is a good human resource manager, but there is no single scriptlet that is representative of these so-called abilities, and indeed it is obvious that they are not "abilities" at all. Rather, they are names for packages of scriptlets, no single one of which may be worthy of comment on its own.

Each scriptlet, whether in a package or not, has the same properties. One needs to learn them by practicing them. When one decides to teach them, however, one must bear in mind their important differences. The ones that stand alone, that are intrinsically rewarding, can be taught by themselves. One can learn to make toast or program a VCR in the absence of any other activity or motivational issue. This is simply not true of packaged scriptlets. A sliding lesson in baseball may be fun for someone who is intrinsically rewarded by getting dirty, but certainly very few people would take a lesson on how to sign a credit card slip, and no one wants to take a braking lesson in the absence of an entire driving lesson. Scriptlets that are part of packages must be taught within the context of those packages. We shall see why this matters later on.

The third category of scriptlet is the one in which scriptlets are learned in order to do something else. This is true of each scriptlet in a package, but it is also true of scriptlets not in a package and of the scriptlet packages themselves. That is, one can learn an intrinsically rewarding scriptlet in order to learn another that is also intrinsically rewarding. Or, one can learn a package that has a goal as part of a larger package that accomplishes a different goal. The idea that a scriptlet is useful only in that it relates to a distant goal is the critical idea in an understanding of what should be meant by curriculum.

We might all agree, for example, that being able to calculate square footage of an area is a useful skill that any adult might need. Schools assume such skills should be taught, but they place such instruction in a course of mathematics. The concept of scriptlets (and for that matter, scenes, MOPs, and TOPs as well) supports my argument that there should not be any courses in mathematics in the early years of school. Rather, mathematics scriptlets, of which the calculation of square footage is one, need to be taught within in a meaningful curriculum. Square footage calculation is not intrinsically rewarding, nor is it a part of a package of scriptlets that depend upon each other; it is a quite independent scriptlet that no one wants to learn for its own sake. It thus presents a serious motivation problem. Perhaps more important, it is also a use problem. Because in such a situation the scriptlet would be learned independently of any real context, it would not be placed within a MOP that connects this scriptlet, and its encompassing scene, to other relevant scenes. Thus, the student, even if compelled to learn the scriptlet, would not be able to find and activate it at some appropriate time in the future. In fact, the student may even have an inappropriate reminding if required to recall the information in a new context (Medin and Edelson, 1988).

One possibility in such a situation is to reconsider whether it is important to learn such a scriptlet. If it is important, a good curriculum must include a situation in which the scriptlet must be learned in order to accomplish a goal that is rewarding. Thus, if the calculation of square footage were important to learn, we might embed it within an attempt to plan and build a treehouse. This calculation would need to be made many times and would be learned through repeated practice. If this situation is rewarding for the student, then he will indeed learn the relevant scriptlets. If, on the other hand, no situation can be found that naturally contains this scriptlet and is rewarding for the student, it is reasonable to assume that it isn't all that important for the student to learn. Not every student will master every scriptlet.

The same is true in business. If we determine that how to read a financial report (really a package of scriptlets) is important to know, we must find a context in which that knowledge matters. Giving the student a decision to make in which the various scriptlets in reading a financial report come into play can make all the difference between a student's really acquiring the relevant scriptlets and his simply learning them in order to pass the test. One thing is important to remember here. It is not simply a question of finding the context in which the scriptlets come into play; they must come into play quite often. Practice is a very important part of scriptlet acquisition. This does not mean repetition of the same scriptlet again and again, as is done in drill and practice situations in school. It does mean finding repeated situations in the curriculum in which the same scriptlet is of use so that the practice does not seem like practice.

Courses, then, should be means by which scriptlets can be acquired when they (or packages of scriptlets) are not intrinsically rewarding by having a situation set up such that every scriptlet is acquired because the student can see that he will need it in order to accomplish a different goal that it enables. The student, in this scheme, must be aware of the progression of goals. He must want to accomplish the goal that drives the scenario itself, must understand the subgoals that lead to the accomplishment of the final goal, and must understand how each scriptlet helps him accomplish the various subgoals necessary. Creating meaningful curricula means creating goal-based scenarios (there will be much more about this idea later) that comprise scriptlets that have been determined to be important to learn.

188

The Role of the Teacher

In designing a curriculum, the aim must be to provide enough relevant experiences to allow for the acquisition of scriptlets and for thinking about difficulties that arise when we are not in a well-rehearsed, scriptlet-based situation. Further, it is important to provide some guidance through various experiences, so that the student can know the difference. That is, the student needs to know when more practice is required or when an exception has occurred and more thought is required (Chi et al., 1989). It is not important for a student to figure out everything for himself, however. A teacher can and should point to knowledge a student may need, or suggest new data to consider or new experiences to try, and, when asked, answer questions by providing facts that are not readily inferable or attainable through repeated experience.[4] The teacher should always be there to guide the student to the right experiences.

Under such a scheme, how do we know the student knows all he needs to in a given situation? We don't. But, we shouldn't care that much, either. A good teacher should have as his goal exposing his student to enough situations so that the student will become curious enough to take his learning into his own hands. In other words, the role of the teacher in a goal-based scenario is to open up interesting problems and to provide tools for solving them when asked by the student to do so. The accomplishment of the goal should be its own reward. The curriculum must be oriented toward, and satisfied with, the idea that the student will learn what he needs to in order to accomplish his goals. Hopefully he will have become curious and will have acquired both oddball cases and routine scriptlets along the way.

If we abandon the idea of easy measurement of achievement, then we can begin to talk about exciting our students with open-ended problems and can begin to create educational goals such as learning to think for oneself. Of course, such things are hard to measure, but one cannot help but feel that we'll know it when we see it. According to this view, the problem of how we teach, how education is delivered, becomes far more important than one might initially imagine. Actual content may not be the issue at all, since we are really trying to impart the idea that one can deal with new arenas of knowledge if one knows

---

[4] Lampert (1995, p. 162) advocates what Brown and Campione (1990) refer to as "guided discovery."

189

how to learn, how to find out about what is known, and how to abandon old ideas when they are worn out (Stasz et al., 1990). This means teaching ways of developing good questions rather than good answers. In other words, it means finding, and teaching, ways to help students learn on their own.

To understand something about why goal-based scenarios matter, let's take a subject that could be done either in the traditional way or in a more reasonable way, and play with the idea. Consider learning about wine. I choose this subject both because I happen to know something about it and because it is an adult subject, that is, one not normally formally taught except to adults who have specifically requested such training and who have typically paid money to attend some training for it.

Let's go to wine school. Not a real wine school, but a wine school where the instruction is done in a way similar to that used in the schools or in many formal training programs. We would start our instruction in wine by handing out four texts. One would be a geography text, teaching about where Burgundy and the wine-growing regions of the United States are, and talking about Virginia, New York, and Texas wineries, for example. The second would be an agricultural text. It would teach about the various grapes, where each is grown and why, and would discuss soil conditions, climate issues, optimal grape picking times, and so on. The third would be a text about the wine making process. Fermentation, storage, blending, and such would be included, as well as a discussion of the wine business, including who owns which chateaus and so on. The fourth would be a history text, answering such questions as, What kind of wine did the Romans drink? Who invented the cork stopper? How were issues of proper storage discovered? Why do the British prefer to drink Bordeaux? Which wine growing regions of France were there in Roman times?

After instruction in these various areas, we would begin testing. What was the best year for Bordeaux in the last thirty years and why? Who owns Chateau Margaux? When did Mouton-Rothschild achieve first-growth status? What grapes are grown in Oregon and why? What was the first French–American joint venture in wine growing? Can you identify the Chateauneuf du Pape region of the Rhone valley on a map?

What is wrong with this picture? It is the way schools teach most subjects. Schools teach information that can be tested. How will they know if you have learned anything if they can't test you? The tests drive the curriculum, and people lose sight of the original purpose.

Notice that no scriptlet (save those of memorization or reading) would really be involved at all in such a course. The goals of the student, which presumably had something to do with a desire to drink wine rather than with the desire to acquire facts, were ignored. I don't think that such a school would stay in business long. Students would vote with their feet. If students in school or training programs could vote with their feet in the analogous situations, they most certainly would.

The school that would stay in business would not involve lectures about wine. Teaching about wine means drinking wine, not memorizing facts about wine. Tasting wines with some help from someone who knows more than you do means that you will learn something. Being able to compare one wine to another, having many different experiences to generalize from, means being able to create new cases (a particularly great wine would be remembered, for example) and new generalizations (seeing a common property that all wines from a certain place or year had in contrast to others from different places or years, for example).

Over time, a learner becomes curious about a wider range of issues. Learning entails, among other things, knowing what questions to ask (Graesser, Baggett and Williams, 1996). This means getting enough cases or scriptlets that one can begin to wonder about them and to seek out new cases and refinements on scriptlets, so that new knowledge can be acquired. It is only in this way that the acquisition of facts is of any interest at all. To put this another way, facts can be acquired in a way that will make them useful only if those facts are sought after by the student for reasons of satisfaction of curiosity.

It took many years of wine drinking before I began to wonder about Rhone wines, or the British preference for Bordeaux (they used to own that region of France). I know approximately when Chateau Margaux changed hands because the quality changed dramatically (down and then back up) the last two times that that occurred and I really like Chateau Margaux and need to know which years to avoid. I visited the famous Chateau Margaux and really appreciated the place and the wine I tasted there, but would not have if I hadn't liked the wine in the first place (a shrine isn't a shrine unless it means something to you). I know where Bordeaux is now because I had to find it on a map in order to get to Chateau Margaux. (I drank Bordeaux for years without really knowing any more about the region of Bordeaux than that it was in the southwest of France somewhere.) All these facts would have been meaningless and easily forgotten had I simply been told them at the wrong time. The right time was when I wanted to know them, a time that could have been determined only by me and not by a teacher.

Disadvantages of Learning by Doing

Learning by doing is the right method for schools to adopt whether those schools are for little kids or for adults. Today, business is becoming more and more invested in teaching its employers to do their jobs more effectively. Nevertheless, businesses tend to copy existing teaching methods, creating so-called corporate universities that are often little more than poor imitations of the defective educational system that caused problems in the first place.

There are few complaints from the employees in these situations, because most adults, being products of our current educational system, are used to learning theories by lecture and to demonstrating their knowledge by multiple choice tests. But it is a bad idea to delude ourselves that this constitutes actual learning. The real learning that takes place in business takes place on the job. The more experience an employee has with a given situation, the more effective he is in that situation. It follows therefore that the best way to teach an employee is to let him work on a job that requires the skills we are trying to teach, and eventually he will pick them up. What then, is the role of training? Why not teach adults by letting them loose on the job and having them learn by doing? Here are some reasons why this can't always work:

1. **Learning by doing can be dangerous.** The best method for learning to defuse bombs, or fly jet fighters, is certainly to learn by doing. But it is imperative that trainees practice in an environment where failure, which is a key element in learning by doing, doesn't mean death or serious injury.

2. **Learning by doing can be expensive.** Not all trainees are best used in their intended capacity right away. Even if using an inexperienced employee in a real job is the best way to train that employee, and even if no physical or grievous financial danger could be caused by the poor performance of the trainee, there is still a very good chance that the trainee will fail to be very useful while he is learning. In cases in which it takes a long time to gather the relevant knowledge on the job or employees tend to not stay in the job for long, the whole idea of prolonged train-

ing is absurd. When failures cost money – through damage to an expensive piece of equipment, or through the loss of business as a result of inappropriate behavior – it is best to allow failures to occur in practice sessions.

3. Learning by doing can fail to provide relevant cases. Training on the job may keep an employee from ever experiencing all that he needs to learn. Real learning by doing can occur randomly in a varied environment. In general, a breadth of experience may not occur in an actual job environment in spite of everyone's desire that it be present.

4. Learning by doing may be inappropriate for children. Children may not be able to do things they would like to be able to do later on in life simply because they are still children. Also, they may be unprepared to spend the large amount of time necessary to learn a skill they may have no use for in later life.

The conclusion from all this is simple. The goal of effective training must be to replicate as well as possible the breadth of experience an employee needs in an as intense, danger-free, inexpensive, and timely fashion (Watkins and Marsick, 1993; Brinkerhoff and Gill, 1994) as possible. Training should look and feel exactly like the job one is being trained to assume.

Education for children, though not specifically job oriented, also should relate to real-world skills. Let children try out adult things they might like to do in life. Children naturally practice such skills, playing house or teacher or doctor or anything they can think up to simulate. We need to start building good simulations that will allow children to practice real-life skills in a realistic manner. We need to determine what these skills are and, with an understanding of what interests children, we need to start creating the learning-by-doing curriculum. Children should not be learning things for which they could not possibly find a use in adult life.

The reason that learning by doing works is that it strikes at the heart of the basic memory processes that humans rely upon. Human memory is based in scriptlets and the generalization of scripts. We learn how to do things and then learn how what we have learned is wrong and right. We learn when our rules apply and when they must be modified. We learn when our rules can be generalized and when exception cases must be noted. We learn when our rules are domain bound and when they can be used independent of domain. We learn all this by doing, by constantly having new experiences and attempting to integrate those experiences (or, more accurately, the memory of those experiences) into our existing memory structures. This integration process relies upon new data. These data are provided by experience. When new data are simply told to us, we don't know where in memory to put them because we don't really understand their use. When we experience the data ourselves, we also experience, at the same time, other sights, sensations, feelings, remembrances of goals achieved and goals hoped for, and so on. In other words, we have enough context to help us know how to characterize what we have learned well enough to find a place for it in memory and to begin the generalization and exception process.

It follows, then, that what we learn when we learn by doing will be details of how to accomplish something in a particular domain (a scriptlet); strategies that are independent of domain (process participation strategies); and the cases that stand alone as exceptions awaiting possible future integration into the memory system. Learning by doing works because it affects all these important memory issues. Learning by doing works because it teaches nonconscious knowledge.

CHAPTER 11

Nonconscious Knowledge

When we begin to think about learning, we begin immediately to ask about knowledge. It is very difficult to think about education without thinking about the knowledge we want to impart to students. We live in a world in which knowledge reigns supreme. In the popular culture, games like "Trivial Pursuit" capture the country's attention; television focuses on "Jeopardy" and other "knowledge games" that test who knows what. Far more important, school focuses on the same sorts of "trivial" knowledge. Schools are driven by tests that focus on fill-in-the-blank and multiple choice questions, thereby making success in school dependent upon memorization of facts. Even outside of school, in the workplace, companies train employees to do their jobs and then worry how to assess what the employees have learned (Brinkerhoff and Gill, 1994). The need to assess has focused everyone on things that are assessable. Thus facts have become "the currency of the educated" because they are so easy to measure.

The problem with all this is twofold. When our institutions of learning focus on test results, it follows that they need to focus on teaching what is testable. This leads to throwing out the baby with the bath water. The question of what to teach gets perverted by the measurements that are already in place, thus making curriculum change impossible. But, perhaps more important, there is a second problem revolving around the issue of our understanding who we are and what makes us tick. As long as we understand ourselves to be a collection of conscious knowledge that we can recite back on demand, we lose an understanding of how we work, of what mental processing is all about, and we begin to become, in a way, disconnected from ourselves. It is hard to know how to make decisions when we are relying upon our conscious understanding of events to guide us while our subconscious minds are merrily going in another direction. What we think we know may not be the same as what we actually know.

Most of the really important knowledge people have that enables them to do things and perform and behave in their daily lives, is not consciously known to them. For instance, we do not know what we know about restaurants. We may know a great deal about the PAYING scene, but this is practical knowledge we can execute, not knowledge that we can (or want to) recite. What currently passes for education in this world, namely the transmission of conscious knowledge from one human to another (Strauss and Shilony, 1994), is, by and large, a waste of time, since what is important to know is actually nonconscious and would not be transmittable in such a direct fashion. We learn how to function in restaurants by going to them, not by being instructed about them.

People perform most of their daily functions in a mindless manner (Langer, 1990). We can't articulate what it is we do when we brush our teeth, drive a car, throw or catch a ball, chew and swallow, compose a sentence, or understand television. We just do these things, following the scriptlets we have for them. When we are asked about what we are doing, even the most articulate of us give answers that would appear as mere hand waving and after-the-fact observations to any serious student of these subjects. Dogs, for example, can catch balls, understand commands, and find lost objects, but it seems unlikely that they have a conscious theory of physics or psychology that explains their behaviors to themselves.

If we believe that conscious knowledge, that is, the kind we can talk (or think) to ourselves about, is at the heart of intelligence, then it follows that we would be upset by a machine that claims to be a product of research in artificial intelligence but could do only what it had been programmed to do. We would be upset that this machine lacked the ability to talk about what it was doing. It is the lack of this latter ability that would make us say that the machine is not an intelligent one. It follows from this that what we appreciate most about ourselves is not what we can do, but what we can say about what we can do. We feel kindly toward our fellow humans because they are able to make commentaries about what they do, and we find fault with machines because they can't do this. The effect of this happiness with the human ability to self-reflect is not harmful as long as we are discussing machines and their possession or lack of intelligence. Unfortunately, these same attitudes have killed our education system. When we run an education system whose basic currency is conscious knowledge, we are, in essence, copying these arguments about intelligence. Conceptions of consciousness that portray conscious knowledge as the sine qua non of humanity or intelligence have the effect of relegating nonconscious knowledge to a nether world of knowledge not worth teaching. As long as we teach what we explicitly know because "what we know we know" is, in essence, what we think of as intelligence, our educational systems will fail.

On the other hand, if we want to teach students to perform, and if explicit knowing about the facts of their performance is unimportant to their performance, then it follows that we are teaching the wrong sorts of things in school. In school, we teach students the knowledge of which we are conscious rather than knowledge that we need in order to perform intelligent tasks, of which we are mostly unconscious. The argument of Bransford et al. (1989) that students should be learning to think "in terms of models" rather than "about" them, highlights the clear split between nonconscious knowledge and the conscious knowledge currently being taught in schools.

It may seem that the idea of teaching unconscious knowledge is an oxymoron. How can we teach what we don't know we know? John Dewey knew full well that performance is the real issue in education, not the demonstration of conscious knowledge. The real question is, Why are we so fascinated by conscious knowledge that we insist on making our educational system beholden to it? What exactly is the difference between conscious thought and nonconscious thought, anyway?

To consider these questions, we need to think about all the times we have had the possibility of viewing the nether world of thinking that is at a level somewhat less than that of conscious thought. We know what it looks like when we consciously think about something (or at least we think we do), but what does unconscious thought look like, and what is its role in performance? The answers to these questions give a surprising view of what thinking is about and what education must therefore be about.

The Illusion of Control

You wake up in the middle of the night and try to fall back asleep, but you can't. Your mind is racing, thinking about what will happen tomorrow, rehashing what happened yesterday, endlessly dwelling on some long-forgotten event. You try to turn your mind off, to relax and go back to sleep, but your mind does not seem to be within your control. You know you could think about these things more clearly in the morning, that the issues you are dwelling upon don't matter that much, but your mind continues to race, on a course of its own, out of control.

What is this phenomenon about? There is a difference between rational thought and nonconscious thought. Most people believe they are capable of reasoning carefully about a subject. They believe they can come to a sensible conclusion based on the facts that will allow them to make the proper decisions in their lives. Further, they believe they are aware of this reasoning process; they can comment on why they reasoned the way they did. Computers, on the other hand, might be able to follow rules people give them that simulate rational thought, but they wouldn't know what they had done and it would be only a simulation, not the real thing. This is how the argument goes, typically.

Yet, there is the other part of us, thinking away on its own, that we only see at night. Certainly, when we dream, we recognize that something seemingly apart from ourselves is doing something in our heads. We feel as if some kind of dream maker is playing with our minds, outside of our own rational selves. Surely, we wouldn't, in "our right minds," imagine that pigs could fly or that dead people could talk to us, or that we tried to move but had no legs. The stuff of dreams does not seem rational. Indeed, it often seems frightening, as if there were something wrong with our thinking process, as if normal thought was being distorted in some way.

When our minds race in the night, however, they do seem to be rational. There are no flying pigs. Nevertheless, this process also seems somehow outside of ourselves. We have no control of it and it seems as if it isn't us doing the thinking. People usually feel that these nighttime phenomena are somehow odd, not part of their real cognitive processes in any serious way. But these are not solely nighttime phenomena at all.

To see that they are not only phenomena of the night, try the following experiment. Put yourself in a darkened room with no external stimuli, and nothing very stimulating to look at. Make yourself comfortable. Now allow your mind to wander. Don't attempt to try to think about anything. Make your mind as clear as possible, concentrating on nothing in particular. Do this for ten minutes. When you are finished, write down what you were thinking about at the end. Ask yourself if you intended to wind up at that point, or in any way could have predicted that you would be thinking about whatever it was you were thinking about.

What you should have experienced in that situation is the daylight analogue of the mind racing that occurs at night. What exactly is this stuff? Is it really such an odd phenomenon? How does it relate to our conscious thinking process?

The claim here is that the racing mind is the real thinking apparatus that humans (and perhaps other animals as well) employ. The so-called conscious mind, where rational thought takes place, is illusory. We do have rational thoughts, but they have a lot less to do with our actual thought processes than we are willing to admit. When we see our minds racing, what is happening is that a window onto our actual thought processes has been exposed to our consciousness (our rational thinking apparatus). Consciousness, the claim is, is not really conscious of all that much of what is going on. When we feel that we can't turn off our racing minds, what is really happening is that we can't close the window. Our minds are always racing or, more accurately, they are always thinking about something; we just aren't always able to look at the process.

We can, of course, make decisions and carry them out, all in a conscious way. We can decide whom we want to marry, what job we want to take, where to take a vacation, and so on. We like to think that all of these kinds of decisions are made by our conscious rational minds. But rational thought is an illusion. We can delude ourselves that the conscious aspects of such decision making typify what thinking is all about. But thinking is a process far more complex than one that makes such simple decisions.

A good way to understand this is by an analogy to breathing. We can decide to take a breath, or to hold our breath. We can alter our breathing in weird ways, breathe through scuba apparatus, hyperventilate, or hold our breaths until we are blue in the face. But, when all is said and done, when we have stopped with the silliness, or passed out from it, all breathing returns to normal. We believe we have control over our breathing, but we do not. We breathe when we are asleep, when we are injured, when we are otherwise engaged, and we are rarely aware of the process. In fact, we don't understand the process at all. (By this I don't mean that physiologists don't understand the process; I just mean that breathers don't.) In fact, the more we think about breathing, the more we can screw it up. When we stop thinking about it, or stop attempting to control it, it goes on its merry way without us.

The same is true of memory and memory structures. We don't think about what we know about how to deal with people, how to close a sale, how to make someone like us, or how to get our way. We just know how to do this stuff, maybe not very well, but we do it. We function in these arenas without thinking, or so it seems. What is really going on is that we have multiple experiences that have been generalized into various MOPs and TOPs that help us deal with a large variety of situations by analogy to prior cases (Ross, 1984; Johnson and Seifert, 1992; Kolodner, 1993; Gholson et al., 1996). We do not often recognize or think about these analogies. They are not conscious, but they are the real stuff of memory and of thought.

Thinking means coming up with explanations, whether conscious or not. To come up with explanations, we must generate and answer questions. No intelligent entity can learn without generating for itself the need to know. However, this need to know doesn't have to be, and often cannot be, conscious. We need to know what the places we are traveling through look like, for example, but we do not consciously make notes on them. Our minds do this "free of charge" without our really thinking about the actual evidence. If we observe that something has changed on a later trip, we often cannot say what. We can recognize but not recall.

Learning depends upon goals (Trzebinski and Richards, 1986; Seifert, 1990). We have the goal of recognizing a friend, and when we see him and think he has done something to his face, we ask if he has grown a mustache, without recognizing that he has shaved his beard. All along, however, we have consciously recognized him. We don't know what we know, because we don't know that the data structure we have stored in memory of his face is a set of procedures in a dynamic memory that we have little access to.

When we say that someone knows a particular fact, we can also say that he is conscious of that fact. When we say that someone knows how to do something, we can also say that he can consciously go about doing that thing. In fact, in most situations in which one is talking about knowledge that people have, one could easily substitute words about their consciousness of what they are doing or thinking. Nevertheless, people don't necessarily "know" what they are doing when they do it, any more than you know how these words transform themselves into ideas when you read them.

Within the broad spectrum of things that we say we know, there is a line between those things that we say we know and can explicitly state as knowledge, and those things we know but don't know that we know. I can say that I know that George Washington was the first president, but this is quite a different kind of knowledge than saying that I know how to ride a bike. I am quite conscious of old George, can picture his face, make conscious associations between his face and the dollar bill, and so on. I know that I know a lot about George Washington and I know that I can tell you what I know. But, with bicycle riding, the story is different. I just know how to do it. I may know some facts about bicycles, but these don't have much to do with what I do when I ride. I may understand some principles about balance and motion, but when I learned to ride a bike I knew none of these explicitly. I am conscious while riding, and I am conscious that I am riding and conscious of what I am doing when I am riding. But, I simply don't know what I know about bike riding. In other words, consciousness and knowledge can be quite different things.

The best exemplar of the phenomenon I am discussing is what happens when we attempt to understand a sentence – when you do what you are doing now, when you are reading this book. You know the meaning of the word *book*, for example. If you were asked to define a book, you probably could do so. The curious thing is that what you would say when asked to define *book* has nothing whatever to do with your knowing the meaning of the word *book* in the context of reading a sentence containing the word. The definitional knowledge is knowledge you have learned in school, or knowledge you can invent for yourself when asked to do so. The knowledge you have about "book" that helps you understand a sentence containing that word is knowledge about what to do when you encounter the word in context, which is knowledge of a very different sort. No one explicitly sets out to learn this kind of knowledge, which we might call language-processing knowledge. We just seem to know it. For example, if you had been asked about the meaning of the word *book*, there is a good chance you would not have mentioned the sense of the word in the following sentence: "That possibility is so likely you could book it." The use of *book* as a verb usually does not come to mind when one is asked to define *book*. Nevertheless, when attempting to understand any sentence with the word *book* in it, one must reject, in some sense, meanings of the word that don't fit in context. To do this, one uses all kinds of language-processing knowledge of which one is rarely explicitly aware.

We must recognize that not all knowledge is conscious knowledge; however, being able to *use* or *apply* that knowledge in context across myriad settings is a valid test of our learning.

What is the meaning of the word *take*, for example? Think about it for a second before you read the next sentence. Did you consider the sense of *take* as used in "John took a bath"? How about "John took an aspirin" or "John took a wife"? You know what these sentences mean without giving them much thought at all. Yet, it is very unlikely that you thought of these senses of *take* when originally asked about its meaning. Further, and more important, even now you would probably have difficulty formulating an accurate definition for *take*. You know how to understand and use the word, but you couldn't say what you knew when asked and, upon further reflection, would still find it difficult to do so. What then does it mean to say you know the meaning of the word?

To understand how to answer this question, we need to know more about different kinds of knowledge. "Knowing" is not the same thing in all cases. It depends upon what you are supposed to know. Here are five ways of looking at knowledge:

1. Rational knowledge: the facts necessary for logical thinking
2. Emotional knowledge: "knowing" how we feel
3. Subconscious knowledge: knowledge we are unaware of having
4. Physical knowledge: knowledge our body uses
5. Nonconscious knowledge: knowledge, used in basic mental activity, that we are unable to articulate

Rational knowledge is the knowledge we can explicitly state. This includes definitional knowledge, factual knowledge, experiential knowledge, and, in general, the kind of knowledge we learn in school or from books. Typically, when I talk about knowledge in this book, I am talking about what I am calling *rational knowledge*.

But what is the knowledge employed by the emotional conscious? For example, I "know" when students understand what I tell them. A man "knows" when his wife loves him. What kind of knowing is this? Clearly this is knowledge of a different kind. Cool, calm, rational, intellectual people are content to say that they know such things without in any way justifying the basis for that knowledge. Are they being crazy or irrational at such moments? Is this their irrational, unmentioned, darker side popping up? Certainly they didn't learn this stuff in school or read it in a book. Where do they get this knowledge then?

Subconscious knowledge is a little more difficult to get at, but people actually do talk about it quite often. In *The Inner Game of Tennis*, for example, Timothy Gallwey talks about two selves who are always in conflict when it comes to playing tennis:

> Most players are talking to themselves on the court all the time...
> "Keep your eye on the ball." "Bend your knees."... One day I was
> wondering who was talking to whom... "I'm talking to myself"
> most people say. But just who is this "I" and who is the "myself?"
> ...The "I" seems to give instructions; the "myself" seems to per-
> form the actions. Then "I" returns with an evaluation of the
> action.

Gallwey goes on to describe how to play better tennis by having the inner self that is being talked to watch what is going on and attempt to imitate it:

> It is possible to hold in your mind the image of where you want
> the ball to go and then allow the body to do what is necessary to
> hit it there.... Suppose for example, that you are consistently
> rolling your racket over on the follow-through... You must give
> (yourself) a very clear image of what you are asking it to
> do....Shut your eyes and imagine... your entire forehand with the
> racket staying flat during the swing.... It is important not to make
> any conscious effort to keep the racket flat.

According to Gallwey, conscious knowledge is more or less useless in playing tennis. The mind doesn't control the body consciously. Rather, the conscious mind can concentrate on actions it wants its body to perform, but deliberate direction is all but useless.

Of course, given that animals have had bodies to control for millions of years but probably have had conscious thought and language for a lot less time, it follows that it is possible to control the actions of a body by means other than by talking to it. Gallwey's point is basically that talking to one's body actually makes things worse. Sometimes the body seems to know what to do without anyone telling it what to do.

Harville Hendrix,[1] writing about love, points out that unconscious decision making is more powerful than conscious decision making when deciding on something as important as a potential spouse. In a

---

[1] Harville Hendrix: *Getting the Love You Want* (1992). I am grateful to Jerry Feldman for pointing me toward this book.

discussion of what he calls the "unconscious marriage," he points out that people often choose mates who reflect the character traits of a parent with whom they had difficulty getting along, unconsciously attempting to cause the same childhood sensations to occur again since they seem familiar. To put this another way, they "know" what they want in a mate but don't know that they know it.

People (outside of educational settings) know that they don't know what they know. For example, in an article in the sports section of the *Chicago Tribune*[2] on why the strike zone in baseball has shrunk, I found the following:

> Pitches that 10 years ago were called strikes aren't called strikes any more... "The hitters are allowed to question every pitch. The pitcher's not allowed to say a word. If the pitcher says something, it shows up the umpire, because he's got to say it to his face. A hitter can look down at the ground and say whatever he wants without all the fans knowing it." "So, over the course of time, what's going to happen on close calls? It's not a conscious thing, but over the course of time it's going to take away a pitcher's pitches."

What is it that Jack McDowell's umpire knows about the strike zone? When asked, he would undoubtedly cite the official definition for the strike zone. Yet he doesn't use it. The strike zone he knows, isn't the one he knows. The rational knowledge a person has can differ on the same subject from what we call his subconscious knowledge. My point here is not to get into the clinical psychology of the subconscious mind. I am worrying about "knowing" here. What does it mean to know one thing rationally and the exact opposite in the recesses of the subconscious mind? Who wins in that case? If it is the subconscious who wins, what does this tell us about real knowledge and where it resides? What would this mean when one is trying to acquire new knowledge? How is the subconscious knowledge acquired? Not in school, that much seems clear.[3] What does this tell us about teaching and learning?

Similar arguments apply with respect to physical consciousness. When we say we know how to hit a tennis ball, what is it exactly that we know? We say things about how to hit the ball, we hear things

---

[2] The quotes are from Kurt McCaskill and Jack McDowell, pitchers for the Chicago White Sox.
[3] For an example, see Strauss and Shilony (1994) on teacher conceptions about their jobs.

about how to do it, we read about how to do it, and yet none of this translates into actually doing it. Gallwey suggests watching a good tennis player and then trying to imitate what he does. Note that he does not suggest trying to characterize in English what that person does and then telling yourself to do what you have memorized. He suggests simply watching and imitating. Obviously this imitative knowledge is an important kind of knowledge; according to Gallwey, it is more important than the verbalization of what you have seen.

From a developmental point of view, it should be obvious that this kind of knowledge is the basis of all other knowledge. Small children do not ask for advice on how to speak their language or how to run or how to throw a ball or build blocks. They copy what others around them do. The core of all knowledge comes when we are not particularly verbal or intellectual about what we are beginning to know. What we know at the beginning is what we have seen; this is later translated into an attempt to imitate what we have seen. In other words, we are operating on prior knowledge, specifically on the prototypical case, which is based on the nonconscious internalization of others' experiences and on our observations, rather than based on our own experiences or our own conscious knowledge. When this works, when we can successfully imitate, we then "know" how to do whatever we have been trying to imitate. But, we don't know what we know, and we are, for the most part, better off for it. Conscious knowledge, as Gallwey points out, is not necessarily helpful for execution.

Although the types of rational knowledge I have been discussing are important, nonconscious knowledge is at the heart of what we know about everything. We do not consciously know how we construct a sentence while we're talking or writing, or how we understand a sentence when we read or listen. We do not consciously know how we find our way or how we show empathy or how we make decisions. Experts in a subject are not conscious of what it is they know about that subject. This last statement is subject to dispute. But the core issues about knowledge revolve around it. Experts spout what they know with some frequency. They write books about what they know and give lectures on it. People who wish to avail themselves of an expert's knowledge buy these books, attend these lectures, or, if they can afford it, hire these experts as consultants. The experts say what they think they know and the listeners hope that they can learn to do what the experts say, or at least that they can understand what the experts say. In some cases, this may indeed happen. But, it is not the norm. Typically it is very difficult for experts to say what they know because, again, they don't know what they know. And typically it is very difficult for listeners to alter their behavior as a result of what they have heard because people learn by doing, not by listening.

Those who believe that what I have said is heretical are typically those who have a great reverence for what has passed as knowledge in the age of the book. As long as books have been the dominant medium of transmission of knowledge, those who have read the most and acquired the most knowledge in this way are the most likely to hold "book knowledge" in reverence. But there are other, less book-oriented people, who do not have the same reverence for rational knowledge.

There is a kind of unspoken war going on these days about the nature of knowledge. It is a war between the young and the old, the rich and the poor, the educated and the noneducated. But, most of all, it is a war between those who are computer involved and those who are computer-shy.[4] Those involved in these verbal confrontations don't usually realize they are fighting about what it means to know something. The arguments take place around the subject of educational reform, or cultural literacy, or consciousness, or what it takes to succeed in society. The arguments are about the value of video games, or the role of the computer, the triviality of television, or the significance of the information highway. But, these arguments are really about what it means to know and what it has meant to know.

The computer has changed our conceptions of what it means to be a knowing entity in the world. Why have there been so many books written about consciousness in recent years? Are we all of a sudden fascinated by our own minds in a way we have not been in previous decades or centuries? Or is it that the computer is threatening what we have always assumed about our own self-knowledge and we feel the need to affirm our own sense of self? As the educated, powerful, and elderly of our society reaffirm their own humanity, a quiet revolution is taking place. It is not the computer revolution that everyone talks about, the one about baud rates and fiber optics and gigabytes of memory. It is the knowledge revolution, the one about what is worth knowing.

Debates about artificial intelligence are only theoretical at this

---

[4] Collins (1991), for instance, argues that schools must inevitably move toward being more focused on computers and computer skills. Further, he argues that this shift will significantly alter the structure of school in general.

point. Very intelligent machines will not arrive next week at Radio Shack. But, what has already arrived in many households across the country and what will continue to arrive at an increasing pace throughout the decade is the nonconscious epistemics of the future. What does this mean? Slowly, without our realizing it, all that we valued about being knowledgeable is changing. Winning at "Trivial Pursuit" in the 1980s or being terrific at quiz shows in the 1950s will no longer pass as a mark of erudition in the 2000s. Facts are becoming an increasingly meaningless currency. The kids of the 1950s argued about batting averages and other meaningless pieces of knowledge because they were brought up in an era when facts were king. Go out and talk to kids today and you will find that they are no longer talking about facts. They are talking about music, or movies, or video games.

Intellectuals decry this change of values. They denounce what is happening to the younger generation. They talk about the failure of the school system, but it is they who have failed. They have failed to observe the change in the currency of knowledge.

A modern intellectual, one who is growing or attempting to grow his breadth of knowledge, does not behave the way his counterpart would have behaved fifty years ago. An example will illustrate this. I had the occasion recently to observe a clinical psychologist expand her knowledge as she expanded her private practice. She took on a patient who was having sexual performance problems. She had never had a patient like this before, so she went to the bookstore and bought a book on the subject. Later she had a patient interested in having a sex change. Again she went to the book store. Later still she had a gay patient. Back to the book store. Eventually she began to see lesbian couples. Again the book store. She couldn't have engaged in this process of just-in-time self-education fifty years ago. These books didn't exist then, and what did exist wasn't always so easy to find. Further, the conception of knowledge of that period did not allow for self-education in this way. Certification was everything and experience counted for little.

Notice that the picture I have described does not involve a computer at all. What would the psychologist have done if these books were available on line? She might not have gone to go the book store. Does this change our conception of knowledge? Of course not. Let's go ahead in time a couple of years. Suppose that, instead of asking for a book on a subject, she could ask a question to the computer and get an answer when she needed it. Does this change our conception of knowledge? It doesn't seem to change it very much. After all, we could always ask questions and get answers, couldn't we?

Actually, we could ask, but we couldn't always be sure that we were getting the right answer. So let's change the game slightly and imagine a world in which she could ask a question and, instead of getting an answer, she would begin a dialogue with one or more of the world's experts on the subject about which she needed information. Proponents of distance learning have suggested that this will be possible on the information highway by dialing up e-mail or video conferencing with these experts. It seems to me unlikely that such experts will make themselves available whenever anyone might need them. What seems considerably more likely is that it will be possible to ask questions that have already been asked of experts and have been videotaped and selected by the computer in response to the needs of the user. The paramount issue in doing this is indexing all this material. There is no value in having a hundred hours of videotape of an expert and being required to watch all one hundred hours to find what you need. Technology needs to be built that can allow a user to ask a question and get an answer. Luckily this is not all that difficult to do. So, a person who needs to know more about a particular subject can ask the best and the brightest, creating debates by accessing those of differing points of view if desired, and then ending the conversation when he feels he has found what he wanted to know.

The systems I am describing exist today, even if they are not generally available. Does the existence of such systems change what it means to know something? I argue that it does. When information is easy to find, the information itself becomes considerably less valuable; what goes up in value is the ability to use that information (Resnick, 1987; Collins, 1991; Murnance and Levy, 1996). This matters because it necessarily changes our conception of what it means to be educated and therefore of what it means to educate. If anyone can engage any expert in a dialogue with relative ease, it is simple (and not very important) to cite what those experts have to say. Being able to use the knowledge those experts conveyed toward some end would become the real issue.

But, of course, today's children already know this. Knowing the facts of the video game doesn't matter; it is being able to use that information in order to win the game that matters. Knowing about bits and bytes doesn't matter; navigating the Internet is the skill worth having. It is for this reason that school is becoming less and less relevant to today's children. They don't need to know the history of man's inhumanity to man when they are participants in these issues through television and real-life experience. They don't need to know anything unless they know its use. Is this wrong?

Certainly, intellectuals of the old school would argue that it is dead wrong. Searle, Chomsky, Wittgenstein, Freud, Kant, and numerous others have very different conceptions of knowledge. In opposition to those scholars stand the researchers in artificial intelligence. In attempting to make intelligent machines, AI researchers discovered what today's kids and our clinical psychologists already knew.

Getting the machine to have knowledge is the key issue in AI. However, factual knowledge is of little use to a machine. Process knowledge, knowledge of *how to do* instead of *what to do*, is the difference between intelligent and unintelligent machines. This is understood easily when one considers the idea that no machine would be considered intelligent if it could not learn. Yet, what is the knowledge of how to learn? People learn but they don't know how they do it. Computers don't learn and thus are unintelligent. How would we make them intelligent? The answer must be by giving the computer the ability to learn.

People have some profound misconceptions about what it means to know. Those misconceptions come about because *what* people know, when they know they know, is facts. They know facts about the world and facts about themselves, so they have assumed that facts are the currency of knowledge and that consciousness is about the self-knowledge that we know what we know. But we don't know how we learn, how we understand, how we come to feel what we feel, or believe what we believe. In fact, all we know that we know we know, are our own sensations, our own thoughts (to a limited extent), and facts. When we see knowledge as being about process rather than about facts, as about doing rather than about reciting, then we can recognize that we don't know what we know at all.

Goals are the key driver of actions in intelligent entities, but they are hardly ever conscious. It is important to recognize this when designing educational systems. All good educational design depends upon a good understanding of students' goals. This understanding is critical both in terms of motivating students (Brinkerhoff and Gill, 1994) and in terms of the focus on goals in people's mental representations (Trzebinski and Richards, 1986; Seifert, 1990). However, students quite often don't know their own goals. In fact, teaching them about their own goals is often a problem to be tackled in educational design. For example, in my role as an undergraduate advisor I once met a student who said she was going to work in the Peace Corps after graduation. I asked her why; she said she wanted to help people. I pointed out that there were many ways in which one could help people and that most of them did not involve going off to a very far away place. I asked her if her real goal wasn't actually to go far away and live in another culture, and I pointed out that that goal could be satisfied in ways other than the Peace Corps. She answered that she didn't know why she wanted to work in the Peace Corps, because she hadn't really thought about it.

This is an example of goals that are nonconscious masquerading as rational knowledge. Often we don't know the difference. We can state our goals, of course, but we are often surprised when our own actions are working toward something else. People who seem to be self-defeating may be just that, or they may be people whose real nonconscious goals and stated conscious goals are quite different.

With respect to plans, the situation is much the same. We plan nonconsciously, but we also plan consciously. Our conscious plans can be more intricate because we can discuss, evaluate, and edit them. This self-reflection is the primary value of consciousness; it becomes most evident in the planning process. The question is, Can we produce nonconscious plans? If one assumes that dogs are in fact not self-aware, then, since dogs can create plans (albeit not complex ones), it follows that planning can be a nonconscious process. But, although planning seems to be a primarily conscious process, the real questions to ask are, Do we come up with good plans in the middle of the night? Do we dream up good plans? Do they come to us in the early morning as we are waking and our minds start to race? If the answers to these questions are affirmative, then we need to consider seriously the idea that we can plan nonconsciously. If this is true, then it tells us a great deal about what kind of education would be needed to help people plan better. It certainly wouldn't be the type of teaching that told people plans or gave people choices of plans. Rather, it would have to entail situations that enabled people to create their own plans and to follow the consequences of those plans in a way that had a real psychological impact. To teach people to plan, we need to teach people to know *how* to plan. Doing this requires serious thought about what it means to plan.

210

The issue then is not about what words we use nor about the physiology of consciousness. The real issue is knowledge. When we talk about what we know, what we should learn, or what we should teach others, we need to know what kind of knowledge we are talking about. You cannot convey knowledge if you don't know what knowledge you need to convey.

CHAPTER 12

Case-based Reasoning and the Metric of Problem Solving

Learning to learn is a very common phrase these days. I don't like it much because we know how to learn from birth. We build MOPs and TOPs effortlessly, and we respond to expectation failures automatically by building explanations. The phrase "learning to learn" refers to the idea that learning to do any *specific* thing is really not all that relevant. The real issue is to get students to the point where they are excited about learning and they want to learn more because doing so is fun. Children (and adults as well) must also believe they *can* learn. This is often a big problem with kids' internalizing failure in school into an idea that they just are not smart enough (Eckert, 1989). They don't need to learn to learn – they simply need to rely upon the natural learning mechanisms they were born with.

Attitude is critical to continued, lifelong learning and to the development of a keen intellect. People who are closed to new ideas and are unwilling to think cannot really be very intelligent; such people may have had dynamic memories but have gradually become impervious to change. In order to understand what intelligence is and what it is not, we need to get away from the problem-solving view of intelligence (which defines intelligence in terms of how well we have learned how to apply rules we were explicitly taught) and move over to one oriented more toward case-based reasoning, which is the natural outgrowth of a dynamic memory.

When intelligence is discussed, the idea of problem solving comes up. Curiously, but by no means by chance, most discussions about, and indeed most work in, artificial intelligence also concern problem solving. For instance, when we want to talk about the intelligence of chimps, the "monkey and bananas problem" is often mentioned (where the issue is how a monkey can get bananas when he can't reach them but has access to some tools, such as boxes to stand on and poles to reach with). Initial work on AI was often about getting computers to solve problems like this. Problem solving usually serves as the major issue in intelligence testing, whether we are talking about chimps, children, or computers. It is important to understand why this is so, and if it *should* be so. As shall be seen, this focus on problem solving has a great deal to do with implicit assumptions about knowledge that, I shall argue, are quite wrong.

In the previous chapter, I mentioned five ways that we typically talk about knowledge. These are rational, emotional, subconscious, physical, and nonconscious. The solution of any formally stated problem usually is presumed to depend upon rational knowledge (of which we are consciously aware). Even though we don't know much about the mental life of monkeys, it is nevertheless interesting to ask if the monkey who solves the monkey and bananas problem knows what he is doing. Darwin thought that higher-order animals were indeed capable of original and rational, and therefore conscious, thinking. If one believes that a monkey who solves an original problem knows how to solve that problem, then it seems to follow that one should also believe that a computer that solves such a problem also knows how to solve it.

But in fact it doesn't follow that a computer knows anything just because it solves a problem by following rules, although most people assume this. They are what I call "fleshists" – people who are prejudiced against any thinking entity not wrapped in flesh. We willingly attribute vast thinking powers to any person doing any mundane task but fail to treat machines with the same largess. "Knowing" is an idea we all have strong views about. Computers we can open up and look inside. We can see what knowledge is there. Curiously, this does not make the critics any more comfortable or any more willing to say that the computer knows something, even when they see that that knowledge is there.

It doesn't follow that the monkey knows anything either. There is no reason to believe that the monkey knows that "a tool is useful for trying hard to reach objects." This is an idea that implies that all real knowledge is rational knowledge. In assuming that, we forget an important thing we know about monkeys, which is often phrased as "Monkey see, monkey do." The issue here revolves around what it means to really know something. Note that although this issue of the monkey's knowledge seems debatable, the situation is even more curious when we start to talk instead about what computers know.

The computer might very well be attempting, if that is the way the programmer wrote the program, to follow logical rules that help solve a problem. To say that the computer "knows" these rules because it can follow them, seems silly. Quite often humans successfully follow instructions on how to do something but then, when left to their own devices without those instructions, they can't perform the same actions. Did the human know how to perform that action and then not know? Or would it be more reasonable to say that the human never knew the rules but could follow them when instructed to do so? Computers can continually follow the same instructions, but this seems different than saying that the computer knows what to do.

These are standard debates from the fields of artificial intelligence and cognitive science and I use them here merely to set the stage for the important questions to follow. The issue is not whether the computer or the monkey seems to be conscious or whether it knows anything. Rather, the question is, What kind of knowledge is necessary to solve the monkey and bananas problem and how does one go about acquiring that knowledge? Clearly the answer is different if you are a computer or a monkey. Certainly the acquisition method would be different. Also, the answer is different if you are a two-year-old person or an adult. Two-year-olds are more like monkeys in that they are imitative, and adults are more like computers in that they want someone to tell them what to do. From an education perspective, we need to think about how to rectify this situation. Perhaps adults have forgotten how to learn (and perhaps computers never knew). It is in examining these differences that we can really begin to understand something about the nature of knowledge.

Why should we assume that an animal who has solved an unusual problem (as in the monkey and bananas problem, or in any of Darwin's examples about how elephants in zoos have been observed to use their trunks as tools in a way they never would have done in the wild) has either done this by instinct or done this by rational reasoning? Isn't there some alternative to these two choices? Isn't it possible that the solution used by the monkey was not knowledge of general rules about problem solving, but was also not instinct? This is not all that radical a statement. After all, a person who follows Gallwey's dictums about tennis playing and watches an expert player, paying close attention to interaction with the ball but not thinking about how to move his own arm, is neither playing tennis by instinct nor using knowledge of how to hit the ball that he can in any way claim to be aware of. Similarly, a person who has a conversation with a friend while driving a car is neither driving the car by instinct nor having a conversation by instinct, but neither is he doing either of these things by use of knowledge about driving or knowledge about conversational structure or language that he is in any sense aware of. In fact, the person in either case cannot report how he did any of these things. Of course, if you ask him, he will make some feeble attempt to make such a report, but as any AI practitioner can tell you, that report will not come close to producing a system of rules that a computer could follow and that would come even close to producing behavior similar to that being described. Indeed, much research has been done in cognitive psychology to try to report the rules that experts follow as a model of their thinking in various domains (Newell, Shaw and Simon, 1958; Newell and Simon, 1972). So, irrelevant reporting notwithstanding, the human is doing something that uses knowledge that is either subconscious, nonconscious, or physical.

Case-based reasoning (CBR) is more or less the opposite hypothesis about expert reasoning from that which is embodied in the notion of expert systems. In a case-based reasoning system, the reasoner relies upon past experiences as a guide for the current situation. CBR became a field for research as a result of the work on reminding in the first edition of this book. CBR involves the normal application of a dynamic memory to issues of everyday reasoning. Expert systems were very much in vogue at the time the first edition of this book appeared. An expert system (e.g., Erman et al., 1980; Lindsay et al., 1980; McDermott, 1982; Buchanan and Shortliffe, 1984; Soloway, Bachant and Jensen, 1987) is a system of rules a computer can follow that are intended to allow that computer to emulate the decision making of an expert. For example, the premise is made that when a medical doctor makes a diagnosis, he is following a system of rules and those rules can be extracted by interviewing the expert. The rules are then given to a computer and the computer has the expertise of the expert. Expert systems are an appealing idea, but they are also quite wrong-headed. It is important to understand why.

It may seem that the attempt to model the mind is no more than the attempt to create a system of rules a computer could follow to enable it to seem intelligent. In fact, this view is the cornerstone of the debate between AI and its critics. On one side, we find people whose view is that the mind is a system of rules and the task of the modeler of mind is simply to find those rules and to make a machine follow them. On the other side of the argument are those who say that the mind is too complex to be characterized simply by a system of rules, and that something else, innate properties, chemicals, or God knows what, needs to be added in to the mix and that this could never be done on a computer. Both sides are wrong.

No system consisting simply of rules will work in modeling the mind. The reason for this is *not* that the mind is too mysterious to understand, but rather that rules do not adequately characterize the subject matter of the mind. What we have come to call the unconscious mind is not the same thing as what we have come to call the conscious mind. Although it is altogether possible that a system of rules could be developed to model the conscious mind, modeling the unconscious mind presents other problems. This whole notion of a division between the two, and the need for scientists to rely upon rational knowledge for their understanding of what it means to know something, are at the root of the problem.

When the monkey solves the problem of getting the bananas for the first time, one is extremely tempted to suggest that he has done something quite intelligent. Solving new problems, that is, ones faced for the first time, always seems like a very intelligent act. I am not interested in debating whether or not this act is intelligent, but it seems to me to be a very interesting question to wonder whether such an act relies upon knowledge that is rationally known. To understand why this matters, consider this excerpt by Newell and Simon (1963) on problem solving.

> GPS is a problem solving program developed initially by the authors and J.C. Shaw in 1957....GPS obtained its name of "general problem solver" because it was the first problem solving program to separate in a clean way a task-independent part of the system containing general problem solving mechanisms from a part of the number of different tasks, and other programs essentially similar in structure have worked on yet other problems....GPS operates on problems that can be formulated in terms of *objects* and *operators*....The main methods of GPS jointly embody the heuristic of means–ends analysis ... Means–ends analysis is typified by the following kind of common-sense argument:
>
>> I want to take my son to nursery school. What's the difference between what I have and what I want? One of distance. What changes distance? My automobile. My automobile won't work. What is needed to make it work? A new battery. What has new batteries? An auto repair shop. I want the repair shop to put in a new battery; but the shop doesn't know I need one.

What is the difficulty? One of communication. What allows communication? A telephone...and so on.

This kind of analysis – classifying things in terms of the function they serve, and oscillating among ends, functions required, and means that perform them – forms the basic system of heuristic of GPS. More precisely, this means–ends system of heuristic assumes the following:

1. If an object is given that is not the desired one, differences will be detectable between the available object and the desired object.
2. Operators affect some features of their operands and leave others unchanged. Hence operators can be characterized by the changes they produce and can be used to try to eliminate differences between the objects to which they are applied and desired objects.
3. If a desired operator is not applicable, it may be profitable to modify its inputs so that it becomes applicable.
4. Some differences will prove more difficult to affect than others. It is profitable, therefore, to try to eliminate "difficult" differences, even at the cost of introducing new differences of lesser difficulty. This process can be repeated as long as progress is being made toward eliminating the more difficult differences.

It is easy to understand how Newell and Simon would look at the monkey getting bananas. Essentially, they see the monkey as solving such a problem by use of means–ends analysis. Means–ends analysis relies entirely upon rational knowledge. When AI researchers worked on programs like GPS, they were attempting to get machines to solve problems in a way that simulates the rational process that they assumed underlies all problem-solving behavior.

It seems more plausible, however, that our monkey is not using means–ends analysis at all, but instead copying some prior behavior, either one of his own or one he saw another monkey do, in order to get the bananas. After all, it is not so farfetched to imagine that every monkey does not need to personally reinvent for himself the idea of tool use. In fact, monkeys do indeed transmit to succeeding generations a "monkey culture" that includes tool use (Jolly and Plog, 1986). So, viewed as a case-based reasoner, our monkey is simply doing case retrieval in this instance. This is not to say that a monkey couldn't invent such behavior; in fact, it seems obvious that he could. He simply doesn't have to.

For a computer, the story could be much the same. We could write programs that do means–ends analysis if we believed that in order to get computers to be good problem solvers they needed to be original, inventive problem solvers. If we believed that in order to get computers to act intelligently we needed to get them to use rational knowledge, then we would indeed try to write programs like GPS.

In fact, GPS did not work all that well as a research paradigm. Eventually, AI researchers began to realize that domain knowledge, rather than general-purpose knowledge about problem solving, is an important issue in problem solving. It might help if the computer already knew something about the domain in which it was trying to solve problems. This was an important realization if one's goal was to create programs that solved problems. It might be assumed that this was indeed the goal of any AI program, but I believe that this was really not the case with GPS.

GPS is a program that comes from an earlier time in AI, a time when the goal of AI was not so much to build programs that were generally useful, but rather to make statements about the possibilities for machine intelligence and also to shed some light on the nature of human intelligence. Indeed, Newell and Simon were quite successful in this latter goal. A great deal of important work in psychology was motivated by what Newell and Simon did on GPS. But, in terms of the claims for machine intelligence, GPS was a disaster.

GPS was a disaster because it did, and indeed still does, influence a great many researchers in the direction of working on problem solving. The reason to do such work is still the same. The goal is to show that machines can rationally solve problems by "thinking" them out, displaying properties that heretofore only humans have displayed. And still, the idea is that humans solve problems by using rational and explicit knowledge about problem solving. There is an inherent belief that original problem solving lies at the core of intelligence.

There are many reasons that these researchers (and many others, too) hold such a belief. We are always impressed by original solutions to problems. We hold in high regard those who come up with answers when others have failed to do so, and there is no reason we shouldn't be impressed by original problem solvers. But, what we should absolutely not do is assume that when people solve the problems, they do so using rational, explicit knowledge known consciously by them.

218

Our monkey could have solved the bananas problem for the first time and still have been copying some other monkey. Or, he could have solved it for the first time for himself or anyone he knew, but still have been only slightly modifying a solution he had used in another time for another situation. The question of originality is key here, and I would like to suggest the assumption with respect to originality that is opposite to that taken by AI researchers working on problem solving.

Real-life problem-solving behavior is almost never original. Almost all solutions to novel problems are adaptations of previous solutions known to the problem solver (Johnson and Seifert, 1992; Kolodner, 1993; Gholson et al., 1996). These solutions, the knowledge of those cases, and the procedure by which those cases are found, is entirely nonconscious. In other words, nearly all human problem solving uses knowledge we are not aware we have.

The case-based reasoning approach to problem solving (e.g., Lebowitz, 1986; Kolodner and Simpson, 1989; Kolodner and Mark, 1992; Kolodner, 1993; Hammond et al., 1996; Kolodner, 1997) views intelligence as depending upon knowledge that is not rationally known to the problem solver. CBR is not necessarily a nonconscious process. Since CBR depends upon reminding, it has the same properties as the reminding process. Sometimes we are vividly reminded and other times we don't sense that we are reminded at all. So, when we enter Sam's restaurant, where we have been many times before, we don't think, "Wow, this reminds me of Sam's!" Similarly, when we need to reason through how to get what we want, we don't necessarily consciously think about other times we have gotten something after desiring it. We internalize these cases and suppress the conscious reminding. This is most clearly true when we are attracted to somebody. We very well may be reminded of our mother, or of a former girlfriend, or of just an image we have. But we interpret this attraction as case-based reasoning.

Actually, attraction is rooted in MOPs and the cases those MOPs point to. When a man meets a woman, one can assume a large variety of MOPs are active, including M–PHYSICAL ATTRACTION or M–SOCIAL INTERACTION. Furthermore, each of these contains pointers to a variety of additional MOPs. For example, M–SOCIAL INTERACTION might include M–HAVE DINNER TOGETHER. Deep down inside this last MOP might be something about dessert ordering, for example, whereby one person might judge another on the basis of whether they ordered one dessert or were willing to share. Who knows where these reactions and needs associated with another person come from, but they are there. For example, when someone takes a bite of what I am eating, I have a defensive reaction. I know this comes from my feelings about eating out with my father when I was a child. However, I also recall nearly falling in love with a woman who buttered my toast at breakfast in a restaurant one day. I have no idea where that came from. The point is, our personal MOPs are typically full of the cases that caused them to be built. Sometimes we have access to those cases and sometimes we do not, but our nonconscious is always using them.

On the other hand, a person may well be aware of the cases he is reminded of and the adaptations he makes to transform what he learned from a prior experience in order to apply that knowledge to the current one. Typically, when people report conscious CBR situations, they are reasoning from one case. And, also typically, they have no idea how they found that one case. So even in one-case CBR, the knowledge that one relies upon, finding what one knows, and deciding if it is relevant, is nonconscious.

For example, imagine a situation in which a college student needs to decide what courses to take. I use this example because it is typical of the kinds of problems people really solve. (I will discuss why this matters later on.) Our imaginary student is a sophomore in college interested in two different subjects. He must meet some school requirements that are in neither of those subjects and must satisfy some prerequisites for courses he wishes to take in the future. In sum, there are more courses that he wants to take than he can take in one semester. How does he decide? He chooses one course because it is a seminar and he likes seminars. He eliminates one course after attending the first day and discovering that the teacher is dull. He has trouble deciding whether to stay in a third course because, although he loves the subject matter, it is not one of his main interests, the class is very large, and he feels he needs special attention. He is thinking about a fourth course where he loves the material and it meets the requirements of the college, but he knows he does very poorly in that subject despite his love for it. A fifth course is great except it has multiple choice tests and he loathes them.

This situation, one fairly typical of college life, is full of case-based reasoning. What does it mean that "he likes seminars," for example? He has probably taken only one or two. He may have liked them, but maybe he liked the teacher or the subject. He has found a case, which he had classified as "seminar" and "therefore enjoyable," and has thus matched his potential seminar to a previous one. What does it mean when he notes that the teacher of another course is dull? Does that mean he shouldn't take the course? It might, if he matched dullness of teacher to his lack of interest in a course. This may be a reasonable match, nevertheless it is another instance of case-based reasoning. It does not necessarily follow that a dull teacher makes for a bad course, although for this student it might. The question is whether he has accurately assessed the situation by looking at all the prior cases of his experiences where the teacher was dull and seeing how this affected his enjoyment of the course.

The student might have been using nonconscious CBR in this instance. Suppose, for example, that our student said "dull" but really what was going on is that the teacher reminded him of someone he loathed, a former teacher, perhaps, or an uncle or childhood friend. Our student might not feel comfortable saying, or even thinking, that he doesn't want to take a course in a subject he wants to take because the teacher reminds him of his uncle. This is subconscious case-based reasoning at work, and it manifests itself in decision making in ways not always obvious or clear to the decision maker.

The student will choose the very large class or the one with multiple choice tests in it by case-based reasoning as well. He will find which courses he has taken that match these assessed characteristics and determine what he should take from how those courses worked out for him in the past. The problem is that he may find "has multiple choice tests" or "is very large" to be the primary characteristics of a course when "in certain classroom" or "has Amy in class" or "uses dull-looking text" may be important assessed characteristics as well. The main point is that the way we choose prior cases to reason from is unknown to us. We can say why we chose a previous case, but we may well be wrong or at best have a very incomplete picture of the matching characteristics. Case-based reasoning relies upon knowledge we do not know we have.

Most of the case-based reasoning in this example is based upon one case. A seminar is a good idea because a seminar worked out well in the past. A dull teacher is a bad idea because a dull teacher was a problem in the past. Of course, the student here may have had more than one case in each instance, but he probably didn't have six hundred. For one-case case-based reasoning, the choice of the prior case is often known by the reasoner. That is, our student may not know how he found the prior seminar to base his decision upon, but he probably knows and can talk about that seminar as the basis of his choice. In one-case CBR, the retrieval characteristics (that is, the indices) are quite often based upon knowledge one knows one has. The reasoner consciously characterizes the new course he is thinking about as an instance of an "X" and then proceeds to ask his memory for any instances of courses that have the index X. Upon finding one, even if there are more actually present in memory, decisions are made by finding the outcome of the prior case and assuming that this will be the outcome of the new case.

In a sense, then, one-case CBR is actually kind of dumb. Although it is true that people reason this way, it isn't rocket science. One reason why AI researchers and people interested in measuring intelligence are not interested in this kind of reasoning is that it isn't very hard to do and it isn't necessarily even good to do. But, it is what people do.

However, most case-based reasoning is not based on one case. An expert in a domain knows hundreds or thousands of cases. Finding the right case is a phenomenally complex process in such a situation, and that process could not possibly be conscious. Thus, it is reasonable to claim that the truly original inventive thinking done by domain experts in a complex situation could not possibly be based upon knowledge they have explicitly acquired via instruction, nor does it use knowledge they can explicitly state.

For example, consider a teacher who has been teaching for twenty-five years. A student comes to see him for advice. He listens carefully and then makes some suggestions. Where does he get his suggestions? He may be able to cite previous students he has known who were in similar situations, or he may have some rule of thumb about life of which he was reminded by the student's story. But, after twenty-five years of teaching and numerous advisory situations, he may simply "know" what to advise without having any idea what particular prior cases he's been drawing upon. This does not mean that he is not drawing upon them implicitly, but the particulars may not come to mind. What we have here is a reliance on the MOPs and TOPs he has built over the years. The experiences from which they were constructed have long since vanished from memory. The original expectation failures and the explanations that resolved them are artifacts of an earlier version of his nascent dynamic memory. What is left is the point of view, not the memories that contributed to it, except for very special and important episodes that are likely still there waiting for explanations

(Patalano and Seifert, 1994; also Slackman and Nelson, 1984; Hudson and Nelson, 1986; Hudson, 1988; Farrar and Goodman, 1992; Hudson, Fivush and Kuebli, 1992).

Recently I was advising an undergraduate who told me he wanted to go into marketing. He was unclear on the reason he wanted to do this, but he did tell me a long story about the divorce of his parents and the difficulties this had caused him. I soon found out that his father was a business man and his mother was a psychologist. I observed that marketing was more or less at the intersection of these subjects and asked if it was possible that he was trying to satisfy both parents at the same time. He agreed that this might be the case. I advised him to find out what he really wanted apart from his parents' desires, and he said what he really wanted was to study marketing.

I use this example to point out what real reasoning is like. The undergraduate had no idea how he reached the decisions he had about his own life. He reasoned using nonconscious knowledge, coming to a conscious conclusion that he could defend with conscious reasoning even though it looked to an outside observer that his real reasons weren't the same as his stated ones.

For my part, I was reasoning, too. I was reminded of a student I had had who quit graduate school in computer science to become a doctor because everyone in his family was doctors and he couldn't take the pressure. I was also reminded of my own view, based on numerous cases, that students' choices are more influenced by their parents than the students realize. I was also aware that when a student comes to talk about one thing (career choice) and winds up talking about another thing (his parents' divorce), the latter thing has an importance in the former whether or not the student thinks so consciously.

Such points of view are conscious in my mind, no doubt. They are the MOPs and TOPs I am aware of. But where did they come from? They came from numerous cases now long lost or only barely memorable. The case-based reasoning I do is not even known to me, although it is clear that I have come to these conclusions based upon a great deal of experience. Bringing up these points of view (or, more accurately, "rules of thumb," but I don't want to confuse the reader into taking the word *rule* literally) is an unconscious process. I hear myself give my advice and it is only at that point that my advice becomes conscious. I think about what I have said consciously. But the original thoughts are nonconscious. The real reasoning, sifting amongst cases to draw conclusions, is a process that is not even open

223

to conscious observation.[1] I have thousands of cases and many ways of interpreting them. I pick and choose amongst them, but I don't even know what they are. Without a case to reason about, I probably couldn't even explicitly state them.

The main point is that I have learned a great deal about students and the choices they make. I learned about each student and drew some conclusions. Some of this knowledge was conscious at the time because I derived it from rational knowledge and reason, but much of it was not. In the same way, much of what we need to concentrate on in education is nonconscious knowledge. Learning itself depends upon, and creates, knowledge of which we are never explicitly aware. I could say that "today I learned X," but I probably learned more than just X on that day. The learning we do comes from an amalgamation of all our experiences all the time, and this turns out to be far more mental work than conscious processing is capable of. This is one reason why we use scriptlets and the other memory structures – to save us work.

Dynamic memory exists in part to relieve us of this cognitive burden, because through these structures we are able to summarize our prior experiences when they were similar in nature (Fivush, 1984; Adams and Worden, 1986; Ratner, Smith and Dion, 1986; Ross and Kennedy, 1990; Ross, Perkins and Tenpenny, 1990; Farrar and Goodman, 1992; Ross, 1996a). We recognize similar situations and thus derive a prototypical representation as an alternative to storing every individual case in memory.

The key issue in intelligence is learning. If problem solving were to be a key issue in examining intelligence, it would have to be key because one would be studying not how someone solved problems, but how he learned to solve new problems, which is a different thing entirely (Reif and Larkin, 1991; Lampert, 1995). In order to solve new problems, students need to learn to use the problem-solving strategies employed by experts (Chi, Feltovich and Glaser, 1981; Reimann and Chi, 1989; Chi and Bédard, 1992). Thus, if we were to measure how people learn to solve problems in novel ways, we would be studying a more critical issue in intelligence than is currently assessed. An intelligent system that repeatedly made the same mistakes, or could not repeat its successes, would hardly be worthy of being called intelli-

---

[1] Gholson et al. (1996) and Johnson and Seifert (1992) on how people reason from cases; also Reiser, Black and Abelson (1985).

gent. We assume that a person who solves a problem in a novel way will recall his solution, for example, when the problem recurs (Gick and McGarry, 1992; Johnson and Seifert, 1992; Gholson et al., 1996). Similarly, a key question to ask about the monkey is not whether he can get the bananas, but whether he will get them without having to solve the problem again – that is, by simply recalling his solution – when he is again confronted with the same situation.

So we see that learning is the key issue in intelligence for people or monkeys. But when it comes to computers, some observers seem to feel that a machine exhibiting medical diagnostic ability would somehow be worthy of the appellation of "expert" independent of the issue of whether that computer can learn from its experience. This seems quite wrong. Expert systems do not learn, indeed cannot learn, because they are systems of rules and not systems of experiences or cases. The monkey who gets smart about bananas next time does so because he can recall the prior experience, that is, because he has stored the "case" away in such a fashion that it can be retrieved and consulted the next time he encounters the same situation. Cases are used, not rules, because much of the knowledge involved is in fact nonconscious and thus, by definition, cannot be entirely rule based.

Three questions arise from this with regard to the issues I have been discussing. First, why can a system of cases learn when a systems of rules cannot? Second, why would a system of rules be part of our rational knowledge, whereas a system of cases would be part of nonconscious knowledge? And, third, what does this tell us about the relatedness of problem solving and intelligence?

The second question strikes at the heart of the difference between conscious and nonconscious knowledge. People can cite rules of thumb (often called heuristics) in which they believe. Not only can individuals cite personal rules they follow, but cultures as a whole have and cite such rules, usually as proverbs. These rules, as I have noted earlier, are really not rules at all, but TOPs. They don't have a logic to them. Rather, they are collocation points for memories that have a TOP in common. In fact, all cultures have proverbs (which are, of course, explicitly conscious TOPs) and these proverbs don't differ all that much from one another. Proverbs are actually very interesting pieces of knowledge. The fact that we can cite them makes it clear that they are conscious knowledge. On the other hand, their actual use in reasoning depends upon the nonconscious knowledge that determines their relevance in a given situation. Understanding this difference is one key to understanding the difference between conscious and non-conscious knowledge.

People give advice to each other all the time, and quite frequently this advice comes in the form of proverbs or (as I mentioned in Chapter 5) in the form of stories. It really doesn't matter whether one tells a story for advice or cites a proverb, since the mental processes are pretty much the same. What happens is that the situation being described by the advice seeker needs to be characterized by the understander in terms of some mental constructs that are indices to information already present in the mind of the understander. From the standpoint of teaching, this means that we need to teach by building upon what students already know (Bruer, 1993; Linn et al., 1994) and by having students construct their own explanations (Chi et al., 1989; Brown and Campione, 1994).

One way to look at this is to recognize that the understander's mind already contains the proverb or story he will later offer as advice and that his understanding process is merely an attempt to find the most relevant story or proverb. Relevance is established by matching commonalities in the advice seeker's story with features in stories that are already present in the mind of the understander. To accomplish this, an understander must decompose what he hears in terms that are precisely the same ones he used at some prior time to store away situations he had heard about or had experienced himself. Either way, the match is made on the basis of these common terms that serve as indices in the mind. As noted earlier, relevant processing structures are activated by the extracted indices, and these trigger recall of past similar experiences precisely because the processing structures are the same ones used for memory storage.

A key question here is, What do the indices look like? It is easy to see something about the nature of such indices by examining any proverb. In "Make hay while the sun shines," the indices are surely not "hay" or "sun." (Of course, a bad indexer could indeed see this proverb as being about "hay." He could recite this proverb whenever issues about hay arise in conversation. But, this would mean that he had misunderstood the proverb, in the sense that he cannot see its applicability beyond haymaking.) Rather, a useful index would refer to the deeper meaning of the proverb – in this case, planning, and, in particular, the opportune time for plan execution being when the conditions for success are right. Ideas like "opportune time to execute a plan" must be the kinds of indices the mind uses to characterize its experiences.

It seems obvious that as critical as such indices are for mental functioning, they are not conscious. One can make them conscious, as indeed I just did, but for the most part people do not realize they have characterized things in this way, do not realize they have stored prior experiences in this way, could not name the indices they use to characterize situations they have experienced, and have no idea which retrieval methods they use to enable them to come up with the right proverb or story and not one they might know that matches less well.

All of these things are part of nonconscious knowledge. We are barely aware of them consciously, although we can be made aware of some of them, as I have shown in the reminding examples sprinkled throughout this book. Case-based reasoning, which depends upon mental indices, is simply not based upon conscious knowledge. On the other hand, we do often consciously cite rules of thumb that we believe in. I might have said, "Take your opportunities when you have them." It would have been a more straightforward thing to say, and it is something I believe. This rule is part of my rational knowledge. It is a rule not unlike "before *e* except after *c*" or "Estimate before dividing." Such rules can be memorized, or invented, and then they can be told to the rational conscious in such a way as to cause them to pop up at the right time. We know many people have such rules, but they do not execute them unless they constantly remind themselves of them. To put this another way, somebody is telling the rules to the conscious. There are some rules by which we reason, but they are not the most "natural" or typical methods for us to use. In fact, we can live well without them.

One might ask, Who is telling these rules to the conscious? This is not unlike what Gallwey describes when he notes that self 1 tells self 2 stuff about how to play tennis. The nonconscious mind talks to the conscious mind, but only in a language the conscious mind can understand. It cannot talk about opportune execution of plans to the conscious very easily (perhaps because such concepts have only recently been given names in human history). So it talks in simpler, everyday metaphors. But, and this is the important part, it doesn't matter at all what the nonconscious says to the conscious because it is the conscious that is doing the mental work and the nonconscious mind simply isn't listening. Posing a question to the nonconscious mind must be done in terms it can understand. We can't ask it to name all fifty states, because it just doesn't have such a list. We can, however, ask it to imagine a map of the United States and then we can try to "read" that map.

Understanding the mental structures used by the mind allows us to interrogate it better.

To use Gallwey's example again, you can tell yourself to hit a tennis ball in a certain way and then still not do it. You can tell yourself that it would be convenient to fall in love with Mary, but that won't make it happen. The nonconscious, though it may understand English (after all, it is responsible for parsing the stuff) cannot be "spoken to" in English, because the belief systems that are entailed in MOPs and TOPs cannot be altered except in the face of expectation failure and explanation based upon cases.

All this is a complicated way to get back to my earlier question about the relatedness of problem solving and intelligence. It seems clear, if one is thinking about the difference between the conscious and the nonconscious minds, that solving problems is an interesting test of intelligence if and only if those problems are case-based reasoning problems. Most problems we see in school or on IQ tests or in AI programs are rule based. One learns to solve them by memorizing the right rules and applying those rules in the prescribed way. When one is being "original" in a rule-based situation, one is trying to use the generalizations behind the rules, as in GPS. But, the problems to which such rule application apply are usually quite artificial. They are not the kinds of problems for which intelligence has developed over millennia.

Given that the natural problem-solving ability of people (and animals) is case based, and given that this ability involves adaptation from prior personal or cultural experience, the fundamental issue is retrieval from prior knowledge. This is a nonconscious problem. People often don't know how they solve this problem, and even if they can find a solution, their ability to do so cannot easily be measured.

The consequences of focusing on conscious, rather than nonconscious, problem-solving ability have been felt in artificial intelligence research, in work on intelligence testing, and, most importantly, in education (in terms of what we teach our children). Each of these fields would have a vastly different history if researchers had properly focused on the dominant role of nonconscious processes in intelligence. I will discuss each of these fields in turn.

Artificial intelligence has been severely set back by the illusion of the primacy of rational knowledge (the old epistemics). This manifests itself in the focus on what I call "artificial problem solving." There has been a focus in AI on cryptarithmetic, the Tower of Hanoi problem, the missionaries and cannibals problem, chess, go, and theorem proving. These problems are rather artificial. Human intelligence evolved over millions of years without ever being tested on them. The kinds of problems that human intelligence evolved to handle necessarily relied upon the use of prior experience. Generalizing from previous situations works well in real-world problem solving, but in artificial-world problem solving, those generalizations need to be about the problem-solving behavior itself. People need to consciously use rules they have explicitly learned in order to become good at artificial problem solving. Explicitly teaching such rules is what schooling is all about. Thus, the solution depends upon the old epistemics – the explicit teaching of rational knowledge.

But, nonconscious knowledge is the core of human problem-solving ability in real-life situations. It is hard to imagine one of our ancestors trying to apply some learned rule when deciding how best to escape a tiger. What worked best last time would be what was worth knowing in such a case. But, the argument in AI has always been that a machine would be intelligent if it performed adequately in a situation that would have required intelligence for human performance. In choosing problems like chess or the Tower of Hanoi, the argument is basically that real intelligence is required to solve these problems, so computers that solve them must have real intelligence.

As far as I am concerned, the real issue is that problems that presumably require less intelligence for humans are harder for computers to do than those that require more. Something must be wrong. For example, a computer that could prove a complex theorem in mathematics would surely not be able to decide between taking a math course or a physics course in college. The kinds of choices the average college sophomore makes would be well beyond its ability. This same computer could not actually understand, nor contribute as a participant or teacher in, a math class in which the very same theorem it could prove was being discussed. Similarly, a program that could play championship chess could not make a single move, nor understand an explanation of the moves, in go.

Those who argue against AI typically are intent on proving that no computer could possibly do these kinds of things and that AI is a waste of time. Clearly I do not believe this at all. What I am saying is that AI has made some serious missteps and that these must be corrected before real progress can be made. Correcting these missteps means getting out from under the burdens imposed by the old epistemics.

The issue is this: If the primary aspects of human intelligence depend upon rational knowledge, then it follows that finding tasks that are difficult to execute that require such knowledge is the main problem for AI. If, on the other hand, the important aspects of human intelligence are nonconscious, then AI must focus on tasks whose performance does not require rational knowledge. In particular, if we were interested in working on how humans solve problems, for example, the question would be whether to work on a problem like the Tower of Hanoi or on a problem like course choice by college sophomores. The solutions for each would be quite different, and the lessons learned about intelligence would be quite different as well. It is because AI has assumed that rational knowledge is an important part of intelligence that it has chosen to focus on problems like the Tower of Hanoi.

The problem with rules is that they are necessarily part of rational knowledge. They represent what people think they do, rather than what they actually do. I am very good at throwing a football, for example. If you asked me how to throw one, I could probably cite all kinds of rules about how to hold the ball, how to release the ball, how to put "touch" on the ball, and so on. I could tell you all these rules, but the likelihood of my actually using them is slim. I simply throw the ball. The knowledge of how to throw the ball is not something I rationally "know." If you ask me to say something that shows off my knowledge, I will oblige you by watching myself throw and then telling you what I see. What I believe about what I know, and what I actually know, are not the same thing. The expert who is interviewed for an expert system will tell the interviewer rules, but the fact is that he probably doesn't follow the rules he details.

A person who does not learn and get better at what he does over time would not be considered an expert. Who would have respect for someone who consistently made the same errors and never improved? Nevertheless, rule-based expert systems must have this property. The reason is simple enough. In a system of rules, when an error is made, the fault is either with one or more rules, or with how certain otherwise-correct rules interact. But, how would you know where the fault lies? If all an expert system has is the rules as elicited from the expert, then when one of those rules fails, the expert must be consulted once again. One can well imagine the expert responding, "Well, yes, I did say that rule but it really applies only under certain conditions, which I forgot to mention."

Expert-system builders had to consistently go back to their experts to find out what the "real rules" were. But, what does a real expert do when he makes a mistake? It is very likely that he does not say to himself, "Ah, this is a problem in rule 356 and I shall have to change that rule." Rather, he stores away the experience of having made an error and hopes that the next time he encounters a similar situation he will remember his mistake and do better. The case-based reasoning done by real experts does not involve rules at all, but, as I have said, involves characterizing experience in such a way as to be able to retrieve it again at the right time.

Case-based reasoning systems can learn, in principle, because they can change over time. They can change over time because they are not, and never could have been, a consistent set of rules. They could not have been such a set of rules because they were nonconscious in the first place. The expert for the case-based reasoning system simply tells cases to the person building the system. It is the job of the case-based reasoning expert to figure out how to characterize those cases, using a set of indices that the system builder must discover. The expert rationally knows only his experience, although nonconsciously he knows how to characterize it, as evidenced by the fact that he can do so when need be.

Let's turn to the issue of intelligence testing. It is fairly easy to get agreement on the idea that IQ tests are a bad idea. But, what is it that is bad about them? In this age of political correctness, the first things that leap to mind are issues of gender equity or cultural bias. And indeed, these problems probably are there in IQ tests, but something much more insidious is wrong with them. The problem with IQ tests is problem solving itself. Robert Sternberg (1991) proposed alternatives to current IQ tests, but these still included problems to be solved. IQ test reformers continue to believe that problems are the key issue in intelligence.

Consider for a minute how real people, not psychologists, judge the intelligence of others. When I interview people, for a job or for graduate school, I am interested in how intelligent they seem. I do not give them a problem to solve in order to determine this. I simply talk to them. The mother of a small child doesn't believe her child is very bright simply because the child can solve a problem. In each case, intelligence assessments are made on the basis of what a person says.

As I pointed out earlier, linguistic behavior uses knowledge we do not know we know. We do not know how we say things, how we understand things, nor are we even aware of what we want to say much of the time. Formal problem solving, on the other hand, uses rational knowledge. We are aware of our own reasoning process when we solve formal problems. The sole exception to this is the case-based reasoning process. We do not know how we find cases or decide that a case is relevant; we retrieve nonconsciously. One could, of course, argue that case-based problem solving would be a good way to measure intelligence, except that there is no way to control which cases a testee would have available for use in a given situation. After all, if one's experience isn't very broad, one would likely solve a problem less well than someone with a wider range of cases to draw upon. That would not mean that the more experienced problem solver is more intelligent, even though he might come up with a better solution. A case-based IQ test would thus be biased toward people who had experience with a lot of cases. This makes sense if what you are testing is who can solve problems best in a given context; but then it is a measure of experience mixed with intelligence, not a measure of intelligence alone.

The question for the IQ test designer ought to be how to measure nonconscious knowledge. To think about how to do this, we should consider how people do it ordinarily. Professors, by way of example, judge the intelligence of their colleagues and their students all the time. They don't do so by handing them tests to take or problems to solve. They do it by talking to them. In the course of an ordinary conversation, it seems, people can make assessments of the intelligence of the person they are speaking with. Similarly, parents assess the intelligence of their children from time to time. Parents are actually quite good at making this assessment unless they base their assessment on how well the children are doing in school or unless they are prejudiced simply because the children being assessed are their own. Parents "know" that one child is smarter than the other, even if their grades in school are similar. How do parents make such assessments? Again, the answer is not by giving out tests or problems to solve.

My mother was once quoted in the *Wall Street Journal* as saying that she knew I was very smart very early on because I had taught myself to understand the calendar before I had learned to read. What kind of assessment is that? It is not original (or complicated) to read a calendar. In fact, it is my assertion that what my mother was noticing was exactly the sort of thing professors (or anyone, really) notices in a conversation when making a judgment about the intelligence of their conversational partner. My mother was impressed, not that I could read a calendar, but that no one had taught me to do so.

We are impressed by someone's intelligence in a conversation when they make a leap that one might not have predicted. The "leap" might be evidence of quick thinking, deep understanding, clever reasoning, or simply an original perspective on a mundane problem or a novel choice of words. The real issue is novelty. We are impressed when we hear things that are new or different in some way, because we make the assumption that the person we are talking to has figured out something on his own. We are considerably less impressed if we hear that what we thought was original was in fact something this person had learned from another. When we consider novelty with respect to intelligence assessment, we are interested in originality.

We can see that this is precisely a question of knowledge we have been told versus knowledge we needed to discover for ourselves. When someone tells us something "novel," we want to know how he did this. If he did it consciously, that is if someone told it to him and he repeated it, we may find it interesting, but we would fail to see it as an indication of intelligence. But, if he came up with this idea on his own, we assume that he did so without consciously trying to do. In that case, we are impressed with the fact that he was original but was not actually trying to be original.

This reminds me of a story about my daughter. She was terribly bored in the first grade, so I decided she should skip to second grade. The school administered some kind of creativity test and said that she scored off the scale in creativity, so she would indeed be skipped. Later I asked her what was on the test. She said they gave her a circle and asked her to make a picture out of it in some way. She drew a moose. Apparently, most children make a human face out of the circle.

With respect to the issues of originality, my daughter satisfied the testers. I am assuming that this test was actually about attempting to assess nonconscious intelligence, so it would seem to be a good measure of that. However, there is an odd end to the story. Some years later, I was talking to my daughter about this test and she remarked that the reason she drew the moose was one of general annoyance with doing things the way that she expected she was supposed to. She said that it was obvious to her that the testers expected her to make "a happy face" and that she simply didn't want to do what she thought they wanted. (This illustrates fairly well her general philosophy of life as far as I can tell.) She drew the moose to be annoying.

One thing I noticed about my own reaction to this story was that I became less impressed with her achievement. It now seemed to me that she was not so much original as she was obstinate. I thus found myself thinking that perhaps the results didn't illustrate creativity at all. On the other hand, it may be that creativity depends strongly on being obstinate in the face of the expected. Of course, the test may be entirely silly in any case. But, I am not interested in the test. I am interested in how people judge intelligence and I found myself judging her intelligence with regard to the moose. As soon as I saw that she had consciously decided to be original, I was less impressed with her intelligence (but was perhaps *more* impressed with her guile).

This is not all that big a deal for a six-year-old who may not understand what is going on in the test, but consider the case of an adult who knew that he was being tested for creativity. We might well expect that an adult who knew he was supposed to be creative would attempt to be different. The issue in our judging him would be, therefore, whether what he did was novel in an interesting way. A moose wouldn't qualify, but something he had done that was phenomenally inventive, surprising in its possibility, would. Why is this? One possibility is that we are hoping for nonconscious inventiveness: We are hoping that our subject is not following a system of rules that he has learned about how to be original. We are hoping the originality is spontaneous in some way. We are hoping that an original and novel idea just sort of "leaped into his mind." That is, we are hoping for nonconscious abilities to come into play.

I am not particularly concerned with IQ tests and it is not my point to evaluate existing ones nor to propose new ones. Rather, I simply want to point out that formal problem solving is not the issue in intelligence. The means we employ to decide whether or not to draw a moose, or to be original in conversation, or to comprehend a complex point being made by another, has nothing whatsoever to do with problem solving. Problem solving is a conscious skill, learned in school for the purpose of performing well in school. Originality in problem solving is almost never the subject of IQ tests. Moreover, if it were, it would be impossible to be fair about it because what is original for one person might not be for another. Given that we are all case-based reasoners, problem-solving ability becomes reduced to what cases you have already had experience with and thus it is not that much of a predictor of intelligence. On the other hand, nonconscious processes, such as an understanding of novel issues and the creation of ideas are very important indicators of intelligence. It is the conscious that everyone interested in intelligence, both testing and modeling, has paid attention to, whereas it is the nonconscious that everyone who isn't doing one of those tasks pays attention to. That is, real people know that it is nonconscious reasoning that matters, and they use observations about people's abilities in that area to make intelligence assessments.

To understand what it means to be intelligent, we must understand not what intelligent people *do* but what ordinary people fail to explicitly *know about* what they do. If we ask about what they *do*, we get answers like "play chess" or "solve the Tower of Hanoi problem." If, on the other hand, we ask what it is that ordinary people *know about* what they do when they perform ordinary tasks, we get quite different answers. First, we find that we really don't know much about the kind of everyday knowledge that is so mundane that it is typically not studied by cognitive scientists. Second, we discover that that knowledge had better become of interest to cognitive science because the other knowledge, the previously highly valued formal knowledge that people have studied and that has previously defined intelligence, has become a commodity all too easy to obtain.

It is trivial to find out the most complex kinds of knowledge (like how to prove a theorem) and quite arduous to find out the most mundane kinds of knowledge (like how we talk). When we design new educational systems, we must recognize that the transmission of mundane knowledge is all too easy to accomplish. Anybody can find ways to deliver information and lots of it, either by lecture, by book, or by software. That is simply not the task before us. Education must be about teaching the more esoteric knowledge about how to do things. We cannot tell people what to do or how to do it. Good educational designs do not use problem solving as a means of measuring intelligence; rather, they use problem solving as a way of teaching implicitly the nonconscious knowledge needed for thinking about those problems. It is not answers we care about, but means. It is not competence we care about, but performance. We need to set up a situation in which performance of the task is used to teach esoteric knowledge about the task that we really have no good way of either quantifying or detailing. And we must accept that there is no good way of quantifying or detailing the learning that follows. So, how will we be able to judge our success as teachers and as learners? The answer is simple: by virtue of getting students to "do" successfully, and by virtue of how able they are to transfer this experiential knowledge to other problem contexts and to other domains.

New teaching methods that we create will need to concentrate on teaching people to do things they need to do, not to know things they can memorize and regurgitate. Education ought not be about explicit knowing – it should be about being able to do. Of course, this idea really isn't all that new. Knowledge was always about doing, or about abstraction based upon doing, until universal schooling changed all that. In contrast, natural learning has always been learning by doing, and natural problem solving has always been case based. It is the school as institution that has permuted our notions of intelligence and education.

CHAPTER 13

Nonconscious Thinking

If we are going to teach nonconscious knowledge, we must understand what this kind of knowledge looks like and where it is used naturally. It is hard to teach what you can't talk about. Nonconscious knowledge isn't all that difficult to see, however. For example, as described in Chapter 11, when people have trouble falling asleep, they report that their minds are racing. Similarly, when they wake up earlier than they would like, and want to fall back to sleep but can't, their minds seem to have a mind of their own. They find themselves thinking about things that seem unnecessary to worry about, or about subjects or problems they have been avoiding.

The sense that the mind has a mind of its own relates strongly to what people refer to when they speak about consciousness. Clearly, we can know what we think. We view ourselves thinking when we're in a semi-wakeful state, and cannot stop ourselves from doing so. We are conscious of our thoughts.

But, if this is indeed what is meant by consciousness, it is an odd situation, to say the least. We may "hear ourselves thinking," but we seem to have no control over the process. We can, of course, interrupt the process, give in to it if you will, and begin to think harder about what our minds were thinking about anyway, eliminating the mind's racing and forcing an order to things. The curious thing is that we have no words to describe these various states.

So, using the vocabulary proposed in Chapter 11, let's ask what this semi-wakeful thinking represents. Certainly it is not rational thinking. It is also not emotional thinking, since that is something directed outward, with respect to another entity. It is not what I have labeled subconscious thinking, since it is not thinking that is directly involved in making subconscious choices. There is nothing physical involved and we are certainly not unconscious while doing it, so this leaves only one possibility from the list, namely, nonconscious thinking. I said earlier that nonconscious thinking is the most basic mental activity. Certainly nonconscious thinking must employ nonconscious knowledge, so this is a good place to start to investigate some aspects of nonconscious knowledge.

I have deliberately cast the view of the racing mind in terms of the semi-wakeful state because it is interesting to ask how dreaming differs from the semi-wakeful thinking that characterizes the racing mind. Scholarly discussions of dreaming often cast it as some oddity that people need to do, which could just as well be eliminated. My argument here is that dreaming is a lot more like normal cognitive activity than we realize. Further, it is important to explore how dreaming is related to semi-wakeful, racing minds since it is my premise that to understand what it means to know, one must understand nonconscious knowledge. Analyzing our thoughts during this particular state is one way, along with analyzing our remindings, that we may gain insight into these otherwise unobservable processes.

As a way of considering some of the aspects of nonconscious thinking that govern our lives, I offer the following story. I was once on a train going from Enschede, The Netherlands, to Amsterdam. The train passed a station whose name was Nord something and suddenly my mind started thinking about a girl I knew in the sixth grade. Her last name was Naarden. Her name was Dutch and drew attention from the other students both because it had those two *a*'s together and because the rest of the class was ethnically rather homogeneous, all with Eastern European last names. I was mulling on this girl and her odd name when we passed the next station. The name of that station was Naarden.

In such a circumstance, one is prone to create one of two possible types of explanations. The first type is a rational explanation: perhaps I saw a sign at the previous station saying "Next station – Naarden" and didn't realize that I had seen it. Or, in the second type, we can go in for the mystical. This type of explanation is fairly common amongst many people, variously labeled as déjà vu, second sight, or ESP. As I was mulling the possibilities for this latter type of explanation, because there was no way I had seen any sign about the upcoming station, I realized that there was a third possibility, one that astonished me.

Two years earlier, I had taken a train from Groningen to Amsterdam. Enschede is in the eastern part of The Netherlands and Groningen is in the north. Amsterdam is in the west, so logically these two trips should not have been on the same tracks. But, geography isn't logical. There is a body of water in the way that causes the two tracks to join up at Amersvoort, something I vaguely recognized on stopping at that station. I thought momentarily about the fact that I had heard of this town without explicitly recognizing that I had stopped at this station before. So, what had happened was clear enough. I had connected Naarden with Amersvoort, and the Nord had reminded me of this.

What is astonishing here is that none of this was conscious. I didn't know that I was on the same tracks, nor did I realize that I had connected Naarden with Amersvoort. In fact, I would have told you that I had never heard of Naarden and didn't know it existed. But, some part of me knew. A nonconscious process was keeping track of details I had consciously only barely paid attention to. My conscious knowledge base was simply different than my nonconscious knowledge base. Although it seems obvious that this would be true for different kinds of knowledge (like process knowledge rather than factual knowledge), it is curious that it seems to be true of factual knowledge as well, and one is prone to wonder why. In fact, it is fairly obvious why this must be the case. At a time when people could not talk (or for animals, who still can't talk), thinking still went on. If we can't talk to others, it makes sense that we can't talk to ourselves either. In that case, how do we go about thinking? The obvious answer is that we do not think in words, although the answer is really more complicated than that.

It isn't just that we don't say things to ourselves in order to think. Rather, thinking is a process we can engage in without knowing that we are doing so. Try not thinking in words for awhile. You'll find, if you succeed at getting all words out of your head, that you are left with images, feelings, attitudes, expectations, lots of stuff. Though it is quite difficult to do this if one is awake and alert, it is possible. In fact, this is what relaxation, meditation, and other "mind clearing" techniques are all about. For those who have not experienced this wordless thinking consciously, there is always dreaming to consider.

People dream all the time, although not always in words. Dreaming is a process that we easily refer to as not being conscious, and, I claim, it is not fundamentally different from any other nonconscious process. In other words, on some other occasion it might not be surprising if I had had a dream about traveling on a train to Naarden. The stuff that composes our dreams is based upon the same nonconscious knowledge we use when we are awake. The difference between nonconscious thinking and nonconscious dreaming is not that great. Dreaming just relaxes the rules of reality in a way that nonconscious thinking cannot.

The nonconscious knowledge of the kind I made use of on that train is an important aspect of the general thinking process. To put this another way, we cannot possibly be conscious of everything we know. But, the interesting difference is that the things we are conscious of are often considerably less critical to our lives than the knowledge of which we are not conscious. (Of course the Naarden knowledge doesn't seem all that critical either, unless one considers that knowing where you are and where you are going is a very basic survival skill.) For example, consider the conscious knowledge tested on drivers license exams concerning issues like how many feet behind a car it is safe to be on a highway. We can learn to memorize answers to such questions, but experienced drivers don't attempt to calculate distances while driving. They just "know" when they are too close. This nonconscious knowledge is based upon other nonconscious knowledge one has about how much pressure one needs to put on the brake to stop the car, how much distance one needs in order to bring the car to a complete stop, how quickly one can react to a sudden situation, and the assessed likelihood of the car's spinning out of control due to excessive braking.

All of this is nonconscious knowledge. We did not learn it in school, we learned it by driving. Knowledge that is never explicitly acquired is not likely to be explicitly recallable either. If you tell a driving student that to stop a car you need one foot per mile per hour that the car is traveling, they can memorize and later recall that fact. If you never tell them how much pressure needs to be put on the brake, they will not "know" it in the sense that they can recall it. But, they will be able to call that knowledge up at the moment they need it in order to make use of it, rather than in order to explicitly state what they know.

In just the same way that I didn't "know" that Naarden was next to Amersvoort, a driver doesn't know how much pressure he needs to put on the brake in order to stop a car. The opposite is also true. If we force students to memorize the location of a city or a numerical fact about stopping distances needed for cars, they may well be able to recall that fact for an exam, but they are also just as likely to be incapable of bringing that knowledge to mind when they actually need it. This is the problem of inert knowledge (diSessa, 1982; Bransford et al., 1989; Reif and Larkin, 1991; Lampert, 1995).

240

For as long as there have been humans, they have had to learn where they are going, how to perform actions of various sorts, how to interact and get along with other people, how to communicate, how to reason, and so on, without "knowing" how they do it. The knowledge by which they do these things is simply not conscious. Writers, teachers, preachers, counselors, and others often attempt to make such knowledge conscious. They tell people explicitly what they may or may not know implicitly. Sometimes learning something explicitly in this way can be helpful. The most important issue, however, is whether one can convert conscious knowledge into nonconscious knowledge because conscious knowledge alone is not of much use. What we see and do on a regular basis is, by necessity, based upon knowledge we don't consciously know we have.

MOPs, TOPs, scriptlets, and scenes do not depend upon conscious knowledge for help in anything important. Expectations are rarely conscious. They are sometimes conscious for adults, but it seems unlikely that they are conscious in small children. There are many reasons for this, not the least of which is the vast amount of knowledge that is needed, knowledge that is very detailed in nature and is needed long before people have been able to talk or think about it. To put this another way, a dog had better be able to find his home, eat, defend himself, maneuver his body, mate, and so on or he won't be alive for long. He does not need to talk about these things or to think consciously about them, he just needs to do them. To do them, he needs nonconscious knowledge and lots of it. The same is true of people, but people, when they examine their own thought processes, do so consciously, so they get confused about the role the conscious plays. To get a sense for how small that role actually is, let's look at nonconscious knowledge in some further detail.

When we understand a sentence – when you read this one for example – we are dealing with nonconscious knowledge. We know that we don't know how we go about attempting to understand a sentence, we just understand it. There is, of course, a big distinction, here as always, between that which we are taught about language (our conscious knowledge of language) and that which we remain blissfully unaware of but use all the time (our nonconscious knowledge of language). So, we can say things about nouns and verbs and parsing and concepts, things we were taught in school, but we really have no idea how we do what we do when we understand; we just do it.

I often use the sentence "John prevented Mary from leaving the room" when I teach about how language understanding works. I ask students to tell me what this sentence means, using only concepts about actions that were specifically referred to. That is, when I ask what John did, and a student says "prevent," I do not allow that answer. "Preventing" is not something we can do. Why not?

One way to answer this is to try to imagine the action or actions the sentence is attempting to depict. So, we can ask what John actually did. Students speculate that maybe John hit Mary, or barred the door, or yelled at her. He might have done any of these things, or he might have done none of them. The sentence simply doesn't say. All it says is "prevent" – and "prevent," I claim, is not an action anyone can directly do.

At this point, students get frustrated. They cannot determine what *prevent* could mean at all. I ask them to tell me what they "know" happened, not what they can guess might have happened. At this point someone usually says that all that is known is that John did something and that, whatever it was, that action had the effect of causing Mary to not be able to leave the room. This is, of course, the real meaning of *prevent*. Further, it is the meaning that everyone "knows" *prevent* to have. But what kind of "know" is this? None of the students knew this meaning of *prevent* when I asked about it. It is always quite difficult to draw it out. Yet, as soon as one student recognizes what's going on, every other student in the class agrees, and they all claim to have known it all the time.

What can this mean? Can these both be right? It is important to point out that there is no doubt the students knew it all the time. They are college students who can and do use the word *prevent* quite frequently in their everyday language. Nevertheless, they did not consciously know its meaning. Our conscious can become aware of knowledge that is nonconscious, by means that I have just demonstrated, but there is still a big difference between these types of knowledge. To see this in another way, consider the meaning of the word *by*.

If you ask these same students what the word *by* means, they are dumbfounded. They cannot articulate anything about *by*. They can only cite examples of its use. But, when I further inquire about trying to understand what John did in the example sentence, after they have all concluded that they don't know *what* he did, they can suddenly recognize that if there were a *by* in the sentence, then they would indeed have known. Thus, if the sentence were "John prevented Mary from leaving the room by offering her ice cream," students would know what John actually did.

Students insist that they of course "knew" that the action John did would be found after the word *by*, and they readily understand that the meaning of *by* is functional. *By* tells us how to properly decompose a sentence into its component parts. The rule is that after *prevent*, *by* indicates the action inherent in *prevent* that is the cause of whatever action is being prevented, which itself is to be found after the word *from*.

This is parsing knowledge. Any speaker of a language has such knowledge. All my students "knew" this stuff, but none knew what they knew. It is all nonconscious. Further, it is all incredibly complex and detailed. The amount of such knowledge we all must have in order to communicate is unknown. However, we do know, from attempts to build computer programs that need such knowledge in order to analyze English sentences (Riesbeck, 1975; Schank, 1975; Birnbaum, 1985), that the amount of such knowledge needed for comprehension is huge.

Much of what we are conscious of about language comes from what we have been explicitly taught. So we are conscious of nouns and verbs, and of poetic ways of talking, or of having heard eloquent speech. But, the mechanics of language, how it works, is unknown to us. One reason we don't consciously know about this is that cognitive scientists haven't officially discovered it; otherwise, it might well have become part of the curriculum. Prior to the advent of computers and the attempt to get computers to use language, this was not an area of science many people concerned themselves with. Thus, students have been spared having to memorize how *by* works and what *prevent* means. Such memorization would be worth no more than the attempts to make everyone parse sentences and understand gerunds, as is done in schools today. Unfortunately, once nonconscious knowledge is made conscious, it often finds its way into what we make children learn.

What comes through loud and clear here is that nonconscious knowledge functions perfectly well without consciousness of it. We don't know what we know and that's okay. There is probably some value in knowing some of this stuff explicitly, at least for communication purposes, but not much. Knowing such things consciously can be useful for some people, but is not typically useful for the students who are taught it.

As an example, consider the meaning of the word *but*. When I ask students what *but* means, I get the same blank stares I get when I ask about the real meaning of any other word. Of course, students can use the word *but* properly, but they cannot articulate what it means. This does not mean they don't know it, of course; it only means they aren't conscious of what they know. However, the nonconscious knowledge of the word *but* that we do have, when made conscious, can be quite useful if we are trying to get computers to understand English.

But means, in actual nonconscious use, that whatever proposition follows *but* is intended to negate the normal implications of the proposition that preceded it. So, for example, if I say, "It was cloudy all day but it didn't rain," I am saying that normally you would have expected rain but it didn't happen. If I say that John hit Mary but she didn't cry, I am implying that I expected that she would cry after being hit. A student of language needs to know consciously the meaning of the word *but* so that he can use this knowledge in attempting to understand what a sentence means. For example, the sentence "John hit Mary but it didn't rain" would be seen as silly. Hitting doesn't imply rain. It is important to know this if we are going to analyze what a word (like *hit*) does mean. For example, if I say that John hit Mary but his hand didn't touch her, we can understand that this might be true, but it seems odd. If I say that John hit Mary but nothing at all ever came in contact with her, then this seems not only odd, but unlikely to be true.

By looking at sentences containing *but* in this way, we can come to know what we know about words. For example, we can see from these sentences that the meaning of *hit* certainly includes physical contact between the object and something, that we can assume it means contact between the hand of the actor and the object, but that this might not be true, and that it implies nothing at all about rain. Becoming conscious of what we know about the meaning of words is very important in studying the mind and how it works. But as we can see, it is unimportant to teach a student any of this, because he *already* knows it. We know what *hit* means – the *but test* shows us that we do. This knowledge is nonconscious and is critical to the basis of what it means to be an intelligent human being. Our conscious knowledge is useful, but being conscious of how language works is not at all important for the user of language.

The conundrum is this: As we become more knowledgeable as a society about the nature of the universe, we believe it is this knowledge that makes us human. We feel, as a society, that imparting this knowledge is what the educational system should be all about (Strauss and Shilony, 1994). If we understand the facts about how language works, we feel we should teach that knowledge to children. But, there is no reason at all to do this. Knowing how things work doesn't make us better at doing them. The person who understands why a curve ball curves will not necessarily know how to pitch, and a pitcher who can throw a great curve ball is more than likely clueless about why the ball does what it does when he throws it. A person who is articulate in his use of language does not possess this ability because he is conscious of how *by* and *from* work. He is articulate because he practices language as a user, not as a scientist. From this it follows that as long as schooling concentrates on conscious knowledge, it is doomed to have little real effect.

Of course, I am not talking only about language here. Everything we know about everything is important to our ability to comprehend the world around us, but we very rarely know that we know any of it. For example, when we enter a restaurant and look for a table and decide what we want to eat, we haven't a clue as to how this all works. We can't say how we recognize restaurants, or how we know who the waitress is, or what is and is not a table. We can move our bodies in such a way that they get to the table and seat themselves, but if anyone ever asked us to describe how to walk or sit down, we would become tongue-tied. Perhaps we can give a rational explanation of why we have chosen what to order, but when we simply feel like having a hamburger, we cannot really say why.

All of what I have described here belongs to the realm of nonconscious knowledge; we use it in thinking, but we cannot say how. We can say why we decided to take an important decision like accepting a new job, or buying a house or a car. We like to imagine that this, at least, is the stuff of conscious thought, but there is plenty of evidence to show that the unconscious influences in such decisions are profound indeed (Tversky and Kahneman, 1981; Langer, 1990; and Freud, 1904).

Our racing minds that keep us awake when we want to be asleep must also be working with nonconscious knowledge. We are sometimes aware of the thoughts we have in these episodes, but often we are not aware of the knowledge upon which those thoughts are based. But, the nonconscious knowledge used in such thinking, such as our views of people or remembrance of events, seems quite different than the nonconscious knowledge we use when we read a sentence or decide how to sit down. We don't know (consciously) that we have to adjust our bodies in a certain way to get them into a sitting position – we just do it (using the unconscious knowledge we have about how to do this). Surely this is something that animals do. Is this really knowledge?

To see what kinds of knowledge we are dealing with, let's again consider driving a car. Animals don't drive cars, and although they might presumably be taught to do so, it is unlikely that they could learn to avoid accidents. (The reason is simple. Accidents damage cars, and damage to a car is bad only if you value that car.) When we teach someone to drive a car, we attempt to make explicit to them in words what we do not really have explicitly represented in our minds. We try to articulate how pressure should be applied to the brake, how the wheel should be turned back after turning, and that the correct way to stop at a stop sign is by inching forward. Although I am sure that professional driving instructors know exactly how to say all this to their charges, I am equally sure that most everybody else does not. I can easily recall, while attempting to teach my son to drive on the streets of Chicago, that I could not properly explain how to go through a stop sign on a crowded city street. I had to watch myself do it later, when he was not in the car, and then remember what I had done, so that I could describe it to him. He was quite annoyed with me when I said that stop signs meant to stop twice, not once, but I was certain we were going to get hit when he insisted on stopping at a stop sign once and then starting back up again.

Am I conscious when I drive? In any standard definition of consciousness, I am. Yet I don't know how I do what I do. I am using nonconscious knowledge. In fact, sometimes I drive where I wasn't supposed to be going because I am not thinking about where I am going. When I do this, I am surely conscious, I am surely thinking, but when I am lost in thought in this way, and a companion asks what I was thinking about, I don't always know. How can this be?

My argument is that what passes as consciousness – our awareness that we have had a thought and can sometimes say what that thought was about – is actually a rather uninteresting part of the human thinking process. The more significant human thinking process, or processes, are nonconscious. We have no control of them and most of the time we are totally unaware of them. But, these processes make up the bulk of what we are talking about when we talk about thinking. Similarly, what passes for knowledge is conscious knowledge, when the really interesting and important knowledge we have is unknown to our conscious selves.

We have some sense of how we acquire conscious knowledge. We read, we listen to what others say, we attend school. All of these experiences attempt to impart rational, explicit knowledge. But we've known for years that people learn far more from doing than they learn from telling (Dewey, 1916). It is reasonable to assume that when people learn from doing, they acquire knowledge. When people dream, they are also learning. Since they are experiencing things (albeit dreamlike things), they are learning from the "virtual" doing in those experiences. What they are learning is difficult to articulate, but it seems clear that they must be learning the same kinds of things they learn from real experiences. Nonconscious knowledge is nonconscious knowledge. It can be acquired in a variety of ways. How it is acquired in dreaming, and what form that knowledge takes, and what role it plays are the subject of a later chapter.

Another form of nonconsciousness is what I have been calling the racing mind. The racing mind occurs in three basic situations. The first occurs when you are not quite asleep, and feel like you are being prevented from sleeping by your racing thoughts. The second occurs when you are calm, alone, and deprived of visual and auditory stimuli, and find your mind taking off on its own. The third occurs when your mind wanders when you are supposed to be thinking or paying attention to something. Often people have difficulty reporting what they were thinking about in such situations; they can sometimes report the last thing they were thinking of, but have often lost the rest.

Typically, people find their racing minds to be annoying. The thoughts of the racing mind seem to be irrelevant and trivial. When our minds go off on their own when we are supposed to be listening to someone else (typically this occurs in school) or when someone is talking too long or too much, we feel that we've done a bad thing, because we aren't absorbing what the teacher is saying. Further, when our minds race, we don't always think anything useful is accomplished; we see ourselves as "daydreaming." But is what we are doing really useless? As one begins to appreciate the issues of the acquisition of nonconscious knowledge, it seems plausible that a student will learn more of value by daydreaming in class than he ever would by paying attention.

An important aspect of the racing mind is its reliance on reminding. It may seem that there is no order to the racing mind's leaping from thought to thought, but this is not always the case. In fact, the very same processes are in operation in this situation as are in operation in case-based reasoning. In order to find a case, the mind must construct an index and then search through cases with that index. This process manifests itself in the conscious mind as "reminding." It also operates in conversation when something someone else says causes us to think of something new to say back. The ideas of other people can remind us of our own as well, as seen in Chapter 3.

When the mind races, the same reminding process is responsible. (This has been referred to as a *stream of consciousness*, except it is really a *stream of nonconsciousness*.) When the mind races, the process is totally internal, but otherwise the process is the same as when an outside situation or statement causes our own minds to look for matching cases. Our own thoughts remind us of more of our own thoughts. These remindings follow an orderly set of rules based upon index construction and index creation. The reminding process is in all cases nonconscious. In order to get reminded, we must have knowledge about cases and about how to characterize and retrieve cases. This kind of nonconscious knowledge is perhaps the most critical stuff we have that helps us reason; I shall discuss it in some detail later.

The phenomenon often referred to as "gut reasoning" may also seem like nonconscious thinking, that is, the kind of decision making that seems rational but really isn't. Often we can say why we decided something if we are asked to explain our actions after the fact. However, although we can use words to make up these explanations, they often have little to do with the decision-making process we went through. The situations I have in mind here have to do with very basic instincts like love, food, or anger. Such basically emotional material can be explained rationally, but this does not mean that decisions about such things are actually *made* rationally. This is why we eat and drink "more than we should have," or make fools of ourselves with someone to whom we are attracted, or can't control our temper when something has made us angry, or "overreact" in an emotional situation. The reason these things happen is that the decisions that comprise these "choices" are not decisions at all. We are not reasoning in any conscious way. What I call "gut reasoning" seems to be more conscious than mind racing, but it really isn't. Often we really don't know the reasons why we have done things on the emotional plane. We do, however, as always, have the ability to reflect on these things consciously and thus come up with an explanation that makes it appear as if we were thinking at the time.

We might want to change how we think about things – how we see the world, for instance. Unfortunately, to change behaviors that depend upon our world view is really very hard. How we eat or how we behave on a date is determined by scriptlets inside scenes inside MOPs that have taken many years to gel into the form that they have for an adult. You can try to alter your behavior consciously, but you will be as frustrated as Gallwey's talking tennis player. Saying "eat less" to a self that needs to clean the plate just isn't likely to have the desired effect. The nonconscious changes slowly over time through habituation that occurs because expectations inside MOPs have failed consistently in the same way, not because we simply decide we should change how we think. Nonconscious knowledge changes when it fails to be correct knowledge after the expectations produced by it fail once too often.

One possible difference between types of nonconscious knowledge revolves around their degree of transparency to the person using that knowledge. When we use nonconscious knowledge, it is possible, although not necessarily easy, to make conscious what that knowledge is. With gut reasoning, however, the situation is quite different. People know they like someone, but don't know why. They manifest signs of nervousness in a situation but deny they are nervous. They make choices about their lives but don't realize they have made them. They avoid risk, or seek out excitement, without knowing that this is what they are doing or why they might fall into such patterns. They "rationalize" their behavior, but the reasons they give often have little relation to what is really going on in their minds. The knowledge employed here seems qualitatively different.

Nonconscious knowledge is critical in decision-making of which we are peripherally aware. When we are driving a car and need to take a defensive action (like deciding to swerve), we need not "think about it."[1] We can just do it. Our basic unconscious decision-making apparatus takes over. We follow its dictates, and then later on we try to consciously explain what we have done. Since we were there and are verbal, we can, in fact, say what happened. But we are describing what we saw (which may include our own thoughts), not reiterating our conscious decision making. Animals do this too, that is, they decide to do something without explicitly thinking about it. Such behavior is very basic to being alive and requires no conscious thought to explain

---

[1] In *Consciousness Explained*, Dennett (1991) also discusses driving (p. 137). He maintains that although it seems that you are unconscious while driving, you really are peripherally aware of "all those passing cars, stop lights, and bends in the road." Note that I am not claiming here that we are unconscious of our perceptions, but of our physical abilities and our cognitive activities.

it. People can do many physical actions without "knowing how they did them," such as running, eating, throwing, or catching a ball. And we can't always accurately describe what we have done. We are viewers of our own actions and have all the flaws of any eyewitness.

A very important nonconscious process is the basic understanding process. When we are attempting to understand what someone is saying, we often suffer under the illusion of consciousness; we believe we understand what has been said to us. The evidence of our understanding ability is clear to us. But, what is it that we do when we understand the individual sentences we hear? We haven't a clue. Most people will say something about nouns and verbs when asked about their understanding, because they learned those words in school. But, the fact remains that this most fundamental of our abilities, the ability to comprehend what is going on around us, is a process that is completely opaque to its users. It is clearly a nonconscious process. We can come up with something to say back when someone tells us something, so surely the ideas behind the response were present in our minds in some way. Where were they? How did we find them? How did we know what to look for? These are questions that only cognitive scientists have a hope of answering in a reasonable way. The average person performs these feats effortlessly and is clueless about them.[2] We know only that we have understood; nothing more of this process is in any way conscious.

Performance tasks can be divided into two types: those we learn to perform with conscious instruction and those we learn without conscious instruction. Both types tend to be opaque, nonconscious processes, but tasks that are learned with conscious instruction confuse us into believing that we are conscious of what we are doing when we perform them. The first category includes walking, eating, observing, navigating, and other such processes we have learned to do, or have innately done, as small children. The latter category includes things like playing the saxophone, hitting a baseball, singing, swimming, or any process we might have taken explicit lessons in. The fact that we might have taken lessons, and that these lessons would have included some authority's telling us the right thing to do, tends to confuse us into believing that, because we hear the voice of our

---

[2] This is one reason why we are so bad at helping kids with learning disabilities; we don't know much about what went wrong with their processing ability. Willams (1993) found what he termed "idiosyncratic" importations in their comprehension of text.

instructor ringing in our heads, perhaps we are conscious of how we perform what we perform. But, of course, we are not. In fact, it is not unreasonable to argue that our instructors weren't conscious of what they did either. They, like me when I was teaching about stop signs, need to review what they do and then articulate what they believe to be the proper procedure for doing it. A student under their tutelage keeps trying their advice, but, more importantly, keeps trying to perform the task, until the performance is not conscious at all. The performer needs to learn well enough that he can perform "in his sleep" without thinking about how to do what he does. This kind of behavior is consciousness rendered unconscious. I will have more to say about this in the next chapter.

For me, one of the most fascinating forms of nonconscious behavior is the process of composition. We talk and write and have the feeling that we know what we are going to say. But, we are often surprised by the words that come out of our mouths. When writing, we need to pause to read what we have written to see what it is we have said. We feel we are aware of what we are saying, but we know we haven't any idea how we decide what to say, and how we find the right words to use. We can edit what we say or write, by pausing long enough to hear ourselves say it (or write it) and then editing. But why the need to do this if the process were conscious? In fact, the process is nonconscious until just before the words are actually generated. At that last instant, there is time for editing, that is, there is time for the intervention of consciousness into an otherwise nonconscious process.

We of course believe that most composition is conscious. For example, right now I am writing. I believe I am thinking about what I am writing and what I have written. This process is conscious in part, but I claim that most of it is not. We have already seen that the proper use of language (including grammar usage, word selection, and such) is certainly nonconscious. But most writers delude themselves into believing that the ideas they are expressing are chosen and expressed consciously. Nothing could be further from the truth.

This is one reason writers experience "writer's block." They need to be in the right mood, the right frame of mind, the right circumstances, in order to write – they need to find a starting point that will activate a string of related remindings. Why would this be the case if writing were a conscious process? You can always engage in a conscious process at will. It is the nonconscious processes over which we have no control. Just knowing consciously what you want to say isn't enough. You also need to have ideas, and the ideation process is non-conscious. We don't know where ideas come from when we have them, but we know it is difficult to generate them on demand. (There are companies who specialize in helping groups of people come up with "original ideas." The ideation process requires some kinds of stimuli and these companies claim to have some idea what those stimuli are.) What I know about the writing process is this: When I write, I find myself saying something that reminds me of something else. Writing helps me have ideas. I find it difficult to have ideas without having ideas. If this sounds circular, it of course is. Nonconscious processes seem circular because we don't have any real sense, consciously, of how they work.

What is conscious is the editing process. In some sense, editing processes are the essence of consciousness. When we can think about what we say before we say it, or think about what we have written after we have written it (but before we have let others read it), we are doing conscious editing.[3] Editing processes are the point of consciousness. They occur in areas other than writing, most significantly in the self-modification of potential behaviors. This is what we mean by mulling something over. If there is an evolutionary advantage to being conscious, and certainly there should be, it must be the ability to not be a slave to one's nonconscious thoughts. A dog cannot, presumably, decide that going for a child's throat is not such a good idea after it has thought it over. A dog cannot self-edit its own potential behavior because the dog is not conscious, by the definition of consciousness portrayed here. Mulling an action over before one performs that action is, then, the very essence of consciousness. And, it is along this line that we can wonder about the consciousness of chimpanzees and gorillas. There is evidence to suggest that these animals do mull actions over (Cheney and Seyfarth, 1990). In any case, whether they do or not, the central question of consciousness is not the issue of knowing what you think, but the issue of being able to alter what you have thought because of a recognition that what you thought was wrong in some way.

We have the possibility of changing our behavior if we use a "mulling time" or reflection period – that is, if we insert a pause between impulse and action and use that time to self-edit. But, this differs some from what Gallwey said. According to Gallwey, conscious knowledge is more or less useless in playing tennis. The mind doesn't

[3] See Dennett (1991) in his criticism of Ryle's work *On Thinking*.

control the body consciously; Gallwey maintains that talking to one's body actually makes things worse. So the question is whether the physical body and the mind are different in this respect. Can we modify mental behaviors where we can't modify physical ones? The answer, I think, is that we can no more change what we think by simply wishing it so than we can change how we perform physically. But between thought and action, it is possible to simply not do what your thoughts tell you to do, because you can self-edit. This may not produce profound changes in behavior, but over time we can change this thought–action link, because we do learn by doing.

There is, of course, some conscious problem solving (like math). This is, in many ways, the main kind of consciousness that people believe. We know rules of deduction, inference, and such, can state our premises and draw conclusions. The irony here is that this is exactly the kind of reasoning that computers can already do. For years, I have been on the side of AI that asserts that programs that simulate such reasoning are of no particular interest, because they tell us so little about natural human thought. People, like machines, have to be taught how to do such reasoning. But people do not need to be taught (nor would they respond well to one's trying to be taught how) to reason about their loves, passions, or philosophy of life. They do not have to be taught how to understand their language, nor how to compose a thought or conduct a conversation. Yet these are precisely the properties of intelligence that AI people have found so difficult to imbue in machines. Machines and people can be taught to follow rules. This is conscious behavior. The stuff that neither machines nor people are easily taught, nonconscious reasoning, constitutes the bulk of what we consider to be intelligent behavior.

There is an illusion that we know why we have thought what we have thought. Psychologists have had a field day with this one, and, in some sense, the confusion here is the basis of much counseling and therapy. People do things for which they do not have easy explanations. Psychologists seek to make conscious what is unconscious. Freud's whole notion of consciousness was that it was a receiver of stuff that had been sent from the unconscious and edited in a way by the preconscious for the purpose of repressing that which the preconscious was trying to avoid making conscious. Although Freud's notion of the role of the conscious and unconscious was focused on neurotic behavior, his ideas can focus our thinking here. The feeling that we often do not know why we do what we do, and that we can create rational explanations of our behavior that may have little to do with what we were actually thinking, is due to Freud. People are perfectly capable of holding contradictory beliefs and of saying one thing and doing another. The goal of therapists is to attempt to help bring to the conscious, unconscious mechanisms that cause people to make decisions with which they are unhappy. Taking this idea one step further, we see that this flow of unconscious decision making and the rationalizing by the conscious need not apply solely to abnormal or problematic thinking. It is quite likely that everyday, normal decision making occurs in this manner as well. One idea that follows from this is that educators could help identify students' naive or intuitive conceptions so that they can surprise the students, that is, cause their expectations to fail, and then help them construct more appropriate conceptions (Minstrell, 1992; Smith, diSessa and Roschelle, 1993).

And last, there is the explicit knowing of what we know or think. This is what is generally meant by consciousness – that we can say what we know and know what we think. This assumption is the basis of our instructional system and our whole conception of learning. And, although there is truth in the idea that we know a great deal that is quite conscious, the amount we "know" that is nonconscious is far more extensive and more significant. We often cannot talk of actually knowing this stuff, however, since the whole idea of "knowing" in this sense is rooted in our conception of consciousness and has nothing to do with nonconscious thinking.

CHAPTER 14

Goal-based Scenarios

Every aspect of human behavior involves the pursuit of goals. Sometimes these goals are rather simple, like brushing your teeth to prevent decay. Sometimes they are quite unconscious, like having your mind search for similar experiences when you encounter some new experience. And, sometimes they are quite complex, like trying to build high-quality educational software as a means to effect change in the school system.

When goals are simple, we really don't think about them much. When they are unconscious, we don't think about them at all. And, when they are complex, we may think about them, but find the going so rough that we hone in on the simplest ones and lose the forest for the trees.

Understanding how people pursue goals is a critical aspect of understanding cognition. For computers to really understand human stories, they would need a complete model of the goals people pursue: the plans, the use, and the complexities that arise. The issue is this: If goals underlie human behavior to the extent that we cannot understand a story or what someone says or wants, without a clear assessment of the underlying goals and the interaction of those goals, then it follows that goals are at the root of human learning. Why would anyone learn anything if not to help in the pursuit of a goal? Why would anyone try to understand anything if not because he had the goal of learning new information from what he was trying to understand? The desire to change one's knowledge base, to comprehend what is going on about him, and to learn from experience, are all pretty much different ways of saying the same thing. And, all of these are goal-directed activities.

Natural Learning

If goals are at the base of the human thought process, then it follows that learning must be a goal-dominated arena as well. This is certainly true of the learning processes of small children, who are quite goal oriented. One-year-olds want to learn to walk because there are places they want to go, or because others around them walk. Their learning to walk follows the goal of walking (which may well be in service of some other goal). Similarly, a two-year-old learns to speak a language because he wants to communicate. Four-year-olds can find any room in their home and they know the neighborhood in which they live; in general, they understand and can plan in their own environment because these plans are in the service of goals the children have.

Children have natural learning mechanisms, ways in which they progress from babies with innate abilities and no actual knowledge to children with a great deal of knowledge about the physical, social, and mental worlds in which they live. And, these mechanisms, like the understanding mechanisms of adults, are goal dominated.

Small children do not have motivation problems. They are excited by learning, eager to try new things, and in no way self-conscious about failure (though perhaps no less surprised by it). In short, they are perfect examples of goal-based learners. Consequently, we never see a two-year-old who is depressed about how his talking progress is going and so has decided to quit trying to improve, or a two-year-old who has decided that learning to walk is too difficult and thus has decided only to crawl.

The natural learning mechanism that children employ is not very much more sophisticated than trial and error. Children learn by experimentation, by failing, by being told, or by copying some new behavior that has better results. Inherent in this model is the idea that children are trying to learn *to do* something, rather than *to know* something. Failure is not frustrating in this context; in a deep sense, learning, until age six, depends mostly upon failure.

But somewhere around age six, all this changes. Children try to avoid having to learn. They fear failure. Their educational goals are no longer in pursuit of some personally motivating goal. Instead, they work to please authority, or they do less work. Furthermore, the instruction they receive is more like thirty-on-one than one-on-one, and tremendous social difficulties inherent to peer group dynamics are encountered. What has happened to cause all this? The six-year-old has started school.

The goals that are the basis of understanding and of learning ought to be the basis of schooling as well, but they are not. In school, natural learning goals are replaced by artificial ones. Instead of trying to learn something because they want to be able to do something (like get places, communicate, or utilize objects), children learn in order to please the teacher (in order to avoid ridicule, get good grades, or get into a good college). In other words, natural learning goals that have to do with increasing understanding or increasing one's power to operate successfully in various endeavors get replaced by artificial learning goals that have to do with acceptance, approval, and socialization. It is simply a matter of intrinsic versus extrinsic motivation.

It follows, then, that the main problem in the schools is the curriculum. Learning in school rarely looks like learning in the real world.[1] Whereas learners in the real world struggle to learn in order to achieve their goals, learners in school struggle to learn material their teachers and school administrators insist they must know in order to achieve the goals of getting good grades and credit for courses and degrees.

Simply put, students are learning the wrong stuff. Why? Because our entire concept of what constitutes an education has been guided by the need for assessment. We don't teach students what they want to know. We don't respond to their real educational goals at all. Rather, we pander to the goals of the system, which usually means finding out who is the best student, who can get into Yale, get the top job, and so on. To make these assessments, we test what is easily testable, which often means looking for knowledge of vocabulary items on multiple choice tests but rarely means looking for knowledge of issues and concepts for which there is no clear answer (but which we'd like students to be able to reason about as they become adult members of society). We decide that every student must know some particular body of knowledge, which sounds fine in principle, but forces one to find ways to make sure that everyone has learned this body of knowledge, which brings us back to simplistic tests. A further consequence of deciding what everyone should know is that we implicitly eliminate other subjects that might genuinely interest a child. There is no time for extra stuff, precisely the sort of stuff that might relate to a child's real goals.

In order to reorganize the schools, then, a theory of what consti-

---

[1] Resnick (1987) and Murnance and Levy (1996) discuss the extreme mismatch between what is taught in schools and what is needed to perform in the work world. DiSessa (1982), Bransford et al. (1989), Reif and Larkin (1991), and Lampert (1995) all offer evidence that students are learning knowledge in schools that they generally cannot apply in their lives.

tutes a reasonable curriculum is necessary. Such a theory ought to be independent of any particular subject matter, dealing instead with principles by which knowledge is acquired and utilized in real life and relating those principles to the schoolroom. Since the assumption that education ought to be goal directed carries with it the idea that education should be self-directed (who knows better what a child's goals and interests are than the child?) rather than imposed by state mandates of what every child should know, we come to the conclusion that the very idea of curriculum is wrong. Built into a curriculum is the idea of "lock-step," each child proceeding on the same course at more or less the same pace. Since natural learning proceeds at its own pace, and since there is no absolutely right set of things that everyone needs to know, this cannot be the right way to proceed. Nevertheless, there are times to bend to reality, and this is one of them. School reform requires clear alternatives, so I will propose a new method for the construction of courses. Courses are important entities in the real world of school and of business training. If we are to have courses, and it seems that they will be with us for the near term at least, then maybe we can have good, high-quality, fun, and goal-directed ones. We can redesign courses using what we know about natural learning and what we understand about the primacy of goals in understanding and learning.

Redesigning Courses

I must begin by discussing what characteristics a course, any course, implemented in any way, should have. The first thing one must realize is that an interest is a terrible thing to waste. People, especially children, come with real interests, things they have a genuine desire to pursue, which, left to their own devices, they would learn more about. Most any interest of a student can be utilized so that it relates in *some* way to the subjects the school wishes to teach. Utilizing this interest would certainly help to capture and maintain the student's attention and help the student leverage off of his prior knowledge in that familiar area of interest. School officials need to consider that what they want to teach may not be so well thought out. Standard courses may need to be seriously reexamined to see if they accomplish the things their designers aim to accomplish. Do we really need to teach logarithms? Why is Dickens so important? Aren't there some everyday social skills that schools might teach that would have more use in the long run?

Courses need to be created within a context that enables students to pursue their own interests for as long as they want to, without disallowing the possibility of switching interests at any time. This means the concept of a curriculum must include an understanding of how materials pertain to specific interests and how they convey general issues independent of a specific context. Once a student selects an interest, accomplishable goals – in terms of visible projects – will be pursued. Much of the kind of knowledge now taught explicitly in school will be taught implicitly, within the context of helping the student achieve the goals of the course he has selected for himself. Teaching will occur as the student discovers his own need to know, in order to accomplish whatever his current task is and in order to serve his higher-level goals.

Designers of these new learning environments would need to understand, and optimally to utilize, the fine differences between skills, cases, facts, subjects, domains, and processes well enough to teach them differently, properly, and cohesively. Most importantly, designers must learn how to construct effective goal-based scenarios (GBSs). Let me define some of these terms.

A *skill* is something you know how to do. If the sentence "John knows how to X" makes sense for a given X, then X is a skill. In general, skills are attained by practice. Reading, addition, driving, doing cost accounting, and plugging in formulas are all skills. Skills have many components, including the strategies that are employed to best utilize a skill. People who are very skilled at something often employ complex strategies that they have learned over time in the course of exercising their skill.

A *case* is a story about one or more events that comprise a whole. The case either may serve to illustrate a point or may, itself, serve as a basic reference point. The point illustrated by a case is usually of significance that is generalizable to other situations. Some cases are simply reference points that are part of the common culture. Thus, the Battle of Gettysburg is a case. It can illustrate one or more military points, or it might tell us something about history, or it might simply be something that all Americans know about.

A *fact* is a piece of information that is often derived from, or serves to summarize, a case (e.g., the fact that the North won the Battle of Gettysburg is actually a summary of the entire case). A fact may be simply a description of a state of affairs that is true apart from any case (e.g., Harrisburg is the capital of Pennsylvania). Often, facts are taught apart from the cases they summarize and tested in such a way as to indicate knowledge of a case that may not be there. For example, we can get students to tell us that the Gettysburg Address was given by Lincoln in 1863, but to what extent would this mean that they understood the issues of the Civil War? I would argue that the Civil War is really rather unimportant to know about; far more important to understand is the effectiveness of war as a means of resolving disputes both between countries and within a country. Teaching facts directly tends to parody the teaching of cases (it just looks like Johnny knows something about the Civil War when he recites what he knows about the Gettysburg Address), and it is very difficult either to remember or to ascertain the significance of facts learned that way.

Subjects are collections of skills and cases that have been grouped together under the same banner for many years. For example, physics is a subject and, like all subjects, it is made up of both skills and cases. There are things to learn to do when one learns physics and there are well-known cases in physics that are worth learning about. Often these two aspects of a subject are confused, so the skills are taught apart from the cases.

A *domain* is an area of interest that can be used as background for the acquisition of skills and cases while one does tasks that teach processes that are used within a subject area. Domains of interest are different from subjects in that they tend to define specialty areas that, apart from various superficial differences, are quite like most other domains. For example, for children, trucks or animals might be a domain of interest. Either of these can be used as means by which subjects such as physics, biology, or history could be taught.

A *process* is somewhat harder to define. When schools try to teach skills and processes, they usually wind up teaching facts instead. For example, reasoning is a process. Since it is difficult to teach abstract reasoning directly, rules for making abstractions or generalizations are often taught as if knowing those rules will help one reason better. Similarly, understanding is a process. But, since understanding is difficult to teach or to assess, we often settle for teaching it within the guise of comprehension tests administered after a paragraph has been read. Since understanding is highly idiosyncratic, this method is actually a parody of the understanding process and is precisely the opposite of memory-based comprehension. Processes are best taught by actually engaging in them, which can often mean, for mental processes, active discussions.

Reconsidering Curriculum

A key factor in education is motivation (Dweck, 1989; Ames, 1990). To the extent that a student feels he has selected for himself what he is going to learn, he can be expected to feel empowered by that selection and be more active about learning. It is important that a student select courses and curricula based upon his own interests. The student's subject matter choices are really irrelevant from the instructor's point of view; if we want to teach reading, for instance, it hardly matters what material is being read. But the more interesting the material is to the student, the more likely he is to want to read it. Similarly, in business, it really doesn't matter what industry a student chooses to study when he studies cost accounting. What does matter is that whatever a student studies must be grounded in some context. As much as possible, students should be using real cases and real situations and should avoid abstractions (Bransford et al., 1989; Cognition and Technology Group at Vanderbilt, 1991; Lampert, 1995). It is important to appreciate the lesson of case-based teaching: real stories, real contexts, told by real people, at the right time. The more the situations being studied relate to the student's area of interest, the more likely it is that the student will want to know more.

The premise is that one can learn almost anything within any context. So, at this point, it is important to consider that loaded question: What should students learn? This is a very tough question, one prone to the creation of endless lists of arbitrary facts. We must consider this question, not from the perspective of facts, but from the perspective of skills and processes.

We have to recognize that just because we choose the American Revolution as a case about revolution, another teacher (or student) might find a different case on revolution to be more enlightening. If we want to teach the American Revolution with respect to common heritage and culture issues, then it should be taught within the context of issues of the governance of our society rather than as history we need to learn from.

The question, then, for a course designer who for his own reasons wants to teach American history is, What skills would a student have that would be enhanced by knowing this case? Put this way, courses can be designed around favorite cases while remaining meaningful to a student.

It is common for students to be taught principles and theories as a substitute for actually engaging in a process.[2] The problem is that most principles, like the Pythagorean theorem and the proper use of gerunds, are not worth knowing. Even when principles are worth knowing, they are extremely difficult to learn without having, in some sense, discovered them oneself. Parents may lament that their children can't learn from the parents' experiences, but there is a very good reason why children can't do so. As we learn, we generalize from our own experiences (Seifert, Abelson and McKoon, 1986; McKoon, Ratcliff and Seifert, 1989; Ross and Kennedy, 1990; Ross, Perkins and Tenpenny, 1990; Farrar and Goodman, 1992; Spalding and Ross, 1994). Only when these generalizations are grounded in actual cases will our memory of a bad or good result reinforce the rule that has been learned. When we try to learn from what others tell us, we may get the generalizations (e.g., the moral of their lesson) but we do not get the rich context of experiencing the episode ourselves and storing it as a fully embodied case in our memories from which to generalize upon. Where do we "put" the lesson? In what scene, as an expectation failure from what scriptlet? How do we generalize, ourselves, when someone else has generalized for us? In such a situation, we end up with some fragment of knowledge gleaned from another person's experiences but which is utterly disconnected from our own idiosyncratic understanding of the world. This memory will fail to be recalled at some relevant later date unless it is grounded in personal experience. Learning is an emotional experience. Without one's own emotional twist, there is little real need to change one's point of view (Read and Cesa, 1991).

Similar difficulties arise when someone tries to teach theory. Schools love to teach theories. However, they often fail to recognize why they are teaching them and thus fail to teach what matters most about them. So we teach the theories of Copernicus or Ptolemy or Einstein because we imagine that students need to learn about planetary motion and the cosmos. Although learning what is known from these experts about the cosmos may be fine for adults who have expressed an interest in this subject, it may not be appropriate for children. Children like to wonder. They hear about the planets and they wonder how to get there and what it's like there. They want to create their own theories and talk about what they are imagining (diSessa,

---

[2] For examples, see diSessa (1982) and Bransford et al. (1989).

1982; Bransford et al., 1989; Reif and Larkin, 1991; Scardamalia and Bereiter, 1991) and how to find out what is reasonable; but instead of teaching them about space exploration and the process of scientific discovery, we teach them about somebody else's theory and make them memorize names and dates. A date has no MOP into which it can be put, no real place to go in memory. To really learn a date, one would need to have a real use for it. Of course, we can make people memorize, but that doesn't mean we can make the knowledge that was memorized available in a context unrelated to the memorization. Real learning takes place inside MOPs, not through memorization.

Teaching reasoning by allowing students to reason about something that interests them is a problem, since students might not all want to reason about the same stuff at the same time. Each child may need a different lesson. But schools can't provide this, so instead students are presented with facts, principles, and theories (all of which they forget later on), even though what we need to be teaching them about is reasoning. There is a big difference between letting students create their own theories and, when these theories seem to fail, allowing them to consider other "official" theories in order to see if they work, and teaching those official theories directly. In the former case, the student's own thinking provides a motivation to learn more. In the latter case, the official theories are objects of learning in themselves and thus of little interest to the student.

What about adults? Do we want to teach theory to them? Here again, I would say no. A communication theory or a reasoning method is just that, a theory, usually unproven, probably wrong. If one wants to train practitioners, then the aim must be to allow students to play with cases, to form their own hypotheses, to learn to reason, and to learn to generalize from their own experiences.[3] Even for adults, theories have only a limited place in the curriculum.

Defining Curriculum

A curriculum is really no more than a domain of interest. When students major in biology in college, for example, they do so (presum-

---

[3] Argyris (1985, 1993), Watkins and Marsick (1993), Brinkerhoff and Gill (1994), and Argyris and Schon (1996) all propose methods for doing this on-line, learning from within the context of work that is currently being done by the learners.

ably) because they are interested in biology. Just as interests drive choices during college, they should do so in elementary school and for adults who find themselves in business training courses. Students should be given many curriculum choices upon entering school – any school. These choices should correspond to the interests a student already has, prior to the school situation, and should build upon those interests. But ultimately, any course a student chooses, on any level, should be constituted as goal-based scenarios embedded within a goal-based curriculum.

Goal-based scenarios allow students to pursue well-defined goals and encourage the learning of both skills and cases in service of achieving those goals. Goal-based scenarios may be quite artificial in the sense that they may, as a way of getting students to understand something, ask them to do something they would never do in real life. It helps if the scenario is something that someone actually does, however. For example, one could teach history by asking a student to play the role of the president of the United States at a particular period and presenting him with decisions that need to be made. Accomplishing this goal would cause the student to need to know certain cases, learn certain skills, and understand certain processes. The idea is that although the student may not ever end up in the Oval Office, he will find use for the reasoning, decision-making, and other skills he learns and practices in this GBS.

Students should know what the goal of a course is, and the designer should construct a course that causes the student to accomplish that goal. As long as the goal is of inherent interest to a student, and the skills needed in any attempt to accomplish the goal are those the course designer wants students to have, we have a workable goal-based scenario.

Learning to communicate, function with others, and reason, are the most important parts of any curriculum. Although it is my view that these subjects should not be taught directly, this does not indicate their lack of importance; everything we design must incorporate them. Every goal-based scenario constructed to teach various skills must, first and foremost, teach communication, human relations, and reasoning.

When we begin to teach subjects in various domains, it is important to realize that a school might decide to devote a classroom and a teacher to each domain. For example, imagine something I refer to as the "truck curriculum." A child could specialize in trucks, learning to read by reading about trucks, learning about economics by examining the trucking industry, learning physics by smashing trucks, and so on. To enable this, a school must have a truck classroom with a truck teacher.

The same pattern could be seen within a business training context. Specialists in a variety of industries would be available so that, for instance, those who wished to learn about the utility industry might have a utility classroom and a utility teacher available to them. Each specialty line would have a specialist teacher. Similarly, each skill that is independent of a domain (for example, using certain repair tools or doing cost accounting) might have a teacher (or a computer program acting as teacher) devoted to it, which could be consulted as needed. Each process would also have a place where it could be worked on. Thus we would expect a human relations consultant (a psychologist, perhaps) to be available. Communications and reasoning would be handled by having specific teachers who would deal with particular problems in these areas.

Students would work in groups when that is feasible, or alone – whichever is better at any given time. Group disputes in joint projects would be adjudicated by the human relations subject teacher and used as a lesson in that subject. Reports would be worked on with the communications teacher and used as lessons in that subject. The subject matter teachers would teach only in response to issues raised in pursuit of a goal in the curriculum.

The primary point is this: Apart from deciding what to teach (which skills, which cases), and apart from deciding which goals best package those skills and cases, we must understand that communication, human relations, and reasoning are the backbone of any educational experience and that they must be taught within the context of every goal we choose to work on.

We can see how this works within the "truck curriculum" mentioned earlier. This is a subject that could easily appeal to a typical five-year-old. But the first reaction of many people to this is, What is a truck curriculum? Children aren't sent to school to study trucks! Of course, that is quite right. But remember that all a curriculum should be is a guise under which goal-based scenarios are grouped. In the truck curriculum, the guise of trucks is used to create GBSs that will be of interest to students who profess an interest in trucks. We are not teaching about trucks in the truck curriculum. We are teaching reading, reasoning, economics, history – even mathematics. The idea is to give the student a reason to want to know about these subjects, given his interest in trucks.

What would happen if a "truck" student suddenly wanted to switch his curriculum? If we have been clever in our design of various curricula, this ought to be easy to do, since the "truck" issue is one of background, rather than one of substance. A student working in the truck curriculum is actually learning to read (about trucks), to understand physics (through simulated truck worlds), to make computations (to help his trucking company do business in simulated truck world), and so on. These same things happen within a traditional curriculum having different (albeit disconnected) subjects. Here though, the curriculum itself remains a ruse, an artifice (although an important one), because it provides motivation. When students are motivated, they learn, so the idea is simply to get natural motivations to drive learning within any sort of curriculum.

This idea works for adults as well, although the curricula for adults need not be play oriented in the way they could be for small children. When adults are asked to learn something, they want to know why they should do so (Brinkerhoff and Gill, 1994). Any adult curriculum should make the "why" clear right from the beginning. The primary role of the goal orientation in goal-based scenarios is to answer the question, why? The goal must be realistic for adults, and exciting for children (actually, both of these characteristics are ideal for both groups). When a student knows where he is going, it helps him focus on learning the skills that will help him get there. His goal serves as a motivator for learning. I am dwelling on motivation here because it is the number two problem in education. It is very difficult to learn about things that you don't feel you need to know and that have no real excitement for you. Notice I said the number two problem. The number one problem is authentic teaching. No matter how interested I am in a subject, I can still learn nothing about it and can be turned off to it by having to listen to a professor who drones on about it and then gives a multiple choice test. Authentic teaching must take place in a context that will allow for MOP and TOP creation by the student – in other words, in a doing environment. Addressing these two problems, teaching in a manner consistent with what we know about human memory's ability to change, and attending to the natural motivations of students, are the key to saving modern-day education.

The concept of curriculum can be seen as an organizer of GBSs. That is, the truck curriculum would contain many GBSs, each of which

266

would be driven by a goal that was intrinsically motivating to a child (e.g., learning to drive or repair a truck, learning to design a truck, learning to operate a trucking company or to be a lobbyist for the trucking industry). Any of these might appeal to children of different ages. The job of the designer of a GBS is to take any of these or similar goals and package within them a set of skills that would constitute the steps that would lead to success in the GBS. Depending upon the goal in question, there are one of two ways in which this can be done. There are two kinds of GBSs, natural and artificial. A natural GBS is something like learning to drive a truck. Although there are many ways to teach this skill, they don't vary all that much. On the other hand, in an artificial GBS, one constructs a fictional goal and uses it to package a skill set. The GBSs listed previously are natural GBSs. Here are some artificial GBSs for the trucking curriculum: increase fuel efficiency on your truck so as to win a simulated truck race; design a truck that can fly if necessary; make a television special about the history of vehicles.

In an artificial GBS, the skill set drives the design of the GBS as opposed to the GBS's driving the design of the skill set. (But, we need to be aware of knowing what it is a student ought to know. Business trainers and school administrators alike often feel they know what their students need to know. Further analysis indicates that they are often quite mistaken.) Simply put, if a student wants to accomplish a goal, there are skills he will need to learn. And if there are specific skills we want to teach, the designer of the GBS must create a goal that packages those particular skills.

A curriculum can consist of either natural or artificial GBSs. It follows, however, that since we often want to teach a set of skills related to a non–naturally occurring goal (because the goal is sometimes just a design for motivating the learning), creating an artificial GBS is necessary most of the time. This would be true both in school (where designing a rocket ship that could get to Mars, and then simulating actually flying it there, might be a great way to teach physics) and in industry (where designing a course that taught proposal writing might be a valuable way of packaging skills but might not be the job for which any one person was being trained). For example, at the most advanced levels of the truck curriculum, a student might have to be able to design and propose legislation that would help the trucking industry, be able to run a trucking company, or be able to design a new, more fuel efficient engine for a truck. GBSs that engage students in these kinds of activities would take some time to accomplish and would be for students who had gotten quite far in the truck curriculum. At intermediate stages, a student might learn how to drive a truck (or a simulated truck), repair a faulty engine, propose changes in the highway system, write a brochure about a trucking company, or make a speech to a truckers' convention. At more elementary stages, a child might learn about the physics of truck collisions, about how to be a dispatcher, or how to efficiently load a truck. A young child might learn about fuel and combustion; he might read about trucks and do arithmetic motivated by trucking issues. He might learn about the life of workers in the truck industry and report on this to students in other curricula. He might apprentice to an older child while he learns to fix an engine, and he might spend time riding in trucks or visiting a trucking company.

The key idea is to embed instruction in such a way that it occurs at the point where the student has developed the need to know what will be taught. When students want to know something to help them in a task, they will be determined to learn what they need to know if their motivation to accomplish the task is strong enough in the first place.

In short, we would want to teach skill sets that are normally packaged under titles such as design, politics, physics, economics, math, reading, history, geography, or biology. Remember that we want to teach the skills needed within these subjects, not the subjects themselves. But because all of these are worthy subjects, the skills they comprise ought to be part of the course designer's skill set and included within one or more GBSs within a curriculum.

In school, curricula ought to correspond to the interests of children of different ages. As a start, and merely as a point of departure for discussion, I propose the following potential curricula based upon my own perception of some of the interests of six-year-old children. It is my contention that any of these curricula could be made to encompass a variety of goal-based scenarios, covering skills encompassed by the subjects and covering communication, human relations, and reasoning. Here are my favorites: dolls, pets, travel, vehicles, food, dinosaurs, sports, music, houses, and clothing. Any of these can teach subject areas discussed earlier. Many other curricula could be devised that would do the same. The issue is finding out what children really want to know about, and using those natural interests as a springboard to teach skills, engage in processes, and kindle new interests.

Goal-based scenarios can be constructed by examining all the skills deemed important and putting them into some natural situation around which a scenario can be constructed. There is no one right format for a GBS. The scenarios can take as long as the instructors want them to, from a day to a year. They can be built into software, or partially instructor led, or completely paper based. Case libraries can come in the form of real live experts or video recordings, in electronic media, or in paper format. Human experts ought to be available for the teaching of processes on an as-needed basis. The point is that skills ought to be taught by the most appropriate method, and that the determining of that method depends on the particular skills. Learning occurs when students want to know. It is the job of the instructional designer and the teacher to do what they can to cause students to care about knowing something.

Conclusion

The intent of a goal-based scenario is to provide motivation, a sense of accomplishment, a support system, and a focus on skills rather than facts. Facts can be deceptive; they give the *sense* of knowing without the *significance* of knowing. Understanding why you are doing something, having a clear goal that is more than the recitation of facts, truly knowing why, and wanting to know more so that one can become curious about more "whys" is what education is all about. Goal-based scenarios, interrupted by well-told, appropriate, and important cases, offer a reasonable framework for courses that are meant to be the means of education. To put this another way: Expectation failure plus storytelling allows for reminding, explanation, and the subsequent reorganization of a dynamic memory. School needs to provide sets of skills that students can learn and that would be skills they would use regularly in real life. Some of those skills students know they need. They may need to be convinced that they need others. This means that the current curriculum is almost entirely without real value.

CHAPTER 15

Enhancing Intelligence

Can we truly educate people? This seems like an odd question for those who believe intelligence is immutable. But for many who study the mind, it is not so odd. One reason our school systems are in such difficulty is that the underlying assumption of "just fill them with facts" comes from an idea that intelligence is not mutable. In this view, people can *know* more, but they can't really change *how they think.*

The dynamic memory view is that intelligence is, of course, mutable. If intelligence depends upon the creation of MOPs and TOPs and other types of generalizations, then it follows that helping students create explanations and generalizations and find patterns helps them to know more and to be more intelligent – not to know more in the "Trivial Pursuit" sense of acquiring facts, but to know more in a deep sense. Knowing more, in a deep sense, is truly a change in intelligence – it is the ability to better comprehend the world in which we live.

Modern educational practice has been greatly influenced by trends in academic psychology. Behaviorism, for instance, inspired a large industry devoted to turning out educational products that put into practice what the theory proposed. Of course, given the inevitable time lag in the popular dissemination of such trends, by the time this industry hit its stride, behaviorism was already in retreat as a theoretical framework for psychology. Unfortunately, by then the damage had been done. Drill and practice, programmed workbooks, memorization, all this is the legacy that behaviorism left the schools.

In the current day we are also faced with educational doctrines structured by followers of positions that make certain claims about the nature of knowledge, its use, and its acquisition, and the results of the application of these claims and positions to education. In this book, I have made claims about knowledge and learning that are substantially different from behaviorism, and that offer grounds to be far more optimistic about the prospect for enhancing intelligence through education.

Knowledge is not cultural literacy or the ability to show what you know, but the ability to demonstrate what you can do. Knowledge for doing is different than knowledge for demonstrating a command of facts that were determined by some committee as worth knowing. These claims form the cornerstone of my proposals for changing education.

There isn't much difference between human intelligence and the intelligence of higher animals. Darwin pointed this out in a number of ways. A cat, for instance, can have expectation failures, and come up with generalizations that allow him to change his behavior in response to events. He can recall cases, or at least he appears to remember previous cases when encountering similar ones.

Intelligence is enhanceable. Artificial intelligence researchers, people who want to enhance the intelligence of machines, have been one of the main groups of people working to understand exactly what enhances intelligence. In contrast, the views of the mind and of intelligence that eminent people such as Noam Chomsky (1980) and John Searle (1983, 1984, 1992) adhere to are inherently anti-education because they both entail, as a central tenet, that what intelligence exists in an entity is completely and inherently unalterable. One can only speculate as to why anyone would take satisfaction in such a view of human beings and human potential.

Through devices such as the competence–performance distinction (invented by Chomsky in 1965, to lay the groundwork for linguistics research by claiming that what mattered was what formal knowledge people had about their language, not the actual communication or memory processes associated with the production and comprehension of language), many scholars have concluded that scientists need be concerned only with "competencies" addressed in a "mathematically rigorous" fashion. This stratagem, and its general acceptance by many linguists, psychologists, and philosophers, has had disastrous consequences for research in these fields. This is a shame, but what is really much worse has been the consequences for our notions of what belongs in a student's education.

To cite one example of these negative consequences, consider the idea of diagraming sentences. Grammar (in particular, diagraming sentences) is a part of many children's education. Although the practice of this particular skill predates Chomsky's theories of linguistics, sentence diagraming and grammar study in general had a considerable resurgence after his work became widely known. Further, the philosophy of education from which follows the idea that school children

271

ought to be diagraming sentences is the same as the philosophy of research from which Chomsky's work follows, namely, that it is the formal, syntactic properties of language that matter, not the use of language as a conveyer of meaning. In school, this gets translated as structure being more important than content. In my terms here, this translates as a problem of establishing certain knowledge as what everyone should know, as opposed to emphasizing performance skills.

To see what I mean, consider five aspects of intelligent behavior: language comprehension, memory retrieval, storytelling, inference, and expectations about effects. While linguists dwell on the nature of language, writing formal rules about the "mathematics" of language and encouraging school children to learn aspects of these rules, these other, everyday problems of language usage remain virtually ignored both in scholarship and in school. Why might this be?

Certainly, no rational person would claim that we can speak or write independently of memory. Yet, Chomsky rules out memory considerations as irrelevant for the study of language, treating memory as something whose main job is to retain sentence structure plans. (Even to refer to these structures as "plans" is to link language to other capacities in a way that many linguists would find unacceptable.) Yet, can we speak of what we don't know? Can we write about events we do not remember or imagine? The process of finding memories and manipulating them to suit our needs for the purposes of communication is just as important a part of the communication process as is language. In fact, there is good reason to consider it to be a far more important part of the communication process since, whether or not dogs have consciousness or chimps have language, it is perfectly clear that both species have memory retrieval capabilities.

Memory retrieval capabilities are not studied in school – no examination of the process, no diagraming of rules, no discussion of the issue. Why not? One might imagine that the answer is that not a great deal is known about them. To some extent this is true, but this cannot be the real reason. The real reason is far more insidious.

The Bias against Content

The greatest discovery of artificial intelligence is a rather simple point: What makes someone intelligent is what they know. What is needed to make intelligent computers is to endow them with knowledge.

This was not the discovery we set out to make. Many of the founders of AI came out of mathematics and physics and were trained in a scientific aesthetic that put primary emphasis on the search for powerful, yet extremely general, principles. (Whether this is how these fields actually operate, of course, is an entirely different question; see, e.g., Lakatos, 1978.) What they aspired to discover was something like the law of universal gravitation for the mind. In retrospect, it would have been far better for everyone concerned if the founders of AI had been trained in biology instead.

The search for general principles is problematic. Scientists love general principles, as do educators. Scientists love them because they are truths of the world and this is what canonical science seeks to discover. Educators love them because they feel that teaching truths is what education is about. Plus, they are so easy to test for. The problem is that, for students, these principles usually don't matter at all. The Pythagorean theorem is, I suppose, my favorite example of these principles. It is taught because it is there. Everyone is supposed to know it, but no one really knows why. It just doesn't come up much in life. What should be taught is how to discover such principles. Learning to make mathematical generalizations may not be a very important task for most people, but it is more valuable than learning to apply a formula when you see a right triangle. To really change education, we need to get over the need to tell students everything we know that is true. They may not care. These truths may not be so important as one might think.

What drove AI researchers to abandon this search for general principles was hard experience. Every project to build intelligent programs, no matter how limited in scope, ended up confronting the same bottleneck: To get the computer to do something interesting, it had to know a great deal about what it was trying to do. Gradually it dawned on people that if this was the functional bottleneck to building intelligent machines, then it followed that knowledge was the central component of intelligence. But not general knowledge, as had been looked for in the General Problem Solver of Newell and Simon (1972). The real issue is domain knowledge. Knowing how to fix a car does not necessarily qualify you to fix an airplane. There may be some general principles in common, but take me to a specialist any time. Specific domain knowledge is what matters when functioning in the real world. General knowledge qualifies you to be a scientist, not a practitioner.

However obvious the discovery that specific, real-world knowledge mattered might seem in retrospect, most of cognitive science (indeed most of AI) still seems determined to avoid its implications. The reason is that the prescription for AI that follows from this discovery doesn't look like science to a lot of people; it just looks like writing down what your grandmother knows. From this can you make a science?

The issue is one of "common sense" or "everyday" reasoning versus "formalistic reasoning." AI researchers wanted to build programs that solved formal problems, or taught LISP programming, or played chess, because they saw these feats as signs of intelligence. Yet, it turned out to be harder to get programs to speak English as well as a five-year-old than it was to have them solve the Tower of Hanoi problem. What is wrong with this picture? The issue is content. To build an intelligent machine, one needs to uncover copious amounts of everyday, real-world, common-sense kinds of information. This doesn't seem like science to most people. Similarly, teaching, or rather helping children discover, the everyday information they really need, just doesn't seem like formal education. This attitude pervades education today, which is a real problem.

The following conflict remains: On the one hand, we have Chomsky arguing that, for example, the common-sense theory of human intentionality necessary to understand the behavior of people around us isn't in the domain of psychology and should be left to literature. Roughly speaking, he endorses the computational view of the mind but rejects as pointless and unscientific, efforts to bring mental content into the computational realm. On the other hand, although Searle clearly endorses the notion that mental content is the essence of intelligence, he believes that creating a precise model of intelligence is impossible. Thus he shares Chomsky's view that efforts to bring mental content into the computational realm are pointless, but for an entirely different reason: not because mental content is "unscientific," but because its essence would be completely missed by such an enterprise. In sum, the attempt to create a clear model of the content *and* functionality of the mind is condemned both for attempting to do semantics at all, and also for doing such a poor job of it. Simply trying to find out how memory works, how a person can learn to do something by building a model of that behavior, is quite often condemned as "unscientific."

Functional Constraints on the Mind

The key issue underlying the discussion of the last section is *functionality*. That is, implicit in my discussion is the notion that no intellectual capacity can be adequately studied without considering the purposes to which it is put by the organism that possesses it. This is exactly what Chomsky denies explicitly, and Searle implicitly. Chomsky simply doesn't care how memory works – he thinks that language somehow can be described apart from memory issues. This is because he doesn't care about language use, he is simply interested in general principles of language. The schools, in picking up this bias, teach rules about the formal properties of language instead of simply teaching people to use language better. It is an issue of "knowing how" versus "knowing that."

Consider, for example, our ability to create novel sentences. The need to reflect this capacity forms the cornerstone of generative linguistics. And yet, it would be very surprising indeed if the generative nature of language were an isolated phenomenon in mental life. After all, if we never had anything new to say, then a simple table, from which we could choose from all possible combinations of words, would in fact suffice to represent the mapping between thought and language. From a functional perspective, therefore, the generative nature of language is necessitated by, and indeed is merely a reflection of, the generative nature of thought itself. It is not our ability to create new sentences that needs explanation – it is our ability to create new thoughts.

The special contribution of artificial intelligence is often supposed to be its emphasis on the creation of process models of mental abilities. In AI, we actually try to build machines that talk, understand, tell stories, and so on. In asking how to do these feats on a computer, we come up with theories of human cognition, like the idea of a dynamic memory. However, this is only part of the story. In fact, what makes AI unique among the cognitive sciences is its stress on functionality – or the idea that the chief constraints on the mind, and hence on models of the mind, must be functional, and must arise from the need to perform realistic cognitive tasks. This is what most differentiates AI models from those produced by the fields of psychology and linguistics. After all, researchers in these fields often build process models of mental phenomena, and sometimes they even implement these models on computers. Yet, why aren't they AI models?

The reason, quite simply, is that they are models of mental phenomena and not of mental abilities. In the hands of linguists and psychologists, computational modeling is simply a novel variant on what is termed, in those fields at least, *mathematical modeling*. It is basically curve fitting by another means. The point of such models is simply to generate the phenomenon of interest. It doesn't matter in the least whether the resulting programs are capable of performing an intelligent task of any sort. The question, What is this program for? makes no sense when applied to these models. From the perspective of computer science, however, this is the very first question that must always be answered about a program.

Because of this fundamental difference in point of view about what computational modeling is, computer scientists working on the problem of artificial intelligence often feel, when contemplating "computer models" produced by other cognitive scientists, that they are looking at Rube Goldberg machines: Computations fly fast and furious, but it is hard to figure out what the point of it all is.

One result of AI's emphasis on functionality is to direct our attention in completely different directions than the focus of cognitive scientists in other disciplines. When a linguist or psychologist looks at a topic in cognitive science, the question of interest is often, What makes this different from other cognitive phenomena? It is more or less assumed that the essence of the phenomenon lies in what makes it unique, that concentrating on this issue is the key to understanding the nature of the phenomenon. From a taxonomic point of view, this is of course a sensible notion. From a functional point of view, however, it is much less sensible. For from a functional perspective, if our goal is to build a model that is capable of carrying out some intelligent task, the issue isn't, How is this task different from all other tasks? but, What is the bottleneck problem here? What is it that makes this task difficult? Often, we find that the underlying functional issue is the same between given tasks, even if the tasks look superficially quite different. Thus, whether the task is learning or language understanding, the key problem is how to represent new ideas in terms of old ones.

What Is Intelligence?

Intelligence is fairly difficult to assess. Many scholars have endeavored to do so by devising different sorts of tests to measure it. But no matter how effective these tests may be, and they are by and large not very effective, they consistently leave us pondering the exceptions. There are always people we know who do poorly at IQ tests yet are "musical geniuses" or "idiot savants." Or, there are people who do well at IQ tests yet seem like idiots socially or even intellectually when we take them to a turf not their own. So, apart from the widely debated issues of cultural bias, and dependence upon multiple choice tests and other intellectual anomalies, a serious issue remains in intelligence assessment, namely, since we don't really know what intelligence is, how can we assess it?

People normally assess the intelligence of one another through conversation. When people understand us readily, they seem intelligent; when they fail to do so, we think less well of them. The mechanisms of intelligence are somewhat more elusive. We can detect a clever insight, but we cannot give a formula for attaining such insights. We understand when we have been understood, but we do not understand how we understand. We can appreciate eloquence, but we cannot define it. We admire analogies from one domain that can be exploited in another, but we cannot tell a computer how to make such analogies.

The nature of intelligence is only barely understood by scientists for whom its nature is of direct concern. Scientists who ought to be most concerned with the subject of intelligence are really most involved in claiming which entities have it, which do not, and which never could. Or they are concerned with elaborating small details of isolated aspects of the process of intelligent behavior – all the while ignoring the functionality and intention of those very aspects.

Darwinian Artificial Intelligence

The issues of intelligence and intelligent behavior were of central scientific concern to Darwin, who needed to state a position on the intelligence of animals as part of his arguments about the descent of man from other species. If animals have no intelligence at all, it is much more difficult to believe that intelligent man could have naturally descended from them. Thus Darwin claimed that "there is no fundamental difference between man and the higher mammals in their mental faculties." (It seems obvious that Chomsky, along with many other cognitive scientists, would disagree with this, because these theorists point to language ability as the fundamental difference between man and animals.) For that reason alone, it is interesting to look at some of Darwin's arguments.

According to Darwin, intelligence is not a uniquely human capability. Thus, one might assume that Darwin would have been comfortable with the idea of a variety of nonhuman intelligences, such as the concept of machine intelligence (from which so many of our ideas on human intelligence have been derived). One important aspect of intelligence, I have noted elsewhere, is the need to generate and answer questions. No entity can learn without generating for itself the need to know. The essence of intelligence is to be found in the need to find out more.

When Darwin writes that "all animals feel Wonder and many exhibit Curiosity," he is putting this forward as the key to the "intellectual faculties" of animals. When he notes that "hardly any faculty is more important for the intellectual progress of man than Attention," he is making the point that in order to learn, one must first know where to look, and then arguing how animals can focus their attention in just this way. Darwin tells a story to illustrate these issues, about a baboon that adopted a kitten and, upon being scratched by the kitten, located the claws of the kitten and bit them off. Darwin used this story to point out that animals cannot have all their behavior attributable to instinct. What kind of instinct would this have been for the baboon? It seems clear enough that the baboon figured out what to do in a situation that was seemingly quite novel. Elsewhere I have written that the cornerstone of the human intelligence process is "the understanding cycle," a cycle of expectation failure, followed by curiosity, followed by an explanation derived from a prior, similar experience by virtue of reminding, followed finally by a revised generalization that will itself fail at some later time – thereby coming full circle through the cycle. The baboon's behavior could be explained in this way, as I feel certain Darwin would have agreed.

Darwin also refers to an elephant in the zoo who "blows through his trunk on the ground beyond (an object) so that the current reflected on all sides may drive the object within reach. These actions of the elephant... can hardly be attributed to instinct or inherited habit, as they would be of little use... in a state of nature." Darwin is arguing, in essence, that figuring something out for yourself is what intelligence is all about. If elephants and baboons are intelligent in that they can figure things out for themselves, then this helps us see that the real question for the creation of intelligent entities (such as intelligent machines and intelligent children) is whether we can enable them to figure things out for themselves, rather than spend our time trying to determine whether or not they are already endowed with this property. In other words, we must ask, Can they learn, and can they be capable of original thought?

The fields of education and AI are asking the same question. For Chomsky and Searle, this is a moot point. They are concerned, instead, with describing aspects of knowledge that are already there in the heads of these creatures, and asserting the specificity of these aspects with respect to one species or another. For Darwin, it would seem that any act of figuring things out for itself would qualify a species as intelligent, and, I am sure, he would not have minded if sea slugs shared this quality to some extent with human beings.

The point is that intelligence is mutable and it is based very much on the acquisition of content. This content is about functionality and performance, not competence. To affect mental processes, we must understand them. We cannot afford the luxury of assuming that they have some mystical properties that make them unanalyzable, or worthy of consideration only if they follow certain general mathematical principles. We must be prepared to discover that intelligence is based upon a hodge-podge of special-purpose behaviors that are learned over time and self-modified through necessity.

What Is Teachable?

The question of what is, and what is not, teachable is significant for two quite different reasons. From a scientific point of view, the question of learnability is quite often the hallmark of the underlying assumptions of a psychological theory. The generative linguists (e.g., Chomsky) came to the somewhat remarkable conclusion in the late seventies that the grammars they proposed were not learnable, that these grammars were innate. They might, of course, have considered the possibility that their theory was wrong, but they failed to do so. That they failed to do so indicates a very strong (if unstated) position on education, namely, that much intelligent behavior is innate and that any education that is intended to affect core abilities is wasted. They think the important stuff cannot be learned. This assumption remains very prevalent in today's educational institutions, and though not necessarily attributable to Chomsky, the ideas are not unrelated, either. Chomsky's views were often stated as being in opposition to the behaviorists, who saw the world as a set of learned stimuli and responses to stimuli. These two opposing views, innateness of complex rules versus the acquisition of simple rules, leave out the key idea that educators ought to have: namely, that education is about the acquisition of complex rules and, thus, that the real issue is in getting children to engage in complex activities that can foster the learning of complex behaviors.

For example, one of the key fallouts from this previous conception of education in American society is attributable to the Educational Testing Service (ETS) and other standardized testing agencies. ETS administers two very important exams that, for all practical purposes, determine the life of every prospective college student: the Scholastic Aptitude Test (SAT) and the individual Achievement Tests. The premise of the SAT is that one cannot study for it. It is supposed to test basic aptitudes. The fact that an entire industry has grown around tutoring for the SAT to do exactly that which ETS claims is impossible to do, does not sway ETS from its position. The Achievement Tests, on the other hand, are supposed to measure what one has learned and hence what is learnable.

Thus, ETS has defined the difference between abilities that are innate and those that can be acquired. Where on this spectrum would something like the Pythagorean theorem go, would you suppose? It is a little surprising to discover that a question that involves knowing the formula derived from this theorem appears on virtually every SAT test. It would seem odd to claim that this theorem is innate, but ETS does claim that one cannot be tutored for the basic aptitudes measured by the SAT. All this may leave us somewhat confused.

The traditional view of intelligence (and modern linguistic theory is completely in line with this tradition) is that knowledge plays a passive rather than an active role. It is simply "grist for the mill." Serious psychological effort must, then, be directed at the mill, not the grist, for it is the mill that captures the universal, necessary essence of intelligence. Moreover, the mill has a clear mechanical structure to be studied and evaluated, whereas the grist just assumes whatever form you put it in. In sum, knowledge is simply too contingent, too atomized, too undifferentiated, to form the core of any serious psychological theory.

One could of course take an entirely different approach to knowledge. Individual facts, considered individually, will necessarily look atomized and entirely contingent. But facts do not arise individually in the world, nor do they exist that way in the mind. Facts, taught in the right way, can be coherent. They can form the very substance of, and be derived from, our systematic theories of the world. We can neither understand, remember, nor utilize isolated facts that we cannot relate in a systematic way to a larger body of knowledge. It is therefore these "larger bodies of knowledge" that must form the core of our study of intelligence. Your grandmother doesn't just know how to make pot roast. She has an unstated theory of cooking, and she uses this theory to understand new recipes, to know how and when it is permissible to substitute ingredients, and to understand why something went wrong with a recipe. In sum, she uses this theory to learn and to adapt.

Cooking may seem like a frivolous matter for cognitive scientists to concentrate on (depending on how you feel about food, of course). But if we look at other competencies people have, such as communicating, planning, making decisions, or designing, it has to be admitted that these form a large part of everyday intelligent behavior. The question is, are these competencies knowledge based in the same way as cooking? And, if so, is formal reasoning really the issue in intelligence or should we be concerned with more everyday activities? After all, isn't the real-world use of knowledge the real issue in intelligence?

It is fairly obvious that some aspects of what is commonly referred to as intelligent behavior are inherently unteachable, whereas others are teachable. The determination of which is the case in particular is somewhat elusive, partly because there is no clear agreement on what constitutes intelligent behavior in the first place. Let me therefore outline some aspects of intelligence that we have learned are critical to intelligent behavior in the sense that no machine could exhibit much intelligence without them. Then, I shall discuss which of these abilities are likely to be human specific. Finally, I will speculate about the teachability of these abilities.

Given the importance of MOPs and scriptlets in human behavior, the key questions concerning them are, Do machines need them in order to exhibit intelligent behavior? Are humans born with them? Do animals have them? Do either humans or other animals learn them? And, can they be taught, to either humans or machines?

From the point of view of AI, the answers to these questions are straightforward. Machines come to processing as a tabula rasa, so there are no innate memory structures. However, such structures can be programmed into machines, enabling them to read and answer questions about texts that depict standard behavior, as well as enabling them to participate in such behaviors. Although there is much in human behavior that is not MOP based, there is much that is. Endowing machines with MOPs enables them to mimic that behavior.

There is no evidence that humans are born with particular memory structures, although there is a good deal of evidence to suggest that they are born with a predisposition to acquire them. Small children seem to create scriptlets at every turn, expecting events that have followed a particular sequence to repeat that sequence the next time, no matter how random the sequence really was.

Animals exhibit the same behavior, as well. They, too, establish sequences at an early age and act as if they expect these sequences to repeat. Although they do not use scriptlets for something as particularly human as language understanding, they nevertheless seem capable of acquiring scriptlets and acting in accord with them for other kinds of understanding. Such behavior has frequently been stigmatized as "just associationism," but it is difficult to understand the "just" here. Surely both animals and people learn to associate one event with another, but their recording of these associations and reliance upon them for future processing are hallmarks of intelligence. The key issue is precisely whether an entity can acquire new MOPs and scriptlets. After all, associating expectation failures with their explanations is a fairly complex mental act.

This raises the questions of innateness and learnability. Not surprisingly, Chomsky and his associates have made big issues of both of these subjects. From their perspective, any scriptlet a lower animal uses is likely to be innate, or built in, and thus would not be considered to be a sign of intelligence. However, if a scriptlet is not built in, if it is learned, and if this learning is critical for intelligence, then it would follow that intelligence is indeed enhanceable.

One memory structure that is clearly not built in is the MOP for M–AIRPLANE. After being a passenger on many flights, we come to understand such things as seat belts, baggage X-rays, boarding passes, tray tables, and luggage compartments. This understanding enables us to avoid thinking hard about what to do on a plane when we are hungry, or enables us to understand someone's comments, such as, "I couldn't sleep because of the cramped legroom." If a dog learned something about behavior on airplanes, we would certainly have to say that it knew some aspect of the airplane MOP. And, in fact, dogs do learn some of the scriptlets contained in M–AIRPLANE, constantly finding certain places to go and ways to behave that are at first novel and then repetitious. Although some MOPs and scripts may have origins in innate animal behavior, clearly some of these are learnable as well. M–AIRPLANE is a collection of small, shareable, *idiosyncratic* units of memory that are quite particular to a specific physical context. These units have been organized together in memory under an artifact of human culture called M–AIRPLANE, which is a learnable structure. It is not innate, and it is not a stimulus–response association. It is what real learning, and therefore education, must be about.

Scriptlets are learnable, as are MOPs. And, more importantly, they are teachable. Children can learn about new behaviors in new situations and can utilize that new knowledge in a variety of ways. One important way this manifests itself is in reading. If you have never been in an airplane, then you cannot easily follow the action that takes place there, especially if you are trying to read a story that assumes that you have that prior knowledge. In fact, a great deal of knowledge is needed to read nearly anything, and such knowledge really must be acquired prior to reading or else we will have large gaps in our understanding. This is important to state here because intelligence, as I define it, is a function of knowledge. One may have the capacity for intelligence but, without knowledge, nothing will become of that intelligence. Acquiring knowledge is thus at the heart of intelligence. In AI, acquiring knowledge is also the main issue. We attempt to build machines that can acquire knowledge on their own, but more often we must hand code that knowledge and place it into the machine manually.

There is no intelligent behavior that is not knowledge dependent. It follows therefore that education means providing knowledge to children. The question is, knowledge of what sort? The difference between animals and humans is in the kinds of knowledge they can acquire. We recognize, for example, that humans can acquire knowledge about mathematics, philosophy, or psychology, and animals cannot. What we fail to recognize is that just because humans *can* acquire such knowledge, it does not follow that such knowledge forms the crux of what they *should* acquire. In fact, it is such assumptions that have ruined the educational system.

It makes sense to concentrate on teaching children the kinds of knowledge they must acquire in order to be intelligent. Similarly, in order to make a machine intelligent, we do not need to teach it about philosophy or mathematics. Machines will never be intelligent unless they learn to do things on their own and learn from the doing of those things. Spoon-feeding them facts does not help. The same is true for children.

We need to teach machines MOPs, how to generalize, how to abandon a MOP, how to understand what is the same and what is different, how to characterize an experience, how to deal with an exception. In other words, we need to teach them to *do*. What is the difference in teaching children? There is no difference. Real-world knowledge that enables an entity to do and to learn from doing is the issue in either case. This knowledge is what is really necessary for intelligence, and yet this is the thing that is consistently left out of the curriculum by the school system. The school system simply ignores functional knowledge. Why is this left out? Two important reasons come to mind. First, educators do not know enough about human psychology and about the lessons learned from AI to put them into the curriculum. Second, the philosophy of the Chomskys and the Searles of the world implicitly prevents these things from being seen as worthwhile, much less critical subjects.

The major lesson to be learned from AI involves issues of the kinds of knowledge upon which intelligence depends. To make children more intelligent, that is, to endow them with more intelligent behavior, which I take as the ultimate purpose of education, we must take seriously the lessons of AI. At the same time, as I've been discussing here, we must also recognize the contributions of philosophy.

Drawing Conclusions

What is it that intelligent humans know, that they should endeavor to teach their children? Here are some of my favorite kinds of knowledge to be acquired:

- **Scriptlets, MOPs, and TOPs**

Children need memory structures. They acquire them simply by living and functioning in the world. They can't help but learn from their experiences. This leaves two questions for educators. First, what kinds of experiences do children not naturally have that would be valuable for them to have, from the point of view of what we hope they will learn? Second, what experiences do they naturally have that they do not fully comprehend or effectively reflect upon, that they would learn better from if there were teaching available? Schooling must be designed around precisely these questions.

- **Connections between events**

When children experience an event, they may not understand how it is related to some other experience that they might have had or that others might have had before them. Good teaching helps students make connections between their own lives and the lives of others, and between events currently being processed and those they have previously processed.

- **How to see an event as "same as"**

To understand the world, we must be able to predict with some accuracy what will happen next. To form effective predictions, we must learn how events taking place in different places at different times can be seen as the same. This is simple enough for recognizing when we are in a restaurant situation, but much harder for recognizing "imperialism" when we see it. Good teaching helps students appreciate similarity across contexts.

- **Outcome prediction**

The key issue is prediction. Explicitly teaching prediction enables students to learn to become good decision makers. We cannot learn to predict without some real experience; the job of the teacher is to provide that experience (not vicariously, if at all possible). Children need to do things, and to learn to think about what they have done and why it worked out the way it did. To do this well, they must have experience planning in a complex environment, and reflecting upon the complexities of achieving their goals. This requires a careful attention on the part of the teacher to making sure the goals children are trying to achieve are ones they are truly interested in achieving.

- **Abstraction**

Underlying these kinds of knowledge is the process of abstraction. One cannot generalize without abstracting common elements from different events. One cannot recognize the applicability of a plan without generalizing between situations. Abstraction is the highest form of thinking, but we cannot teach it directly. Rather, students need to reflect on commonalities, to discuss abstractions they see, or to hypothesize. Again, there is a dependence upon real-world experiences and upon real-world goals that drive those experiences.

- **Self-awareness**

One of the key real-world experiences we can examine is our own thinking process. This is very hard to learn to do, and indeed most people are quite bad at it. We often don't know why we do what we do, and we fail to understand what we want and what we should do to get what we want. This self-reflection ought to be the stuff of schooling because it is so important to all the other processes and to becoming a healthy person .

- **How to understand scriptlet and MOP violation**

When scriptlets and MOPs fail to predict behavior correctly, we need to know what has gone wrong. Quite often we resort to the idea that someone else has made a mistake and that we can simply ignore what has gone awry. Children need to understand that their preconceptions can be wrong and that they must be constantly vigilant to avoid assuming that the memory structures they have are the same ones everyone else has. We can change our own conceptions only when we are prepared to admit they were in error.

- **Exception handling**

Seeing exceptions as things worthy of interest is what separates the curious from the self-satisfied. We need to account for exceptions. Indeed, we need to revel in them. Appreciating differences and explaining them is part of what intellectual growth is all about.

- **Recovery from failure**

We cannot let failure get us down. Lack of understanding can be a beautiful thing because it allows for creative thought. Students need to learn to revel in their failures. Having things not work out the way you expected is what starts the creative juices flowing. School should be about causing expectation failures and helping students to recover well.

- **Case absorption**

Knowledge resides in cases (and in interconnected memory structures), not in facts. Students need to learn cases. They need to have a library of experiences to draw upon and to examine when they are looking to generalize, to predict, to abstract, and to explain. We need to learn cases from our own experiences and also from the experience of others. Teaching cases is an art, and it is one teachers need to learn to do effectively. Teachers need to be good storytellers, and they need to help students become good story analyzers. A student with a large set of cases is prepared to understand the world in all its complexity.

286

- **Generalization**

Obviously I believe that generalization is the key to understanding. Oliver Wendell Holmes said that "no generalization is worth a damn, including this one." It is a quote I have always liked. We are taught to avoid generalizations, when in fact we ought to be taught to make them. We understand the world through our various attempts to make and to abandon generalizations.

- **Explanation**

All of the processes I've been discussing depend upon explanations. We explain the world around us all the time as we create the memory structures that contain those explanations. Teaching children to accept the explanations of others and then later to venture out and make explanations of their own is what real teaching is all about. When we stop creating new explanations, when we are self-satisfied and rely upon all the old explanations we were taught or those we created for ourselves when we were young, that is when we have stopped learning. Good teaching and effective schooling depend upon putting students in situations that require explanation and then letting students come up with explanations on their own. Being wrong doesn't matter as much as learning to rely upon one's own thought processes. Schools stress being right. They should stress having an opinion of one's own that is founded on solid thinking.

The more intelligent a person is, the better he is at all of these skills, and it is impossible to acquire new knowledge in a useful way without having these skills. The fact that, in general, we do not teach the basic stuff of human intelligence, the stuff that allows us to acquire, absorb, and integrate knowledge, comes from the fact that the school curriculum was designed when no one understood what this was and how it works. We know a lot more now. It is time to rethink what we teach, why we teach, and the way we teach.

There is also, of course, another set of behaviors and skills that are important in determining intelligence and knowledge acquisition and that are less easy to enumerate. This set includes playfulness, interest, attention, perception, rule breaking, and individuality. These behaviors and skills are idiosyncratic. They are critical in the acquisition of new knowledge, and it is differences in these arenas that account for many of the differences in human intelligence and the ability to learn. These reflect a given student's personal characteristics and his particular learning style. It is, of course, possible to enhance these capabilities to a certain extent, but one must recognize their significance first.

In short, we must teach students to absorb and analyze their experiences. We must value their observations, generalizations, and creative points of view. We need to deemphasize the idea that there are right answers and to take careful heed of the idea that any individual has his own way of seeing the world. We must come to understand that human memory has a wonderful, mutable quality and that a teacher's job is to help memory evolve and grow.

References

Abelson, R. 1980. Common sense knowledge representations. *De Psycholoog,*
15, 431–449.

Adams, L.T., and Worden, P.E. 1986. Script development and memory organization in preschool and elementary school children. *Discourse Processes,*
9, 149–166.

Ames, C.A. 1990. Motivation: What teachers need to know. *Teachers College
Record, 91,* 409–421. Cited in J. Bruer, 1993, *Schools for Thought: A Science
of Learning in the Classroom.* Cambridge, Mass.: MIT Press.

Anderson, S.J., and Conway, M.A. 1993. Investigating the structure of autobiographical memories. *Journal of Experimental Psychology: Learning,
Memory and Cognition, 19(5),* 1178–1196.

Argyris, C. 1985. *Action Science.* San Francisco: Jossey-Bass.

Argyris, C. 1993. *Knowledge for Action.* San Francisco: Jossey-Bass.

Argyris, C., and Schon, D. 1996. *Organizational Learning II: Theory, Method, and
Practice.* New York: Addison-Wesley.

Bain, R. 1986. Case-based reasoning: A computer model of subjective assessment. Ph.D. thesis, Department of Computer Science, Yale University.

Barsalou, L.W., and Ross, B.H. 1986. The roles of automatic and strategic processing in sensitivity to superordingate and property frequency. *Journal
of Experimental Psychology: Learning, Memory and Cognition, 12,* 116–135.

Bauer, P.J., and Mandler, J.M. 1990. Remembering what happened next: Very
young children's recall of event sequences. In R. Fivush and J.A.
Hudson (eds.), *Knowing and Remembering in Young Children,* pp. 9–30.
New York: Cambridge University Press.

Bédard, J., and Chi, M.T.H. 1992. Expertise. *Psychological Science, 1,* 135–139.

Berntsen, D. 1996. Involuntary autobiographical memories. *Applied Cognitive
Psychology, 10,* 435–454.

Birnbaum, L. 1985. Lexical ambiguity as a touchstone for theories of language analysis. *Proceedings of the Ninth IJCAI,* 815–820.

Bower, G.H. 1978. Experiments on story comprehension and recall. *Discourse
Processes, 1,* 211–232.

Bower, G.H., Black, J.B., and Turner, T.J. 1979. Scripts in memory for text.
Cognitive Psychology, 11, 177–220.

Bransford, J., Franks, J., Vye, N., and Sherwood, R. 1989. New approaches to
instruction: Because wisdom can't be told. In S. Vosniadou and A.
Ortony, *Similarity and Analogical Reasoning.* New York: Cambridge
University Press.

Brinkerhoff, R., and Gill, S. 1994. *The Learning Alliance: Systems Thinking in Human Resource Development*. San Francisco: Jossey-Bass.

Brown, A.L., and Campione, J.C. 1990. Communities of learning and thinking or a context by any other name. *Human Development, 21*, 108–125.

Brown, A.L., and Campione, J.C. 1994. Guided discovery in a community of learners. In K. McGilly (ed.), *Classroom Lessons: Integrating Cognitive Theory and Classroom Practice*, pp. 229–270. Cambridge, Mass.: MIT Press/Bradford.

Bruer, J. 1993. *Schools for Thought: A Science of Learning in the Classroom*. Cambridge, Mass.: MIT Press.

Buchanan, B.G., and Shortliffe, E.H. (eds.). 1984. *Rule-based Expert Systems: The MYCIN Experiments of the Stanford Heuristic Programming Project*. Reading, Mass.: Addison-Wesley.

Carbonell, J. 1979. *Subjective Understanding: Computer Models of Belief Systems*. Technical Report 150. New Haven, Conn.: Yale University, Department of Computer Science.

Cheney, D., and Seyfarth, R. 1990. *How Monkeys See the World*. Chicago: University of Chicago Press.

Chi, M.T.H., Bassok, M., Lewis, M., Reimann, P., and Glaser, R. 1989. Learning problem solving skills from studying examples. *Cognitive Science, 13*, 145–182.

Chi, M.T.H., Feltovich, P.J., and Glaser, R. 1981. Categorization and representation of physics problems by experts and novices. *Cognitive Science, 5*, 121–152.

Chi, M.T.H., and VanLehn, K.A. 1991. The content of physics self-explanations. *The Journal of the Learning Sciences, 1*, 69–105.

Chomsky, N. 1965. *Aspects of the Theory of Syntax*. Cambridge, Mass.: MIT Press.

Chomsky, N. 1980. Rules and representations (including responses). *The Behavioral and Brain Sciences, 3*, 1–61.

Cognition and Technology Group at Vanderbilt. 1991. The Jasper Series: A generative approach to improving mathematical thinking. In *This Year in School Science*. American Association for the Advancement of Science. Cited in J. Bruer, 1993, *Schools for Thought: A Science of Learning in the Classroom*. Cambridge, Mass: MIT Press.

Collins, A., 1991. The role of computer technology In restructuring schools. *Phi Delta Kappan, Sept. 1991*, 28–36.

Conway, M.A., and Bekerian, D.A. 1987. Organization in autobiographical memory. *Memory and Cognition, 15(2)*, 119–132.

Crowder, R.G. 1976. *Principles of Learning and Memory*. Hillsdale, N.J.: Lawrence Erlbaum and Associates.

Cullingford, R. 1978. *Script Application: Computer Understanding of Newspaper Stories*. Technical Report 116. New Haven, Conn.: Yale University, Department of Computer Science.

De Graef, P., Christaens, D., and d'Ydewalle, G. 1990. Perceptual effects of scene context on object identification. *Psychological Research, 52*, 317–329.

DeJong, G.F. 1977. *Skimming Newspaper Stories by Computer*. Technical Report 104. New Haven, Conn.: Yale University, Department of Computer Science.

Dennett, D. 1991. *Consciousness Explained.* London: Penguin.

Dewey, J. 1916. *Democracy and Education.* New York: Macmillan Company.

diSessa, A.A. 1982. Unlearning Aristotelian physics: A study of knowledge-based learning. *Cognitive Science, 6,* 37–5.

Dweck, C.S. 1986. Motivational processes affecting learning. *American Psychologist 41,* 1040–1048.

Dweck, C.S. 1989. Motivation. In A. Lesgold and R. Glaser (eds.), *Foundations for a Psychology of Education.* Hillsdale, N.J.: Lawrence Erlbaum and Associates.

Dyer, M.O., and Lehnert, W.G. 1980. *Memory Organization and Search Processes for Narratives.* Technical Report 175. New Haven, Conn.: Yale University, Department of Computer Science.

Erman, L.D., Hayes-Roth, F., Lesser, V., and Reddy, D. 1980. The HEARSAY II speech understanding system: Integrating knowledge to resolve uncertainty. *Computing Surveys, 12(2),* 213–253.

Farrar, M.J., and Goodman, G.S. 1990. Developmental differences in the relation between scripts and episodic memory: Do they exist? In R. Fivush and J.A. Hudson (eds.), *Knowing and Remembering in Young Children,* pp. 30–65. New York: Cambridge University Press.

Farrar, M.J., and Goodman, G.S. 1992. Developmental changes in event memory. *Child Development, 63,* 173–187.

Fivush, R. 1984. Learning about school: The development of kindergartners' school scripts. *Child Development, 55,* 1697–1709.

Freud, S. 1900. *The Interpretation of Dreams* (1995 translation by A.A. Brill). New York: Modern Library.

Freud, S. 1904. *The Psychopathology of Everyday Life* (1965 translation by Alan Tyson; edited by James Strachey). New York: Norton.

Galambos, J. 1986. Knowledge structures for common activities. In J. Galambos, R. Abelson and J. Black (eds.), *Knowledge Structures.* Hillsdale, N.J.: Lawrence Erlbaum and Associates.

Gallwey, W.T. 1974. *The Inner Game of Tennis.* New York: Bantam Books.

Gholson, B., Smither, D., Buhrman, A., Duncan, M.K., and Pierce, K.A. 1996. The sources of children's reasoning errors during analogical problem solving. *Applied Cognitive Psychology, 10,* S85–S97.

Gick, M.L., and McGarry, S.J. 1992. Learning from mistakes: Inducing analogous solution failures to a source problem produces later successes in analogical transfer. *Journal of Experimental Pscyhology: Learning, Memory and Cognition, 18,* 623–639.

Graesser, A.C. 1981. *Prose Comprehension Beyond the Word.* Berlin: Springer-Verlag.

Graesser, A.C., Baggett, W., and Williams, K. 1996. Question-driven explanatory reasoning. *Applied Cognitive Psychology, 10,* S17–S31.

Graesser, A.C., Gordon, S.E., and Sawyer, J.D. 1979. 3D recognition memory for typical and atypical actions in scripted activities: Tests of a script pointer + tag hypothesis. *Journal of Verbal Learning and Verbal Behavior, 18(3),* 319–32.

Graesser, A.C., Woll, S.B., Kowalski, D.J., and Smith, D.A. 1980. Memory for

291

typical and atypical actions in scripted activities. *Journal of Experimental Psychology: Human Learning and Memory, 6,* 503–515.

Granger, R. 1977. FOUL-UP: A program that figures out meanings of words from context. *Proceedings of the Fifth Annual Joint Conference on Artificial Intelligence,* Cambridge, Mass.

Granger, R.H. 1980. Adaptive understanding. Technical Report 171. New Haven, Conn.: Yale University, Department of Computer Science.

Hammond, K.J., Seifert, C., and Gray, K. 1991. A good match is hard to find. *The Journal of the Learning Sciences, 1(2),* 111–152.

Harel, I., and Papert, S. 1991. Software design as a learning environment. In I. Harel and S. Papert (eds.), *Constructionism: Research reports and essays 1985–1990,* pp. 41–84. Norwood, N.J.: Ablex.

Hendrix, H. 1992. *Getting the Love You Want.* New York: Harperperennial Library.

Hudson, J. 1988. Children's memory for atypical actions in script-based stories: Evidence for a disruption effect. *Journal of Experimental Child Psychology, 46,* 159–173.

Hudson, J., Fivush, R., and Kuebli, J. 1992. Scripts and episodes: The development of event memory. *Applied Cognitive Psychology, 6,* 483–505.

Hudson, J., and Nelson, K. 1983. Effects of script structure on children's story recall. *Developmental Psychology, 19(4),* 625–636.

Hudson, J., and Nelson, K. 1986. Repeated encounters of a similar kind: Effect of familiarity on children's autobiographic memory. *Cognitive Development, 1,* 253–271.

Hue, C.W., and Erickson, W. 1991. Normative studies of sequence strength and scene structure of 30 scripts. *American Journal of Psychology, 104,* 229–240.

Hull Smith, P., Arehart, D.M., Haaf, R.A., and deSaint Victor, C.M. 1989. Expectancies and memory for spatiotemporal events in 5-month-old infants. *Journal of Experimental Child Psychology, 47,* pp. 210, 235.

Jackson, S., Stratford, S., Krajcik, J., and Soloway, E. 1994. Making dynamic modeling accessible to precollege students. *Interactive Learning, 4(3),* 233–257.

Johnson, H.M., and Seifert, C. 1992. The role of predictive features in retrieving analogical cases. *Journal of Memory and Language, 31,* 648–667.

Jolly, C., and Plog, F. 1986. *Physical Anthropology and Archaeology.* New York: Knopf.

Kafai, Y., and Resnick, M. (eds.). 1986. *Constructionism in Practice: Designing, Thinking, and Learning in a Digital World.* Hillsdale, N.J.: Lawrence Erlbaum and Associates.

Kolodner, J. 1993. *Case-based Reasoning.* San Mateo, Calif.: Morgan Kaufman.

Kolodner, J.L. 1997. Educational implications of analogy. A view from case-based reasoning. *American Psychologist, 52,* 57–66.

Kolodner, J.L., and Mark, W. 1992. Guest editors' introduction: Case-based reasoning. *IEEE Expert, 7(5),* 5–6.

Kolodner, J.L., and Simpson, R.L. 1989. The MEDIATOR: Analysis of an early case-based problem solver. *Cognitive Science, 13(4),* 507–549.

Koton, P. 1989. Using experience in learning and problem solving. Ph.D. thesis, Department of Computer Science, MIT.

Lakatos, I. 1978. *The Methodology of Scientific Research Programmes*. Cambridge: Cambridge University Press.

Lampert, M. 1995. Managing the tensions in connecting students' inquiry with learning mathematics in school. In D.N. Perkins, J.L. Schwartz, M.M. West, and M.S. Wiske (eds.), *Software Goes to School*. New York: Oxford University Press.

Langer, E. 1990. *Mindfulness*. New York: Addison-Wesley.

Lebowitz, M. 1986. Concept learning in a rich input domain: Generalization-based memory. In R. Michalski, J. Carbonell, and T. Mitchell (eds.), *Machine Learning: An Artificial Intelligence Approach*, Vol. 2. Los Altos, Calif.: Morgan Kaufmann.

Lehnert, W. 1979. *Text Processing Effects and Recall Memory*. Technical Report 157. New Haven, Conn.: Yale University, Department of Computer Science.

Lindsay, R.K., Buchanan, B.G., Feigenbaum, E.A., and Lederberg, J. 1980. *Applications of Artificial Intelligence for Organic Chemistry: The DENDRAL Project*. New York: McGraw Hill.

Linn, M.C., diSessa, A., Pea, R.D., and Songer, N.B. 1994. Can research on science learning and instruction inform standards for science education? *Journal of Science Education and Technology*, 3(1), 7–15.

McCartney, K., and Nelson, K. 1981. Scripts in children's memory for stories. *Discourse Processes*, 4, 59–70.

McDermott, J. 1982. R1: A rule based configurer of computer systems. *Artificial Intelligence*, 19, 39–88.

McKoon, G., and Ratcliff, R., 1992. Inference during reading. *Psychological Review*, 99(3).

McKoon, G., Ratcliff, R., and Seifert, C. 1989. Making the connection: Generalized knowledge structures in story understanding. *The Journal of Memory and Language*, 28, 711–734.

Medin, D.L., and Edelson, S.M. 1988. Problem structure and the use of base-rate information from experience. *Journal of Experimental Psychology: General*, 117, 68–85.

Metcalfe, J. 1993. Novelty monitoring, metacognition, and control in a composite holographic associative recall model: Implications for Korsakoff amnesia. *Psychological Review*, 100(1), 3–22.

Minsky, M. 1975. A framework for representing knowledge. In P.H. Winston (ed.), *The Psychology of Computer Vision*. New York: McGraw-Hill.

Minstrell, J. 1992. Facets of student knowledge and relevant instruction. In R. Duit, F. Goldberg, and H. Niedderer (eds.), *Research in Physics Learning: Theoretical Issues and Empirical Studies*. Kiel, Germany: University of Kiel.

Murnance, R., and Levy, F. 1996. *Teaching the New Basic Skills*. New York: The Free Press.

Myles-Worsley, M., Cromer, C., and Dodd, D. 1986. Children's preschool script reconstruction: Reliance on general knowledge as memory fades. *Developmental Psychology*, 22, 22–30.

Nelson, K. 1979. How children represent their world in and out of language. In R.S. Seigler (ed.), *Children's Thinking: What Develops?* Hillsdale, N.J.: Lawrence Erlbaum and Associates.

Nelson, K., and Gruendel, J.M. 1979. At morning it's lunchtime: A scriptal view of children's dialogues. *Discourse Processes, 2,* 73–94.

Newell, A., Shaw, J., and Simon, H. 1958. Elements of a theory of human problem solving. *Psychological Review, 65,* 151–166.

Newell, A., and Simon, H. 1963. A GPS program that simulates human thought. In E.A. Feigenbaum and Feldman (eds.), *Computers and Thought,* pp. 279–296. New York: McGraw-Hill.

Newell, A., and Simon, H. 1972. *Human Problem Solving.* Englewood Cliffs, N.J.: Prentice-Hall.

Patalano, A., and Seifert, C. 1994. Memory for impasses during problem solving. *Memory and Cognition, 22,* 234–242.

Pressley, M., Symons, S., McDaniel, M., Snyder, B., and Turnure, J. 1988. Elaborative interrogation facilitates acquisition of confusing facts. *Journal of Educational Psychology, 80,* 268–278.

Ratcliff, R., and McKoon, G. 1988. A retrieval theory of priming in memory. *Psychological Review, 95,* 385–408.

Ratner, H.H., Smith, B.S., and Dion, S.A. 1986. Development of memory for events. *Journal of Experimental Child Psychology, 41,* 411–428.

Read, S.J., and Cesa, I.L. 1991. That reminds me of the time when...: Expectation failures in reminding and explanation. *Journal of Experimental Social Psychology, 27,* 1–25.

Reif, F., and Larkin, J. 1991. Cognition in scientific and everyday domains: Comparison and learning implications. *Journal of Research in Science Teaching, 28(9),* 733–760.

Reimann, P., and Chi, M.T.H. 1989. Human expertise. In K.J. Gilhooly (ed.), *Human and Machine Problem Solving,* pp. 161–191. New York: Plenum.

Reiser, B.J., Black, J.B., and Abelson, R.P. 1985. Knowledge structures in the organization and retrieval of autobiographical memories. *Cognitive Psychology, 17,* 89–137.

Resnick, L. 1987. Learning in school and out. *Educational Researcher, 16(9),* 13–20.

Riesbeck, C. 1975. Conceptual analysis. In R.C. Schank, *Conceptual Information Processing,* pp. 83–156. Amsterdam: North-Holland.

Ross, B.H. 1984. Remindings and their effects in learning a cognitive skill. *Cognitive Psychology, 16,* 317–416.

Ross, B.H. 1996a. Category learning as problem solving. *The Psychology of Learning and Motivation, 35,* 165–192.

Ross, B.H. 1996b. Category representations and the effects of interacting with instances. *Journal of Experimental Psychology: Learning, Memory and Cognition, 22,* 1249–1265.

Ross, B.H., and Kennedy, P.T. 1990. Generalizing from the use of earlier examples in problem solving. *Journal of Experimental Psychology: Learning, Memory and Cognition, 16,* 42–55.

Ross, B.H., Perkins, S.H., and Tenpenny, P.L. 1990. Reminding-based category learning. *Cognitive Psychology, 22,* 460–492.

Scardamalia, M., and Bereiter, C. 1991. Higher levels of agency for children in knowledge building: A challenge for the design of new knowledge media. *The Journal of the Learning Sciences, 1,* 37–68.

Schank, R.C. 1972. Conceptual dependency: A theory of natural language understanding. *Cognitive Psychology, 3,* 552–631.

Schank, R.C. 1975. *Conceptual Information Processing.* Amsterdam: North-Holland.

Schank, R.C. 1981. *Reading and Understanding: Teaching from the Perspective of Artificial Intelligence.* Hillsdale, N.J.: Lawrence Erlbaum and Associates.

Schank, R.C. 1986. *Explanation Patterns.* Hillsdale, N.J.: Lawrence Erlbaum and Associates.

Schank, R.C., and Abelson, R. 1975. Scripts, plans, and knowledge. *Proceedings of the Fourth International Joint Conference on Artificial Intelligence,* Tbilisi, USSR.

Schank, R.C., and Abelson, R. 1977. *Scripts, Plans, Goals and Understanding.* Hillsdale, N.J.: Lawrence Erlbaum and Associates.

Schank, R.C., and Wilensky, R. 1977. A goal-directed production system for story understanding. In *Pattern-directed Inference Systems.* New York: Academic Press.

Searle, J.R. 1983. *Intentionality, An Essay in the Philosophy of Mind.* New York: Cambridge University Press.

Searle, J.R. 1984. *Minds, Brains, and Science.* Cambridge, Mass.: Harvard University Press.

Searle, J.R. 1992. *The Rediscovery of the Mind.* Cambridge, Mass.: MIT Press.

Seifert, C. 1990. Content-based inferences in text. *The Psychology of Learning and Motivation, 25,* 103–122.

Seifert, C., Abelson, R., and McKoon, G. 1986. The role of thematic knowledge structures in reminding. In J. Galambos, R. Abelson, and J. Black (eds.), *Knowledge Structures.* Hillsdale, N.J.: Lawrence Erlbaum and Associates.

Slackman, E., and Nelson, K. 1984. Acquisition of an unfamiliar script in story form by young children. *Child Development, 55,* 329–340.

Smith, E.E., Adams, N., and Schorr, D. 1978. Fact retrieval and the paradox of interference. *Cognitive Psychology, 10,* 438–464.

Smith, J., diSessa, A., and Roschelle, J. 1993. Misconceptions reconceived: A constructivist analysis of knowledge in transition. *The Journal of The Learning Sciences, 3(2),* 115–163.

Soloway, E., Bachant, J., and Jensen, K. 1987. Assessing maintainability of XCON-in-RIME: Coping with the problems of a very large rule base. *Proceedings of AAAI-87.* Los Altos, Calif.: Morgan Kaufmann.

Spalding, T.L., and Ross, B.H. 1994. Comparison-based learning: Effects of comparing instances during category learning. *Journal of Experimental Psychology: Learning, Memory and Cognition, 20,* 1251–1263.

Stasz, C., McArthur, D., Lewis, M., and Ramsey, K. 1990. *Teaching and Learning Generic Skills for the Workplace.* Berkeley, Calif.: National Center for Research in Vocational Education, University of California, Berkeley.

Sternberg, R.J. 1991. Are we reading too much into reading comprehension tests? *Journal of Reading, 34,* 540–545.

Strauss, S., and Shilony, T. 1994. Teachers' models of children's minds. In S. Gelman and L. Hirschfeld, *Mapping the Mind: Domain Specificity in Cognition and Culture.* New York: Cambridge University Press.

Trzebinski, J., and Richards, K. 1986. The role of goal categories in person impression. *Journal of Experimental Social Psychology, 22,* 216–227.

Tversky, A., and Kahneman, D. 1981. The framing of decisions and the psychology of choice. *Science, 211,* 453–458.

Watkins, K.E., and Marsick, V.J. 1993. *Sculpting the Learning Organization.* San Francisco: Jossey-Bass.

Wattenmaker, W.D. 1992. Relational properties and memory-based category construction. *Journal of Experimental Psychology, Learning, Memory and Cognition, 18,* 1125–1138.

Wilensky, R. 1978. *Understanding Goal-based Stories.* Technical Report 140. New Haven, Conn.: Yale University, Department of Computer Science.

Wiley, J., and Voss, J. 1996. The effects of "playing historian" on learning history. *Applied Cognitive Psychology, 10,* S63–S72.

Williams, J.P. 1993. Comprehension of students with and without learning disabilities: Identification of narrative themes and idiosyncratic text representations. *Journal of Educational Psychology, 85,* 631–641.

Further Reading

Abbott, V., and Black, J.B. 1980. *The Representation of Scripts in Memory.* Cognitive Science Technical Report 5. New Haven, Conn.: Yale University, Cognitive Science Program.

Abelson, R. 1973. The structure of belief systems. In R.C. Schank and K.M. Colby (eds.), *Computer Models of Thought and Language.* San Francisco, Calif.: Freeman.

Abelson, R. 1976. Script processing in attitude formation and decision making. In J. S. Carroll and J. W. Payne (eds.), *Cognition and Social Behavior.* Hillsdale, N.J.: Lawrence Erlbaum and Associates.

Barron, B.J., Schwartz, D.J., Vye, N.J., Moore, A., Petrosino, A., Zech, L., and Bransford, J. 1986. Doing with understanding: Lessons from research on problem- and project-based learning. Session 21.35 AERA Annual Meeting, San Diego, Calif.

Buchanan, B.G., Smith, D.H., White, W.C., Gritter, R.I., Feigenbaum, E.A., Lederberg, J., and Djerassi, C. 1976. Automatic rule formation in mass spectrometry by means of the Meta-Dendral program. *American Chemical Society, 98.*

Burton, R., Seely Brown, J., and Fischer, G. 1984. Skiing as a model of instruction. In B. Rogoff and J. Lave (eds.), *Everyday Cognition: Its Development in Social Context.* Cambridge, Mass.: Harvard University Press.

Charniak, E. 1977. A framed painting: The representation of a common sense fragment. *Cognitive Science, 1,* 355–394.

Cohen, D.K. 1988. Educational technology and school organization. In R.S.

Nickerson (ed.), *Technology and Education: Looking toward 2020*. Hillsdale, N.J.: Lawrence Erlbaum and Associates.

Davis, R. 1976. *Application of Meta Level Knowledge to the Construction, Maintenance and Use of Large Knowledge Bases*. Technical Report AIM-283. Stanford University, Palo Alto, Calif.: Artificial Intelligence Laboratory.

Duchastel, P.C. 1990. Cognitive design for instructional design. *Instructional Science, 19(6)*, 437–444.

DeJong, G.F. 1979. Prediction and substantiation: A new approach to natural language processing. *Cognitive Science, 3*, 251–273.

DeJong, G.F. 1979. *Skimming Stories in Real Time: An Experiment in Integrated Understanding*. Technical Report 158. New Haven, Conn.: Yale University, Department of Computer Science.

Eckert, P. 1989. *Jocks and Burnouts: Social Categories and Identity in the High School*. New York: Teachers College Press.

Feigenbaum, E.A. 1977. The art of artificial intelligence: I. Themes and case studies of knowledge engineering. *Proceedings of the Fifth International Joint Conference on Artificial Intelligence*, Cambridge, Mass.

Fivush, R., and Slackman, E. 1986. The acquisition and development of scripts. In K. Nelson (ed.), *Event Knowledge: Structure and Function in Development*, pp. 71–96. Hillsdale, N.J.: Lawrence Erlbaum and Associates.

Fivush, R., Kuebli, J., and Clubb, P. 1992. The structure of events and event representations: A developmental analysis. *Child Development, 63*, 188–201.

Hammond, K.J., Fasciano, M.J., Fu, D.D., and Converse, T. 1996. Actualized intelligence: Case-based agency in practice. *Applied Cognitive Psychology, 10*, S73–S83.

Kolodner, J.L. 1980. *Retrieval and Organizational Strategies in Conceptual Memory: A Computer Model*. Technical Report 187. New Haven, Conn.: Yale University, Department of Computer Science.

Kolodner, J. 1981. Organization and retrieval in a conceptual memory for events. *Proceedings of the Seventh International Joint Conference on Artificial Intelligence*.

Kolodner, J.L. 1983. Maintaining organization in a dynamic long-term memory. *Cognitive Science, 7(4)*.

Kolodner, J.L. 1983. Reconstructive memory: A computer model. *Cognitive Science, 7(4)*.

Langer, E. 1998. *The Power of Mindful Learning*. New York: Addison-Wesley.

Lebowitz, M. 1980. *Generalization and Memory in an Integrated Understanding System*. Technical Report 186. New Haven, Conn.: Yale University, Department of Computer Science.

Malt, B.C., Ross, B.H., and Murphy, G.L. 1995. Predicting features for members of natural categories when categorization is uncertain. *Journal of Experimental Psychology: Learning, Memory and Cognition, 21*, 646–661.

Nilsson, N. 1980. *Principles of Artificial Intelligence*. Palo Alto, Calif.: Tioga.

Rosch, F., and Mervis, C. 1978. Family resemblances: Studies in the internal structure of categories. *Cognitive Psychology, 1*, 573–605.

Ross, B., and Bradshaw G. 1994. Encoding effects of remindings. *Memory and Cognition, 22,* 591–605.

Sacerdoti, E.D. 1975. *A Structure for Plans and Behavior.* Technical Report 119. Menlo Park, Calif.: SRI Artificial Intelligence Center.

SCANS Commission. 1991. *What Work Requires of Schools: A SCANS Report for America 2000.* Washington, D.C.: The Secretary's Commission on Achieving Necessary Skills, U.S. Department of Labor.

Scardamalia, M., Bereiter, C., McLean, R.S., Swallow, J., and Woodruff, E. 1989. Computer supported intentional learning environments. *Journal of Educational Computing Research, 5,* 51–68.

Schallert, D.L. 1991. The contribution of psychology to teaching the language arts. In J. Flood, J.M. Jensen, D. Lapp, and J.R. Squire (eds.), *Handbook of Research on Teaching the English Language Arts,* pp. 30–39. New York: Macmillan.

Schank, R.C. 1978. *Interestingness: Controlling Inferences.* Technical Report 145. New Haven, Conn.: Yale University, Department of Computer Science.

Schank, R.C. 1980. Language and memory. *Cognitive Science, 4,* 243–284.

Songer, N. 1996. Exploring learning opportunities in coordinated network-enhanced classrooms: A case of kids as global scientists. *The Journal of The Learning Sciences, 5(4),* 297–327.

VanLehn, K. 1988. Toward a theory of impasse driven learning. In H. Mandl and A. Lesgold (eds.), *Learning Issues for Intelligent Tutoring Systems,* pp. 19–41. New York: Springer-Verlag.

VanLehn, K. 1989. Rule acquisition events in the discovery of problem solving strategies. In *Proceedings of the 11th Annual Conference of the Cognitive Science Society.* Hillsdale, N.J.: Lawrence Erlbaum and Associates.

Wilkes, A.L., and Leatherbarrow, M. 1988. Editing episodic memory following the identification of error. *Quarterly Journal of Experimental Psychology, 40A(2),* 361–387.

Index

abstraction 122, 285
Advise Project 169
anomaly 93–5, 153
artificial intelligence 206, 209, 212,
    214–15, 228–30, 253, 272–6,
    279, 281, 283–4
  reseachers 271, 273–4
assessment 257
  of intelligence 277
authentic teaching 266

behavior modification 159
beliefs 94, 96–8

case-based reasoning 174, 212,
    215, 219–23, 227–8, 231–2
case-based teaching 261
cases 174, 177, 191, 194, 200,
    219–20, 222–5, 232, 247, 286
  within goal-based scenario 259,
    261, 264–5
Chomsky, Noam 271–2, 274–5,
    277, 279, 282
*Community Partnering for
    Environmental Results* 168
competence–performance distinc-
    tion 271
competencies 271
computational modeling 276
conscious knowledge 196–7,
    201, 203, 205, 225–8, 240–1,
    243–6

courses 181–2, 188, 258–9
curriculum 184–5, 187–9, 193, 195,
    257–9, 261, 263–9, 284

Darwin, on intelligence 277–9
distance learning 208
domain, within goal-based sce-
    nario 260
dreaming 238–40, 247

editing 251
  process 252
educational design 209–10
Educational Testing Service 280
Emerging Economies 171
episodic memory 22, 27, 47, 56,
    77, 102, 116
epistemics 228–9
  nonconscious 207
expectation failure 17, 31, 56, 59,
    74, 76, 84, 94, 108, 111, 113,
    117, 125, 130, 151, 154, 156–7,
    159–61, 164–5, 173, 228, 269,
    271, 282
expectations 79–80, 154–6, 162,
    238, 241
expert systems 215, 225, 230–1
experts 167
explanations 58–60, 62–3, 67, 74,
    153, 164, 269, 287
  kinds of 68–70
  process 152–3

extensibility 14

facts 191, 195, 197, 209, 280–1, 286
  within goal-based scenario 259
failure-driven learning 166
failure-driven memory 45, 55
frame selection problem 139
Freud, Sigmund 253–4
FRUMP 10, 129
functionality 275–6

general problem solver (GPS)
  216–18, 228, 273
goal-based scenario (GBS) 181,
  188–90, 259, 264–6, 268–9
  natural 267
  artificial 267
goals 61, 139, 147, 156, 166, 175–6,
  188–9, 191, 194, 200, 209–10,
  255–7, 259, 285
generalizations 121, 152, 154–7,
  160, 174, 262, 270–1, 287
gut reasoning 248–9

in order to learning 185
index 85–6, 94, 96–7, 108, 144–8,
  159, 161–2, 164–5, 167, 226,
  247
  anomaly-based 95
  extraction 92
indexing 44, 51, 90, 150–1, 167,
  208
innateness 282
Institute for the Learning Sciences
  168
intelligence 196–7, 212, 225, 228,
  230, 234–5, 270–1, 274, 276–81,
  283–4
  testing 231, 277
interest 258
Invitation to a Revolution 171
IQ tests 231–2, 234
  designer 232
Is It a Rembrandt? 170

knowledge 206–7, 209, 211,
  213–14, 220, 231, 233, 236,
  239–40, 270–1, 273–4, 280–1,
  283–4, 286
  domain 218
  emotional 202, 213
  inert 240
  physical 202, 204, 213
  rational 202, 204, 206, 210, 213,
  216–18, 227, 230, 232
  revolution 206
  subconscious 202–4, 213
knowledge structures 4–5, 11–13,
  81, 83, 118, 126, 128, 160, 162

language understanding 4–5
learn by doing 31, 165, 167, 171–3,
  175–6, 192–4, 236, 247, 253
learnability 282
learning 200, 224
  nonconscious and conscious
  172–3
  process 42
  to learn 212

means–ends analysis 216–18
memory 102, 107, 118, 141–2, 148,
  177, 193, 200, 284
  indices 64
  organization 65, 123
  reconstructive 16–17, 118
  short and long term 15–16
  story-based 105
Memory Organization Packet
  (MOP) 112–137, 145, 148,
  155–66, 158, 160–6, 168, 171,
  173, 175, 177, 186–7, 200, 212,
  219–20, 222–3, 228, 241, 249,
  263, 266, 270, 281–3, 286
  personal 124, 128, 132–3
  physical 123–8, 131
  societal 123, 128, 131
memory structures 12–13, 17–18,
  23, 27, 31–2, 75, 80, 100, 107–8,

110–12, 116, 121, 125, 127, 130, 140, 145–7, 155–6, 159, 166, 175, 186, 194, 200, 224, 281–2, 286–7
monkey and bananas problem 212–14, 225
morals of stories 37–8
motivation 71, 167, 185, 261, 266, 269

nonconscious knowledge 194–7, 202, 205, 213, 223–6, 228–9, 232, 237–41, 243–9
Nutrition Project 170

performance tasks 250
planning failures 70–1
plans 7–8, 146–7, 150, 210
practice and learning 47
prediction 75–6, 285
problem solving 212–13, 218–19, 225, 228, 231–2, 234–5
process, within goal-based scenario 260, 265
processing structure 80–1, 112, 146, 155, 226
proverbs 141–2, 148–9, 225–6

racing mind 199, 237–8, 245, 247–8
reasoning 274, 281
reconstruction process 121
reminding 21–5, 27, 40, 44, 46, 51–2, 55, 74–6, 87–8, 91, 98, 107–8, 150, 152–3, 160, 162, 164–5, 174, 177, 215, 219, 235, 247–8, 269
  across contexts 36–7, 79, 88
  cross-contextual 140
  culturally shared 150–1
  dictionary-based 28–9
  expectaion failure–based 150–1
  failure-driven 56, 79, 84, 87
  goal-based 33–35
  in school 39

intentional 38–9, 143
outcome-driven 80, 82, 86–7
plan-based 35–6
processing-based 28, 30–2
visually based 29–30
role-playing 165, 171
rules 215, 225, 227, 230–1, 248, 253, 280

SAM 5, 8–10, 129
scene 18–19, 111, 113–25, 129–32, 155–65, 175, 187, 241, 249, 262
script 4, 6–15, 19, 25–6, 30–2, 44–9, 51, 55, 60, 89, 108, 110–15, 128–9, 158, 163, 174, 193, 282
  acquisition 47–8
  building 47
  generalized 13
  personal 108–10
  sketchy 10
scriptlet 115, 117–18, 121–2, 125, 129–30, 132, 155–7, 160, 163–4, 175–87, 189, 191, 193–4, 196, 224, 241, 249, 262, 281–3, 286
  cognitive 177–9, 184
  perceptual 177–9
  physical 177–9
Searle, John 271, 274–5, 279
semantic memory 102–3
semantic/episodic memory distinction 102
simulation 136, 166–8, 171, 198
skills 177–9, 181, 186, 192–3
  within goal-based scenario 259, 261, 264–5, 267, 269
skill-set 179–80
stories 89, 91–2, 96, 97, 99–100, 102, 105, 226
story creation 100
storytelling 89, 101, 106, 135, 269
subject, within goal-based scenario 260

teaching of facts 166
teaching of theories 262–3
teaching methods 165–6, 168
Thematic Organization Packet
    (TOP) 81, 83–5, 121, 137–55,
    160, 165–6, 168, 170, 173, 177,
    187, 200, 212, 222–3, 225, 228,
    241, 266, 270
thinking 237
    types of 237

Tower of Hanoi problem 229–30,
    235, 274
training
    role of 192
    goal of 193
truck curriculum 264–8

understanding 27, 97, 99, 287
understanding cycle 278
understanding process 92, 98, 250

Printed in the United States
79902LV00005B/57